# GBC

## GOVERNMENT BEYOND THE CENTRE

### SERIES EDITOR: GERRY STOKER

The world of sub-central government and administration – including local authorities, quasi-governmental bodies and the agencies of public – private partnerships – has seen massive changes in recent years and is at the heart of the current restructuring of government in the United Kingdom and other Western democracies.

The intention of the *Government Beyond the Centre* series is to bring the study of this often-neglected world into the mainstream of social science research, applying the spotlight of critical analysis to what has traditionally been the preserve of institutional public administration approaches.

Its focus is on the agenda of change currently being faced by sub-central government, the economic, political and ideological forces that underlie it, and the structures of power and influence that are emerging. Its objective is to provide up-to-date and informative accounts of the new forms of government, management and administration that are emerging.

The series will be of interest to students and practitioners of politics, public and social administration, and all those interested in the reshaping of the governmental institutions which have a daily and major impact on our lives.

*Published*

Richard Batley and Gerry Stoker (eds)
**Local Government in Europe**

Clive Gray
**Government Beyond the Centre**

John Gyford
**Citizens, Consumers and Councils**

Richard Kerley
**Managing in Local Government**

Desmond King and Gerry Stoker (eds)
**Rethinking Local Democracy**

Steve Leach, John Stewart and Kieron Walsh
**The Changing Organisation and Management of Local Governance**

Arthur Midwinter
**Local Government in Scotland**

Christopher Pollitt, Johnston Birchall and Keith Putman
**Decentralising Public Service Management**

Lawrence Pratchett and David Wilson (eds)
**Local Democracy and Local Government**

John Stewart
**The Nature of British Local Government**

John Stewart and Gerry Stoker (eds)
**Local Government in the 1990s**

Gerry Stoker (ed.)
**The New Management of British Local Governance**

Gerry Stoker (ed.)
**The New Politics of British Local Governance**

David Wilson and Chris Game
**Local Government in the United Kingdom** (2nd edn)

*Forthcoming*

Stephen Cope
**Local Government Finance in Britain**

---

**Government Beyond the Centre**
**Series Standing Order**
**ISBN 0–333–71696–5 hardcover**
**ISBN 0–333–69337–X paperback**
(*outside North America only*)

You can receive future titles in this series as they are published by placing a standing order. Please contact your bookseller or, in the case of difficulty, write to us at the address below with your name and address, the title of the series and the ISBN quoted above.

Customer Services Department, Macmillan Distribution Ltd
Houndmills, Basingstoke, Hampshire RG21 6XS, England

---

# The Nature of British Local Government

John Stewart

MACMILLAN

First published 2000 by
MACMILLAN PRESS LTD
Houndmills, Basingstoke, Hampshire RG21 6XS
and London
Companies and representatives
throughout the world

ISBN 0–333–66568–6 hardcover
ISBN 0–333–66569–4 paperback

A catalogue record for this book is available
from the British Library.

This book is printed on paper suitable for recycling and
made from fully managed and sustained forest sources.

10   9   8   7   6   5   4   3   2   1
09  08  07  06  05  04  03  02  01  00

Printed in Hong Kong

 Published in the United States of America by
ST. MARTIN'S PRESS, INC.,
Scholarly and Reference Division
175 Fifth Avenue, New York, N. Y. 10010

ISBN 0–312–22639–X (cloth)

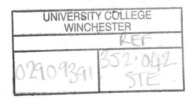

# Contents

## PART II  THE INSTITUTIONAL SETTING

## PART III  CHANGE AND THE WORKINGS OF
##           LOCAL GOVERNMENT

# Acknowledgements

This book has only been made possible by help from a variety of sources. It draws upon visits to local authorities made on behalf of the Local Government Management Board (and its predecessor, the Local Government Training Board) over the period between 1983 and 1998. I am grateful for their support for my work over the period and to the local government councillors and officers who assisted with this work. It draws, too, on over thirty years' work with and for local authorities at the Institute of Local Government Studies. I am indebted to the Leverhulme Trust for their support enabling this material to be worked on.

I am grateful for all the support and advice I have received from the staff of the Institute of Local Government Studies, from academic colleagues and from the world of local government – of special importance have been Michael Clarke, Steve Leach, George Jones, Stewart Ranson, Judith Hunt and of course Kieron Walsh, whose stimulus is sadly missed. Eileen Dunstan played a valuable role in assisting me with research. Kathy Bonehill, Tracy Mallin and Dot Woolley have assisted me greatly with typing material and arranging visits. From my wife Theresa, I have learnt much about political leadership and much else about local government as well as having continuing support. Steven Kennedy and Gerry Stoker have played a helpful role on all the problems of this book. To these and many others, my thanks.

JOHN STEWART

# 1 Introduction: Uniformity and Diversity and Continuity and Change

## Diversity within a national system

This book is a contribution to understanding the nature of local government in the United Kingdom. In the study of local government one can emphasise the degree of uniformity in the policies and practice of local authorities. Equally, one can emphasise the degree of diversity, for there are in the workings of local authorities forces both for uniformity and for diversity. To understand the nature of local government one has to recognise both.

It is easier to write about uniformity than about diversity. In books about local government it is natural to concentrate on the shared features, but that can conceal the diversity within, and diversity is inherent in the nature of local government. Local authorities are constituted with a capacity for difference both in the policies they follow and in their way of working. If it were not for that capacity there would be little point in local government as opposed to local administration. The local elections on which local government is based are an act of choice by voters between candidates and in many cases between political parties. Were there no capacity for difference there would be no point in local choice. Local government is the government of difference, responding to different needs, and realising different aspirations. As Hasluck wrote in defining local government, 'there must be a definite power to do things in a different manner from that followed in other areas within the same national or State area. If some local body has it in its power to govern in a different manner from other local bodies, there we have Local Government' (Hasluck, 1936, p. 6).

Yet local government is set within a national system of government so that the capacity for difference is constrained. It is not necessarily that local authorities adopt a common approach because they are required to, although sometimes that will be true, but it can be because their choices lead that way. Local authorities will make their own choice in their own circumstances. Because of shared conditions and shared views, the choices made by individual local authorities can lead to relative uniformity but because of different conditions and different views they can lead to relative diversity. The pattern of choices made by local authorities creates patterns of uniformity and patterns of difference or rather patterns in which both uniformity and diversity are to be found.

Uniformity and diversity can be found in the outcomes of the policies adopted by local authorities. Such patterns have been studied and attempts made to explain those differences by the environmental conditions faced by local authorities. If all the variations were explicable by the environment, then local authorities would be conveyor belts automatically turning environmental inputs into service outcomes.

> In this model the representative process was, in effect, a kind of transmission belt in which the political mechanisms as such had little independent effect on public policy since they merely performed the task of reflecting in policy terms the presumed wants derived from the socio-economic structure of the participative citizenry. Politics, therefore, did not matter, since what a government did was to all intents and purposes predetermined by factors outside its control, factors such as per capita income, age structure, or population density. (Sharpe and Newton, 1984, p. 204)

Sharpe and Newton reject the transmission process as an explanation of the policy-making process and assert the primacy of the political conditions and the political process.

> We fully recognise, of course, that socio-economic structure has a close bearing on some outputs... But we also assume a largely autonomous decision-making system in which **all** outputs are viewed as being a product of the political process. Some

outputs are likely to be more predetermined by the structural characteristics of the society concerned, but seldom, if ever, solely predetermined by them. To be logical – and resolve once and for all the long and by now somewhat gamy debate as to whether politics matters – the procedures of output studies should be transformed so that all outputs are assumed to be the product of the political process. This assumption would only be relaxed to the extent that factors that are external to the policy process itself are shown to have a significant association with the output in question. (Sharpe and Newton, 1984, p. 206)

If one accepts that conception of the policy process, it will include not merely the role of councillors and the pressures upon them, but the role of officers in advising on and implementing the policy. The organisational processes of the local authority – its structure, its culture, its way of working – have a significant impact on the outcomes.

This book focuses on the organisational processes including the political processes of party, of pressures and of the public, the role of officers and the interaction between officers and councillors. The book aims to fill a gap left by many works on local government. It examines what is unexplained in most output studies by examining the organisational processes of local government. It will depart from those works on local government which focus on uniformities, by recognising the diversity as well as the uniformity in the workings of local authorities.

*Forces for uniformity but yet diversity*

Legislation has its necessary impact. Ministerial pressures and departmental guidelines can influence the workings of local authorities beyond the simple requirements of legislation. Forces for uniformity also reflect the shared problems and the shared aspirations within society. Because all local authorities are set within a common society and economy, it is inevitable that they face similar demands and pressures. The national media raise issues and concerns not for one authority alone – although from time to time they may do that – but for all.

Within local authorities there are forces for uniformity in the workings of the organisation and in the political processes. Political parties and professions are national institutions to which most councillors and most chief officers belong. National influences play directly on local authorities through the political process and through the professions. That national influence can yet allow diversity. While the national parties will be found in most local authorities, there are considerable variations in the nature of the party from authority to authority. There are new Labour councils and old Labour councils. There are Thatcherite and traditional Conservative groups. There are many varieties of Liberal Democrat groups. Within groups there can be a range of views and approaches. While the national party label may place limits, the extent of variation is significant. There are Labour groups that have supported contracting out or the externalisation of services, while there have been Conservative groups opposed to them.

Professionalism is a powerful force in ensuring common standards and common approaches across authorities. Yet professionalism can be a spur to innovation and hence to diversity. The model that underlies many strands of professionalism is of the individual professional exercising his or her own judgement. Professional reputation is established through individual initiatives leading to innovation, albeit innovation that is within established lines of professional development.

There is a world of national negotiations and provincial councils that has its own rituals. Its language and its procedures are known by personnel officers and chairs of personnel committees. It has its special culture of elaborated structures and procedures beloved by the aficionados, creating its own enclosed world. The products are detailed agreements covering in carefully specified clauses not merely wages and salaries but also conditions of service. The result is inevitably a pressure for uniformity and in some cases limitation on change. However, within the elaborate agreements there is always scope for variation. Such agreements can never cover every possibility. Recently there have been changes to bring about greater flexibility and some authorities have abandoned national pay and conditions.

Trade unions are an established part of the workings of local authority, although their role has changed over time. The unions as national bodies, each with their own policies and procedures, are a force for uniformity in the workings of local government, giving a particular form to staff relations. The unions are also a source of diversity, since the local branch can be a powerful actor in the workings of a local authority and local branches vary in militancy and in involvement in the political process.

Local authorities belong to a national world of local government formed in part by shared experience and shared folkways. 'The local government press (both the general and professional outlets), the functional services associations, and their publications and activities, the apparatus of local government professionalism and the regular conferences, seminars and meetings which play such a large part in the nationalisation of local policy change – all these define the boundaries of policy consideration and debate, in local authorities as a whole' (Dunleavy, 1980, p. 106). Within local government there are shared beliefs about how a local authority should act, about the ways to conduct its business and about the attitudes it should adopt. Although the statutory framework allows considerable discretion as to how local authorities are organised, common patterns develop. Thus it has been assumed almost without question that a local authority requires a committee system or that the council meeting should follow established practice centring on committee reports or minutes. At least until recently it was assumed that each department should be headed by a chief officer drawn from the appropriate profession. Yet such mind-sets can never totally confine and can be broken through as the record of organisational innovation shows.

Organisational innovations can move rapidly through local government, sometimes encouraged by government action or guidance but often independently of it. Concepts like customer care or devolved management can be seen as the product of innovation by exemplar local authorities, as can previous movements to establish chief executives or to build corporate management. The spreading of such innovation is assisted by the networks of communication that mark the national world of local government. Key reports – Maud in the 1960s and Bains in the 1970s – had their impact as did those of the Audit Commission more recently. However, the existence of innovation is itself a product of the capacity for diversity.

*The diversity of locality, but yet within uniformities*

Local authorities are multi-functional authorities responsible for a defined area and constituted by local election. Those characteristics are shared but are a source of diversity since areas vary in their nature and elections vary in their results.

While there are uniformities of practice in the committee system and in the nature of professionalism there are differences in ways of working. There are differences between authorities in the number of committees and of departments and in the frequency of committee meetings and of group meetings. Party groups vary in their approach to group discipline. The pattern of decision-making in hung authorities, where no party has a majority, differ from those where the conventions of majority rule prevail, and differ between authorities.

Yet these formal differences are limited when compared with the differences in the ways of working and in culture. As one visits authorities, one is struck by the differences in their character often reflecting the nature of the locality. These differences are found in attitudes to innovation and to change, the nature of political leadership, the relative role of officers and councillors, the perception of the role of the authority, the nature of councillor–officer relations and the dominant attitudes. The relationship between locality and local authority is complex. The local authority can be described as governing and being governed by locality. In complex interaction local authority and locality are moulded by each other, as was recognised in the nineteenth century. Brodick wrote:

> No anatomical resemblance of outward structure can assimilate the inner municipal life of quaint old cathedral cities with that of new and fashionable watering-places, that of sea-ports with that of inland towns, that of manufacturing or mining settlements with that of market towns in the midst of agricultural settlements. (quoted in Smellie, 1957, p. 101)

Lowndes wrote more than one hundred years later:

> Objective characteristics of a locality, its social and economic character, its geography, its demography and settlement patterns – placed particular demands (and opportunities) upon a local authority; so too did 'subjective' elements of the local environment, like political and civic traditions, local conventions and the culture of different communities. Locally-specific

'ways of doing things' were sometimes formally articulated and vigorously promoted as part of a local authority's identity and heritage; sometimes they impacted subtly and informally on perceptions of what was possible and impossible, desirable and undesirable. (Lowndes, 1999, p. 16)

Consider:

- The proud city council with its civic tradition in which the authority sees itself as the expression of that tradition.
- The local authority in former mining areas, in which strong trade union values are still sustained and inform the workings of the authority.
- The Welsh rural authority committed to preservation of the Welsh language and the Welsh culture.
- The rural authority seeking the maintenance of rural values and therefore continuity of established practice.
- The new town authority carrying forward habits of innovation and intervention inherited from the rapidly growing new town.
- The London Borough with its mixed social composition caused by a combination of gentrification, old rented accommodation and housing estates, leading to complex internal politics.

So the list could continue, reflecting in the authority the impact of locality and, to an extent, the impact of the authority on locality.

The relationship between local authority and locality is expressed more through the political process than through the officer structure. The political process is embedded in the locality and councillors come from the locality. While councillors are drawn from national parties, their political experience will in many cases be formed in the locality. The careers of chief officers will normally have involved work in several authorities. Their training will have been in professions that owe no particular loyalty to any one authority. Much of their working and professional experience may well therefore have been beyond the locality. The officers are more likely to be cosmopolitans, while the councillors are more likely to be locals, although the distinction should not be pushed too far.

**Continuity and change**

Cross-cutting the dimensions of uniformity and diversity are dimensions of continuity and change. Forces for uniformity and forces for diversity are forces both for change and for continuity. National legislation sets a continuing framework, yet is a means for change. Within the national economy and society are forces for continuity and for change which can be expressed through national politics. The national world of local government maintains a continuity of practice yet provides for the dissemination of innovation. The relationship of a local authority to locality is a force for continuity and yet for change as localities change. Local politics and the impact of individual officers and councillors have their impact both in sustaining continuity and in stimulating change.

History, or the inherited pattern of behaviour, is a powerful force in the transmission of continuity both in its impact at the national level and in the internal workings of local authorities. History is transmitted through established procedures and the pattern of accepted ideas which form the experience of the main actors within local authorities. They identify the ways of working they have come to know as *the* way of working. After all, they may know no other. There is not merely continuity of processes but of ideas about the role of local government and of its ways of working. In different authorities different arguments are acceptable. In some the search is for innovation, yet in others caution is required. Prestige projects can excite in some authorities, but in others there are no such aspirations.

The transmission process for continuity is through accepted and acceptable discourse but these are not necessarily fixed for all time. Change can be brought about by a change in the political composition of the council, in the personalities involved or in the challenges faced. If history mediated through experience is a force for continuity, experience can challenge that continuity. If discourse can sustain present practice, discourse can change it. To understand local government in continuity and in change it is necessary to plot the history of practice and the history of discourse about local government, for they enable both continuity and change to be understood.

The book is about the interaction between forces for uniformity and forces for diversity, taking account of their impact for continuity and for change. The themes laid down in this chapter will be explored throughout this book and their interaction analysed.

## The structure of the book

Local authorities are set within a wider system of community governance (sometimes called local governance); community governance being the complex processes by which local communities are governed, involving many organisations and many relationships. The focus of the book is upon local authorities, but as part of that wider system, in which the role of local authorities in community leadership is being increasingly recognised.

The book is divided into three parts. The first two parts describe the conditions which have formed and form local government. The third part describes the workings of local authorities during the period of challenge and change that has marked the last two decades and is likely to mark the next decade, a theme that is turned to in the concluding chapter.

Part I is concerned with the impact of history both on local government generally and on particular authorities, reflecting both forces for uniformity and forces for diversity. Chapter 2 explores how history is carried forward into the present. Chapter 3 shows how in that history there have been different roles emphasised, giving rise to continuing discussion of key themes. The relative emphasis given to the role of local authorities as political institutions constituted for local choice and local voice or as agencies for service delivery is identified as critical. Chapter 4 sets out the assumptions inherited from history about the way of working of local authorities. It describes the conditions that reflect those assumptions of the inherited world.

Part II focuses on the institutional setting within which the workings of local authorities take place. By the institutional setting is meant both the legislative framework that structures local authorities and the impact of the system of community governance upon them. Chapter 5 describes the main elements in that setting, with the exception of the central–local relationship, which because of its importance is dealt with separately in Chapter 6. Part II shows that while the institutional setting reflects uniformities of legislation, the areas of local authorities as defined in that setting provide the basis for diversity.

Part III focuses upon the workings of local authorities. It begins by describing in Chapter 7 the challenges faced by local authorities in recent years as a result both of legislation and of changes in society. The remainder of this part describes the workings of local authorities, showing the impact of these challenges and of the inherited world of local government.

The starting point for this description is Chapter 8 on the changing politics of local government. Chapter 9 describes the workings of the political processes. Chapter 10 turns to change in management processes, followed in Chapter 11 by a discussion of the impact on officer structures. Chapter 12 brings together the political and management processes in an exploration of councillor–officer relations.

Chapter 13 deals with the relationship of the local authority to its locality. The chapter argues that relationship is a major factor in the diversity of local authorities and of their ways of working. It discusses the forms taken by the relationship with the publics of the authority through which locality has its impact, and shows how those forms are changing. The movement to the development of the role of local authorities in community governance is seen as the culmination of those changes, reinforcing diversity. This role expresses the concern of local authorities for the well-being of the locality beyond the impact of their own services and is a re-assertion of the role of local authorities as political institutions constituted for local choice and local voice.

Part III draws on more than 300 visits by the author to local authorities in all parts of England and Wales between 1983 and 1998, as well as material from other researchers, to illustrate the diversity to be found within the workings of local authorities. The findings of the visits represent snapshots taken at particular moments of time. I often use the past tense to describe them, being conscious that the visits took place during a period of rapid change. For similar reasons, I describe Liberal Democrats and their predecessor parties by the label used at the time of the visit. During the visits I received much information which has to be treated as confidential. I have therefore made some descriptions anonymous, while naming authorities where that was appropriate. The visits can best be seen as a journey in search of local government, which continues as local government continues to change.

In the concluding Chapter I highlight both diversity and uniformity and continuity and change and the likely impact of the Labour government programme, for the reform of local government. That programme which is described in Chapter 7 represents a new challenge for local government. How the programme affects the workings of local authorities will be influenced by established attitudes, even where the programme is designed to change them, which makes the experience set out in this book relevant to the future. There will be both continuity and change as well as there will be diversity within uniformity.

# PART I
# THE IMPACT OF HISTORY

# 2 The Carriers of History

## From history, to the present

The nature of local government has been shaped by its history. Shared understandings that have developed over time have become part of the assumptive world of local government. They have formed beliefs about the role of local government, and its ways of working. Because these beliefs are widely held, they support the uniformities that enable one to speak and write of the shared world of local government. But from history also comes diversity. Assumptions about the roles and ways of working are built up that reflect the experience of particular authorities. History is written into the practices of the authority and into the attitudes that have been formed by them.

Broad patterns differentiate authorities. There is a tradition of urban government centring on towns and cities expressing civic pride and marked by a strong sense of identity and intense councillor involvement. There is a different tradition of county government, which is about the continuity of an established way of life, a sense of county background and more limited councillor involvement giving expression to geographical distance, which meant that county government was originally 'government by horse and trap' (Stanyer, 1989, p. 69). In nineteenth-century towns and cities, status was established and expressed through the council. In the counties, status was given by history and society. City and town government and county government have greatly changed from the days when city government was in the hands of city merchants and industrialists and county government in the hands of 'social persons', as Lee has called them, and changed even more from the county society they replaced (Lee, 1963). Yet past styles have their impact in current working. The intensity of city politics contrasts with the more relaxed style of the county. As

Robin Wendt wrote in his last article as Secretary of the Association of County Councils:

> First and foremost is the county style of quiet and efficient administration. They are calm and fairly dignified places in which people normally go about their business in a measured and effective way. (Wendt, 1997, p. 13)

Other histories lead to different traditions. There is the unsung story of district councils, themselves the product in many areas of amalgamations of smaller district councils, accustomed to a councillor focus on detail. There are the distinctive traditions of Wales and Scotland. In both the mining area of South Wales, with its dominant Labour and trade union traditions, and the rural North Wales, with its politics of Independents, there has been detailed councillor involvement reflected in, for example, selection of chief officers by the whole council, and education committees consisting of all councillors. In London, councils see themselves as different from the rest of the country, changing in style often and rapidly in the intensity of metropolitan politics, but with different cultures in the inner city and outer suburbs.

These traditions will be explored in later chapters. This chapter focuses on how history is carried forward from the past to the present and into the future.

## Buildings

The buildings in which the business of the authority is conducted express in the present the history of the authority, and also express both uniformity and diversity. Each Victorian or Edwardian town hall has its own distinctive architecture, but there is a shared style in what can almost be regarded as the 'cathedrals' of the nineteenth-century entrepreneur. Buildings set in the centre of cities remain symbols of the perceived self-importance of the council, expressing the urban manufacturing and commercial leadership's pride in its achievements. Buildings reflected power and, in their size and scale, centralised municipal power. In the town hall important decisions were made.

There are different styles of building in other authorities. Those counties that retain their old shire halls – and there are fewer of them than of the town halls – are grounded in different traditions. They were associated with the administration of justice or with older feudal regimes. In Oxfordshire and Cambridgeshire, the county hall adjoins the old castle mote. In other authorities the county council shared a building with the courts. If one had lunch with the chief executive one shared it with barristers pleading cases at the county court.

The shire halls were often to be found in the county town, even where the county town was a county borough and therefore outside the county's jurisdiction – at least until 1974. After local government reorganisation a number of counties built new buildings, but the site then was normally – as in Berkshire, Leicestershire or Hereford and Worcester – outside the county town but close to it, representing a balance between town and country in the workings of the authority. County halls have normally never had the proud architecture of town halls. The county had less need to assert itself. The subdued architecture reflects the on-going certainty of the county, although perhaps Wales was different: West Glamorgan offices (now inherited by Swansea unitary authority) has 'the finest view of any Council in England or Wales' with the members' lounge looking across the Bristol Channel.

The buildings of district councils (apart from those based on former boroughs) and of London boroughs were designed for smaller authorities, leading in a number of cases to the perceived need for new buildings. Often the buildings inherited by district councils were modest, reflecting acceptance of a lesser status. In London, it was difficult for a metropolitan borough to assert its position, when it was merely a small part of London. That was left to the London County Council, whose location almost opposite Parliament was an assertion of status – an assertion increasingly resented in the latter days of its successor, the Greater London Council.

It is not merely the outward appearance and location of the council buildings that carry history. The interiors tell much of the way of working. Council and committee rooms bring their own messages down the years. They are rooms for formality. When one enters a committee room, there is a pervading sense of committee procedure. I have often run seminars for councillors, designed to encourage the free flow of discussion. If I have been allocated a committee room, I know it will be an uphill struggle against the formalities embedded in the decoration and layout of the room and written into the experience of the participants, as they assume their places around the committee table. The table and the chairs can be moved but the room has its own meanings in the experience of councillors.

The council chamber has its own messages. Status in the scale and decoration of the room is often added to formality in layout. The semicircle is a more common model than the adversarial layout embedded in the House of Commons, although the semicircle has not prevented the development of adversarial politics. The layout of the council chamber has messages about relations with the public. Space is provided for only a few and often in ways that emphasise their exclusion from council debates.

Council offices and the arrangement of rooms tell their own story of hierarchy and of status within the officer structures. There can be and have been changes. Rooms have been amalgamated or divided. Victorian and Edwardian buildings are often shells used for change within. The space allowed for councillors' rooms has expanded. In several, leaders have taken over rooms formerly held by county clerk or town clerk.

In the buildings will be found many signs of history. Portraits of past mayors or lord mayors give way to photographs of more recent ones. In old cities, such as Chester or Norwich, lists of mayors can be found going back to the fourteenth century. There are sheriffs of Nottingham today, although they are now councillors. Local councils are conscious of past traditions to which they attach themselves, and that past is reproduced in the present.

There are legendary figures who may still be remembered. Joseph Chamberlain reappears again and again in Birmingham rhetoric, and his former house, with titles on the doors of rooms such as 'Mr Neville', is now used by the council for some civic occasions. One recent Labour leader in the chequered history of Hackney, installed a photograph of Herbert Morrison in his room. In the director of education's office in Cambridgeshire the bust of Henry Morris was to be found. The present leader of Coventry told me that every councillor should be given the autobiography of Alderman Hodgkinson (Hodgkinson, 1970) whose influence on post-war Coventry with Alderman Stringer remains part of local political folklore. The legendary figures of the past have representation in the present.

*Ways of working*

In buildings, history is given physical representation in the present. They are not the only means by which history is transmitted from past to present. The ways of working and structures have continuity over time. They can be changed and often are, but normally those changes are limited in form and in impact. Thus the committee structure may be changed but still remains a committee structure, and the way committees conduct their business often continues unaffected by structural change.

The committee cycle of meetings setting a regular rhythm to the business of the council, the formal agendas supported by reports, and the standing orders governing the conduct of business – all are part of experience, shaping councillors' perceptions of their roles. The council meeting considering reports or, in some cases, minutes from committees, has been routinised by history. The lord mayor (or mayor or chairman) presides in ways established over time. The structures and procedures of council and committees are for councillors their formative experience. They define their role and 'the way it is done here'. They can be changed but that requires effort whether generated by internal actors or stimulated by external requirements. Unless and until that happens the procedures carry forward past experience into the present and in doing so form future experience. For councillors and officers the procedures of the authority are powerful carriers of history. For officers, at least for senior officers, professional practice inculcated both by training and experience is a carrier of history forming departmental ways of working, influencing both councillors and officers. The way of working depends upon officers and councillors 'socialising each other over a long period of time' (Stanyer, 1975, p. 49).

*Culture and beliefs*

Ways of working are supported by the culture of an authority or the set of beliefs and attitudes that underlie a way of working. Culture is conveyed over time by a combination of experience and by accepted discourse. Experience is carried forward through the gradual turnover of councillors and officers and by the continuities 'of the way things are done here' which newcomers find they have accepted before they have had the opportunity to challenge them. Discourse expresses that experience as the accepted way of thinking about the authority. 'That was a committee decision', 'the next cycle', 'the chief officer' become part of the language through which councillors and officers talk about their work. Words may have particular significance to particular authorities, expressing the desired pattern of working. Experience expressed in discourse is a powerful carrier of culture, reinforced and supported by structures and processes.

Culture reflected in discourse expresses beliefs and attitudes both about how the authority should behave, the way of working and the proper role of local government. In one Welsh county the discourse was about the Welsh language even though most of the area was English-speaking. Although the discourse was about language, much more was implied. A model Welsh family is conjured up from the past, but in the present was described to me as 'living on a hill farm or in a market town, Welsh-speaking, believing in education – with their children accumulating endless O-levels, A-levels and a degree – an interest in Welsh literature, radical but conservationist, still attached to the chapel, maintaining high standards'.

Past history is reflected in present culture. Kingston-on-Thames sees itself as more than just another London suburban authority. It is 'the royal borough' with a sense of history – the Saxon Kings' Stone is in the grounds of the council offices. In South Somerset it was said 'Monmouth's rebellion lives on in Somerset'. The new town and parish councils built on the old towns and villages express that sense of independence and are important in the life of the council. The paternalist tradition of the Great Western railway was carried forward by the Swindon council (later Thamesdown council) until it adopted a community development approach (Broady and Hedley, 1989). History was remembered when I visited Hereford and, it was claimed, they built the first council house one hundred years ago.

More recent history can have an impact. Councils in new towns have their own distinctive culture; for long they were the junior partners, whose activities were almost submerged beneath the activities of the dominant and resource-rich new-town corporation. The presence of the corporation set an example of innovation. Now the local authorities are inheritors of the role of the corporation. In

Harlow the chief executive is called general manager, the authority has adopted a social development role, and has innovated in
its approach to decentralisation. The cultural changes brought
about in the Wrekin and the developments in community governance in Stevenage are examples of new-town experience establishing a culture of innovation.

Local authorities may have a blame-culture, for the culture of
an authority should not be assumed to be positive. In such a culture, blame is placed by councillors on officers for any error or
public criticism and blame is passed downward. Passing the blame
is then the automatic response to any difficulty. Local authorities
may be officer-led, where the presumption in practice, if not in
words, is that officer advice is normally followed. The culture may
be departmentalised and may remain so against endeavours to
assert a corporate culture.

The way roles are played will be an expression of culture as well
as of the individual playing the role. There will be an expectation
as to how a leader will behave, or a chair, chief executive or chief
officer. The processes of the authority will be geared to those
expectations. The mayor plays a role that is rarely laid down in
any formal procedures or standing orders. There are however a
series of understandings about the role. Thus it is understood that
the mayor will not play a political role in his or her year of office.
In Birmingham, when one lord mayor began to disregard those
understandings by seeking an active political role, action was
taken by the leader to ensure the role was played as it was understood it should be played. Nor is it just within the authority that
the role is understood. The social role of the mayor in the community is not prescribed in law but is carried forward from year to
year, in authority after authority.

The culture of an authority expresses beliefs about how a local
authority should act. I saw a proposal in Coventry, proud of its
record of innovation, attacked by the then town clerk as an
untried innovation, arguing that this time the council should let
others test it out. Put forward as an argument against, it became
an argument for the proposal. Councillors saw the authority and
indeed the city as a leader in innovation.

Local authorities have a self-image which encompasses both
their area and the council. That image has a life of its own and
may represent the past rather than the present. Conservative

councillors in Harrow saw it as a collection of villages with Pinner being the largest village in England and saw their role as village defenders. In Rotherham the leadership spoke easily about mining, in which they had all worked, as though it was still a mining area. Many rural authorities see themselves as councils of farmers, and the farmers on the council speak for its values, although farming has ceased to be dominant in the rural economy. In Somerset, Woods found an 'agrarian-centred discourse' of rurality drawn from the past as still influential (Woods, 1997).

Authorities have a certain perception of themselves which may or may not correspond to reality. They may see themselves as a high-performance authority, although the evidence may be hard to find. They may see themselves as innovating, although what they regard as innovations are to be found in other authorities. Sometimes the basis of an innovatory reputation lies in the past rather than in the present, since the authority will long have been overtaken by others. Authorities that were once in advance of others can easily become complacent. Birmingham in the 1960s still valued its nineteenth-century description as the 'the best-governed city in the world'.

An authority's culture can be challenged, not least by political change, and the role played by officers is a key part of the culture. 'It has all become too cosy here' is an expression of that challenge – which may be directed at perceived officer domination or what are seen as too close relations between the parties. In the words of the challenge the power of culture is recognised.

Some elements in the culture are shared within the national world of local government and are hard to challenge. That shared culture is reflected in common patterns of behaviour and in beliefs about the organisation of local government. Thus committee working with its regular cycle and its agendas conforms to patterns found throughout local government. The belief that officers have a duty to the whole council, while recognising, where it exists, a duty to the majority party, guides behaviour generally. The professionally-based department was established in the shared culture rather than in legislation. Some beliefs about the institution of local government are widely held and are products of history. These beliefs are so widely accepted that they are rarely argued against or even for. Debates lie in the past and local government has taken over the conclusions as basic beliefs, as Chapter 3 will illustrate.

*Legislation*

Legislation provides the framework within which local authorities act, setting the limits of the possible and determining forms to be followed. Legislation is a carrier of the past into the present. Legislation continues over time, and even when new legislation is introduced it often carries forward provisions from previous legislation. Parts of the 1972 Local Government Act reproduced in the twentieth century the provisions of earlier legislation.

Even where legislation is changed, habits induced by previous legislation may be carried forward into the future. Thus although most of the legislation requiring local authorities to appoint specific committees has been repealed, the habit of committee working continues almost as though legislation required it. Indeed many within local government believe the committee system is part of the statutory framework within which local authorities act. The life of legislation is extended by beliefs built by the past.

## Uniformity and diversity

The carriers of the past are forces for both uniformity and diversity. There are carriers which enhance uniformity. Legislation can have an impact, even after it is repealed. Professions, political parties and trade unions each form the attitudes of actors within authorities. Each is a carrier of history and that history is in part a national history.

The national world of discourse about local government is a source of uniformity reflecting past history. In that discourse, attitudes are cultivated and beliefs established over time. Professions, national societies of chief officers and the local authority associations with their histories provide settings where there are areas for shared discourse. Local government journals have a long history, with the *Local Government Chronicle* being over one hundred years old. They are carriers of attitudes and beliefs, as are books about local government. A series of writers have helped to shape discourse about local government. Writers such as Mill, Redlich, Finer, Hasluck, Robson and others can be described as the classic writers whose influence can be found in discourse, and embedded in the structure of local government.

But the carriers of history reflect the experience of a particular local authority and locality. That experience is written into the buildings, procedures and the culture of the local authority. It is common to speak about 'our way of working' to distinguish the local authority from others. That way of working will be expressed in discourse and in patterns of acceptable behaviour. Officers and councillors are socialised by their experience both of the national world of local government and of their own local authority.

## Continuity and change

History is a force for continuity, but can itself be challenged by forces for change. Thus change can be brought about by national legislation, by change in regulations or by change in government policy. Yet the extent to which they bring about change may vary from authority to authority. Legislation differs in the extent to which it requires organisational change and enforces it.

Changes in society generally or in the framework of ideas that govern the polity can challenge past experience. The growth of the welfare state and the recent emphasis on market forces can both be seen as powerful in their impact on authorities, although response varies. There are changes too in the ideas about the working of authorities that affect the shared discourse. In the 1950s an organisation and methods report on Coventry led to an emphasis on its precepts in many other authorities. The Bains report with its stress on corporate management, the later search for the enabling authority or the aspiration to community govern-ance all led to changes in discourse.

Continuity can be broken and the carriers of history apparently shattered by local government reorganisation, but appearances can be deceptive. Local government reorganisation amalgamated authorities and abolished county boroughs in 1974, yet it could not abolish the experience of history. The impact of history can be seen in the struggle by many towns and cities for the restoration of their powers. Attitudes, beliefs and even ways of working are carried by local government officers and councillors over the divide of reorganisation.

There are changes brought about in and through the diversity of local government. A new party gains control; there is a change in group leadership; a new chief executive or chief officers can have their impact, as can local economic and societal change. Particular events can have an impact. There are many forces for change, but they are mediated through existing ways of working, themselves the product of history. The tale is one of both continuity and change.

# 3 Differing Roles and Continuing Themes

## Introduction

Local authorities are responsible for the provision of a series of services, many of them required by national legislation. Yet local authorities are also political institutions constituted by local elections with a capacity for local choice and local voice. Within the parameters set by these conditions, different emphases can be given to the role of local government. Local authorities can be seen as agencies for the delivery of a series of services. Jackson wrote in 1958, 'Local government is essentially a method of getting services run for the benefit of the community' (Jackson, 1958, p. 1). They can, however, be seen as political institutions constituted for local self-government with a concern for their area that extends beyond the services provided, as Sir Jeremy Beecham was to urge on the Hunt Committee: 'We do not see local government simply as a vehicle for the delivery of a series of services. We see an over-arching strategic role in civic and community leadership' (Hunt, 1996b, p. 41). Within the boundaries set by these emphases there are many intermediate positions.

The emphasis on the role of local government in the delivery of services is a force for uniformity, modified in as far as there is local choice on the nature and level of services. The emphasis on the role of local authorities as institutions for local self-government supports diversity, modified in as far as the choices made reflect shared perspectives.

Issues about the role of local government have underlain recent discussion about the future of local government. That discussion will be covered in Chapter 13 in which the emphasis on local self-government will be represented by the movement to community leadership within community governance. Although discussion about the role has gained prominence in recent years, different

26

positions about it have been held at different periods. Those positions have given rise to themes that have run through the history of local government. In this chapter the positions dominant at different periods will be outlined and recurrent themes highlighted.

## Roles explored

### *The civic tradition*

Loughlin argues that 'Local institutions emerge not simply as creatures of the central state, but as representations of historic communities within a structure of national laws to which the crown and localities are bound. It is in this sense that we may call the English inheritance a tradition of local government rather than a system of local administration' (Loughlin, 1996, p. 23).

Here, discussion of the role of local government begins with the authorities set up by the Municipal Corporations Act 1835. It created the elected municipal corporation which has through the civic tradition had a powerful influence on thinking about the role of local government. The municipal corporations had a limited role although the Act imposed a general duty of 'the good rule and government of the Borough' (s. 90). Many of the functions carried out at local level remained with special-purpose organisations. The new corporations inherited the limited role of the small closed corporations distinguished as much by inactivity as by activity. On many councils 'economisers' were dominant who did not wish for extended functions and the imposition of burdens on the rates, seeking to limit expenditure to that covered by the inherited municipal estate.

There was the potential for a wider role in the concept of the municipal corporation. The 'burgesses as citizens are members of the corporation . . . The constitution of an English municipality is based upon the community of its members and its members are essentially inhabitants' (Redlich, 1903, vol. I, p. 244). Later in the nineteenth century the potential of the municipal corporation was realised through a recognition of a wider role of local government. That change reflected both urban problems and civic pride. The pressures of industrialisation brought many problems to towns and cities. Disease created needs for sanitation. Industry and commerce had their requirements for an adequate infrastructure. As well as problems there was pride in towns and cities as dynamos for economic and social progress, and councils gained a new sense of their role in promoting that change.

The municipal gospel proclaimed in Birmingham by the Reverend George Dawson gave expression to that role. It was a doctrine inspired not merely by economic achievements but by a vision of the good city, leading to

> the discovery that perhaps a strong and able Town Council might do almost as much to improve the conditions of life in the town as Parliament itself. I have called it a 'discovery', for it had all the freshness and charm – it created all the enthusiasm – of a good discovery. One of its first effects was to invest the Council with a new attractiveness and dignity... The November ward meetings assumed a new character. The speakers, instead of discussing small questions of administration and of economy, dwelt with growing enthusiasm on what a great and prosperous town like Birmingham might do for its people. They spoke of sweeping away streets in which it was not possible to live a healthy and decent life; of making the town cleaner, sweeter and brighter; of providing gardens and parks and music; or erecting baths and free libraries, an art gallery and a museum... Sometimes an adventurous orator would excite his audience by dwelling on the glories of Florence and of the other cities of Italy in the middle ages, and suggest that Birmingham, too, might become the home of a noble literature and art. (quotation from Dale's life of George Dawson and other writings, in Gill, 1952, p. 382)

In speeches and sermons, Dawson proclaimed the municipal gospel and Joseph Chamberlain as mayor gave it expression in action. Under Chamberlain the council used private bill legislation to take control of and develop the water supply, to municipalise the gas supply and to undertake a major improvement scheme for the development of the city centre. This period was not of privatisation, but of municipalisation. Local authorities were to be the means for creating the conditions for the health, welfare and prosperity of the town. On this basis Chamberlain declared that 'he was inclined to increase the responsibilities of the local authority and would do everything in his power to constitute these local authorities, real local parliaments supreme in their special jurisdiction' (Garvin, 1932, p. 188). He argued, 'local government is near the people. Local government will bring you in touch with the masses' (quoted in Young, 1989, p. 8).

Joseph Chamberlain was only one of several such leaders in Birmingham and their record was matched by 'Fit and Proper Persons' (Hennock, 1977) on the councils of other towns and cities providing the same emphasis on municipal enterprise. As an American writer at the time wrote, 'great towns are remaking themselves physically, and providing themselves with the appointments of civilisation, because they have made the great discovery that their masses of population are to remain permanently. They have in practice rejected the old view that the evils of city life are inevitable, and have begun to remedy them' (Shaw, 1895, p. 9). The nineteenth century established a model of city government, which has had a deep and continuing influence. It can be seen in Birmingham's transformation 'from a badly administered city into what an American observer described as the Best-Governed City in the World' in an article that appeared in *Harper's Monthly Magazine* in 1890 (Briggs, 1952, p. 67).

That model gave expression to a role of local government concerned with the welfare of its area. It generated a belief that city government led by a multi-purpose authority grounded in the civic tradition was the model for local government. This model led to two themes which remain of continuing importance in local government: that size and efficiency are associated, and that the all-purpose authority was the ideal model for local government.

*A parish tradition*

There are other traditions, but nineteenth-century history was on the side of the towns and cities in their period of industrial growth and success. Indeed only in the towns and cities was there effective elected local government. The counties had their history, but until 1889 the government of counties was in the hands not of elected councillors but of justices of the peace. Beyond that, local government was in the hands of parishes. Because of scale, parishes could not aspire to the role of local government developed in the cities. Many saw them as inevitably limited in role, reluctant to develop significant functions. That was not the view of Toulmin Smith who, writing in the middle of the nineteenth century, saw in local government generally, and in parishes and vestries in particular, a tradition dating back to Anglo-Saxon times, in which people came together to govern themselves. He dismissed criticism:

> 'Local jobbing', and the influence of 'local interests', are often held up as bugbears. But each of these, wherever it be found, exists, and only ever can exist, because true Local Self-Government is not there found; because the discussion and management of matters is practically left in the hands of a local clique or oligarchy – under the form and name, it may be, of a Town Council or otherwise, but without the practical activity of that other part of the Local Institutions which the spirit, the letter, and the long practice of the common Law and Constitution of England require, namely, the Folk and People themselves meeting in frequent, fixed, regular, and accessible assemblies, as matter of individual right and duty, and discussing, and hearing discussed, the matters which the local body, entrusted to administer in their behalf, has done or is doing. (Smith, 1851)

Toulmin Smith has often been attacked as putting forward views that had no basis in history. Yet he advocated a theme that recurs in the continuing debates about local government. He spoke for the small against the large, and for the town or parish assembly against representative democracy.

Advocacy of the parish as the basis of local government was an important element in the nineteenth-century debates over the future structure of local government. Such advocacy came from very different sources from those represented by the conservatism of Toulmin Smith. Radicals wanted to see 'smaller discrete units of local government in place of municipal despotism' (Fraser, 1976, p. 177). Gladstone argued in 1889 that they should 'go still nearer to the door of the masses of the people, to avail ourselves of the old parochial divisions of the county and to carry home in the mind of the peasants and the agricultural labourers the principles and the obligations, and to secure to them the benefits, of local government' (quoted in Poole and Keith-Lucas, 1994, p. 27).

However, the dilemma was seen that if 'the parish, as a unit, is to be an effective unit of local government it must be enlarged;

but if the average parish is enlarged then it is no longer a parish' (Lipman, 1949, p. 163). The parish option was rejected as the basis for local government. The choice then made was critical, separating off developments in English local government from much of Europe, where the commune remained the basic unit of local government. Advocacy of the parish was a theme in discussions of local government, although never a dominant theme. The Redcliffe-Maud Commission was impressed by parish councils and its report was described as 'a fanfare for parish councils' (Poole and Keith-Lucas, 1994, p. 202). It did not, however, 'see them as having statutory responsibility for any local government service', but rather as focusing 'opinion about anything that affects the well-being of each community, and to bring it to bear on the responsible authority' (Redcliffe-Maud, 1969, para. 370).

*Other traditions*

In the reforms of local government stretching from 1888 to 1895, new elected local authorities were established. County boroughs were created as 'all-purpose' authorities drawing on the civic tradition. County councils took over the functions previously exercised by the justices of the peace, with non-county boroughs, urban and rural districts carrying out other functions. In London, the London County Council was created along with metropolitan boroughs.

The county councils did not aspire to a wide-ranging role. Their functions were limited. The needs seemed less pressing. County councils in most areas were dominated by the landed estate or by business people who moved out from towns and cities to the suburbs and beyond as new means of transport developed. They were less concerned with the issues faced by councillors in urban areas. In many ways the main concern of the counties was territorial preservation against the growth of urban areas and of urban government as towns claimed county borough status and county boroughs claimed more territory.

When the legislation for county councils was proposed their role was envisaged as an intermediate tier of government capable of assuming 'many of the duties now performed by central departments, and in some cases by Parliament' (speech by C. T. Ritchie, the Minister introducing the bill, quoted in Young, 1989, p. 16). The bill provided a mechanism for achieving decentralisation by orders in council, initiated by the county councils themselves. Amendments made in the course of legislation required a further bill to confirm such orders, but that bill failed to obtain parliamentary support. 'The brightest hopes of a sweeping decentralisation of powers had been dashed' (ibid, p. 18). A more limited role for the counties had been established.

The non-county boroughs were largely formed by municipal corporations that did not achieve county borough status. Many, especially where population growth favoured it, sought that status and some succeeded. They joined the 'big league' – the county boroughs – in the Association of Municipal Councils. Their model of local government expressed the aspirations of the civic tradition.

The urban and rural district councils were the newcomers. Although based on the previous sanitary authorities, they lacked the heritage of history, and perceived themselves, and were perceived by others, as junior partners. Smaller size and limited powers gave them a lower status, although they were close to their areas and to those they represented. In much writing on local government they have been neglected, and even condemned for what was perceived as narrow and parochial views.

The London County Council saw itself as a metropolitan authority with wide aspirations dominating in its scale and in its scope the metropolitan boroughs. Its scale set it apart and the size of the metropolitan boroughs meant they were often seen as relatively unimportant.

*Municipal socialism*

In the early days of the Labour movement a doctrine of municipal socialism developed. The London programme, as set out by Sydney Webb, set out an ideal for London based on municipalisation to achieve the socialist dream.

> All this relates more to the comfort than to the maintenance of life, and indeed, it is probable that public ownership of the means of enjoyment will, for a long time, outstrip public ownership of the means of production. But when London's gas, and water, and markets are owned and controlled by its public authorities; when its tramways and perhaps its local railways are managed, like its roads and parks, not for private profit, but for

public use; when the metropolis at length possesses its own river and its own dikes; when its site is secure from individual tyranny, and its artisans' dwellings from the whims of philanthropy; when, in short, London collectively, really takes its own life into its own hands, a vast army of London's citizens will be directly enrolled in London's service. The example of short hours of labour, adequate minimum wages, and regularity of employment set by this great employer of labour will go as far to extinguish the 'sweater', as it will have done to supersede the demoralising scramble for work at the dock gates. The example of the municipal artisans' dwellings and common lodging-houses will co-operate with a drastic administration of the sanitary law in securing for even the poorest London worker at least as good a home as it provided for the meanest of its cab-horses. With decent housing, short hours, regular work, and adequate wages the worker will at last have been placed in a position really to take advantage of the opportunities for civilisation which life in the capital of the Empire should imply. London, clothed, and in its right mind, may at length come to take its proper place in the history of cities, pre-eminent, no longer only in size, but also in all the civilisation rendered possible by the 'higher freedom' of collective life. (Webb, 1891, pp. 213–14)

This represents not just the Chamberlain dream of civic leadership and industrial progress, but of the transformation of society by municipal collective action. The ideals of municipal socialism were given expression by Alfred Salter in Bermondsey, who sought to use the often limited power of the metropolitan borough to change the conditions of working life, not least in health and housing (Goss, 1988). Herbert Morrison in his leadership of the London County Council also gave expression to these aspirations (Donaghue and Jones, 1973). A challenging approach was adopted by Poplarism, as Lansbury and his fellow councillors defied government in the level of payments of national assistance (Branson, 1979). There were even a few authorities that were 'little Moscows' (Macintyre, 1980).

## The growth of national legislation

Starting in the later nineteenth century and continuing over the twentieth century, the role and responsibilities of local government became defined by national legislation. One of the effects was to strengthen the forces for uniformity, although within the legislation there was considerable scope for choice on the level and nature of the services.

The change reflected an extension of the role of central government in social welfare and of the role of local government as its agent. In the nineteenth century the main role of local government focused on the physical environment and to that extent was inevitably locally based. Its new role increasingly reflected national requirements. Schulz described the 1902 Education Act as the 'decisive turning point which divides the nineteenth century local authority which administered services... mainly directed towards the benefit of the neighbourhood and protecting and maintaining property, from the twentieth century which is in addition the agent for numerous personal social services initiated and controlled on a national level' (Schulz, 1948, p. 69). Over time a new model of the role of local government began to emerge. The local authority became increasingly an organisation for the delivery of a series of services prescribed in national legislation.

*Physical development*

In the post-war period, in the urban areas which had suffered severe bomb damage, the planning role assumed a new importance and gave a wider role to urban local authorities. In cities like Coventry, Bristol and Southampton the redevelopment of the city centre was a major challenge, although, given the variety of local government, 'while all three councils recognised that the bombing had provided a golden opportunity for comprehensive re-planning, their approaches were strikingly different' (Hasegowa, 1992, p. 126). In many authorities, it was a limited approach focusing on physical change, neglecting social consequences or economic needs. There was a concept of the role of community leadership, struggling to establish itself, but it was limited in scope.

This emphasis on physical redevelopment in urban areas was associated with the dominance of the professional in the workings of local authorities. The professions of planner, architect and engineer produced the development plans of the 1940s. The councillors' trust was placed in the professionals as guardians of expertise. In the name of the best professional practice, city centres were rebuilt, and redevelopment pursued. Later, disillusion was to grow as the hopes raised were not fulfilled.

## The impact of the welfare state

In the post-war period up to the 1970s, local authorities tended both to lose and to gain functions, and to see existing functions grow and expand in scope. As a major instrument for the delivery of the welfare state, local authorities increased their responsibilities for education, housing and for social services. They gained major responsibilities for town and country planning, but lost responsibilities for health services when the national health service was created and when community health services were transferred to health authorities. They also lost responsibility for major public utilities when gas and electricity were nationalised, and later water.

The period from 1945 to 1975 was a period of growth in local government expenditure financed largely by central government grant. Revenue expenditure rose in real terms from £3,592 million (in 1975 prices) in 1950 to £12,253 million in 1975. Capital expenditure rose even more rapidly from £331 million (in 1975 prices) in 1950 to £4,075 million in 1975 (Foster *et al.*, 1980).

Local government became a major agency in the welfare state with growing responsibilities in education, housing and social services. Whereas in the nineteenth century much of the focus of the local authority was on the infrastructure and on local action to create the physical conditions for healthy urban living, the emphasis was now upon the delivery of services as part of the welfare state. Local authorities were still concerned with the physical conditions of the city, in post-war reconstruction, in slum clearance and in town-centre development. Even in these activities, local action came to be seen as part of a national programme. The building of high-rise flats using systems building dominated the development programmes pursued in many towns and cities, more because such developments were encouraged by the grant structure, by commercial advocacy and by a professional consensus, than because they were the product of local political choice (Dunleavy, 1981).

To a large extent, local authorities had become and saw themselves as agencies for the delivery of a series of separate services on well-established lines. The main task for the local authority was the management of services, and councillors gained their satisfaction from growth in those services. There was a general acceptance of the need for growing services, and the response required was clear, resting on an acceptance of professional expertise. On that basis a consensus was established which governed the policy networks linking central and local government (Rhodes, 1988). Thus, a commonplace of the times was to describe education as 'a national service locally administered', reflecting consensus more than the application of detailed controls.

There were still initiatives taken by local authorities. Sheffield pioneered initiatives for clean air. Birmingham sponsored free bus passes for the elderly, and although this action was held by the courts to be beyond its powers, it later led to general legislation. While such examples could be multiplied they remain exceptions to the general tendencies.

The 1970s were to see a challenge to the post-war settlement which was to grow in the later years. It was given expression in policies of expenditure constraint and in the legislative programme of the Conservative government, and reflected changes in society and in the economy. These challenges are discussed in Chapter 7.

While in the post-war period the emphasis has been on the role of local authorities as agents for the delivery of services covered by national legislation, there have been earlier periods when particularly in urban authorities the emphasis was on local authorities as a political institution expressing local self-government. The civic gospel and municipal enterprise, aspirations of municipal socialism and, to a less extent, authorities' leadership in physical redevelopment in the post-war period all gave expression to that emphasis.

**The recurrent themes**

Certain themes, reflecting choice about roles, run through the development of local government.

*Powers and duties*

In the early part of the nineteenth century, national legislation imposed few duties upon local government and there was little need for central government involvement with local authorities.

Under the influence of Edwin Chadwick, the social reformer, there was a tendency, as with Poor Law reform, to by-pass local authorities and to set up separate bodies. This tendency recurred in the post-war period, reaching its apogee in the Conservative government of 1979 to 1997, except that in the nineteenth century, what were created were not appointed boards, but separately elected boards, each with its own constitution. It led to what Goschen described as 'chaos as regards authorities, a chaos as regards rates and a worse chaos than all as regards areas' (quoted in Lipman, 1949, p. 79), leading to pressure for multi-function authorities. Local authorities gradually accumulated powers and duties which had belonged to such bodies and became recipients of new powers and duties.

However, before that growth of powers and duties on a national basis, local authorities used their own initiative in seeking powers. Some local authorities could claim a competence that came from their charters; its scope was uncertain and was gradually narrowed by the doctrine of *ultra vires*. That doctrine emerged in cases dealing with railway companies, but was extended to local authorities. In one sense the doctrine was not new. Any organisation exercising public authority had to show the basis for that authority. What the doctrine of *ultra vires* did was to give that general requirement a particular application, preventing any development of a power of general competence, which is prevalent in Europe.

In the absence of such a power, local authorities had to seek specific powers to act. Local authorities promoted private bills in Parliament to give them the powers they lacked. This process meant that in the nineteenth century the main relationship of local authorities at national level was with Parliament and not with central government, since Parliament was where local authorities brought problems and issues, and petitioned for powers to resolve them. Over time, private legislation for an authority accumulated, giving it a particular local set of powers. Even when public legislation was passed, it was often in the form of adoptive acts which local authorities could choose to follow, rather than imposing duties on all authorities.

In addition to private legislation and adoptive acts there was the 'legislative function' of local authorities. Redlich wrote about the possibility of 'sub-legislation' in a local authority, distinguishing between regulations which governed its own actions and bye-laws

which governed the activities of its citizens (Redlich, 1903, vol. I).
The municipal corporations had general powers to make bye-laws
for the 'good rule and government' of their areas.

The combination of private legislation, adopted acts, and bye-
laws gave expression to the role of local self-government, responding to local needs. Dependence on private legislation created a
burden for local authorities and for Parliament. 'The enormous
amount of private business which takes up the time of parliament
and the thoughts of its individual members, distracting them
from the proper occupations of the great councils of the nation, is
felt by all thinkers and observers as a serious evil, and what is
worse an increasing one' (Mill, 1904, p. 264). Gradually national
legislation which lay down duties became more important, emphasising the role of local authorities as providers of a series of national
services. Private legislation became of less importance, and even
where undertaken, subject to scrutiny by central government
departments to ensure it conformed to accepted principles. Bye-
laws had normally to be approved by central government departments, conforming to models laid down. As a result, bye-laws are
barely discussed in works on local government and few writers
today would describe them as giving a legislative role to local
authorities. Yet a bye-law remains 'a law which operates over the
area of the authority' (Bailey, 1997, p. 157), embodying in however constrained a form the role of local authorities as local
government.

Despite the dominance of national legislation there remained
scope for local choice. Much legislation governing local government was framework legislation:

> The duties cast on local authorities have generally been drafted
> in broad and often highly subjective terms. Thus the basic duty
> of the local education authority was to 'contribute towards the
> spiritual, moral, mental and physical development of the com-
> munity by securing that efficient education . . . shall be available
> to meet the needs of the population of their area'. This general
> form is quite common.

> The logic of this legal framework, which both conferred sub-
> stantial powers of local authority action and extensive powers of
> central supervision is revealed only once it is appreciated that

its function was to establish a broad framework of inter-dependent relations within which the centre and the localities would be obliged to negotiate and bargain over the manner in which these various governmental responsibilities were exercised. (Loughlin, 1996, pp. 62–3)

Although the dominant emphasis was on the role local authorities took in the delivery of a series of national services, scope for local choice remained. In this way forces both for uniformity and for diversity were sustained.

The issue of wider powers to sustain the role in local self-government has not disappeared. The case for a power of general competence was made by the Redcliffe-Maud Commission. A limited step in that direction was taken by the Local Government (Financial Provisions) Act 1963, which enabled a local authority to incur expenditure up to a 0.4p rate for any purpose which in its opinion was in the interests of the area or its inhabitants, provided such activity was not subject to other statutory provisions. The power was slightly extended in s. 137 of the Local Government Act 1972.

## The structure of local government

Local government reorganisation has been a recurring theme. In the nineteenth century the dominant issue was the creation of elected local government, finally resolved in the last two decades of that century. That did not remove issues of local government structure from the agenda as urban authorities sought extended boundaries or higher status. A Royal Commission on Local Government wrestled with the issue from 1925 to 1929. The Local Government Boundary Commission set up in 1945 was dissolved because its proposed approach was seen as too radical. A later commission was dissolved to make way for the Royal Commissions on Local Government for England and Scotland set up in 1966, while London was subject to reorganisation in 1965 following the Herbert Commission. New structures in Scotland, Wales and England were based on two-tiers with varying distribution of functions in London, the metropolitan counties and the shire counties in England. That did not resolve the issue and further re-organisations were undertaken by the Conservative government creating unitary authorities first in London and the metropolitan counties and later in Scotland, Wales and parts of England. The issue of local government structure absorbed much energy in local authorities. Lee's studies of Cheshire County Council could almost be described as a history of territorial defence (Lee, 1963; Lee *et al.*, 1974).

The issue raises questions about the role of local government. Lipman distinguishes between two broad purposes of local government: 'its function as an instrument of civic self-education' and 'the administration of public services for the benefit of the citizens whether of a particular locality or of the nation as a whole':

> Since local administrative areas have to serve the ends of local government, they can be studied in the light of these two broad classes of purpose. To these classes of purpose there correspond two tests, as criteria of the suitability of local administrative areas. For the fulfilment of the educative purpose of local government, the administrative area needs to approximate to that of a social community, so that civic consciousness may be stimulated and the forces of local interest and sentiment be harnessed to the task of local self-government. On the other hand, for the operation of public services efficiency and economy are the primary requisites. In the choice of suitable areas the desire to give administrative autonomy to a social grouping or community may conflict with the need to obtain the most efficient unit of administration for the provision of public services. (Lipman, 1949, p. 1)

The tension between these requirements runs through the discussion of structure. It was present in the differing requirements placed on Commissions which emphasised both the requirement of community and the effective delivery of services. The instructions of the 1945 Boundary Commission stressed community of interest and related factors, but also had to be guided by the governing principle 'to ensure individually and collectively effective and efficient units of local government administration'. The Redcliffe-Maud Commission had to have 'regard to the size and the character of areas in which these [functions] can be most effectively exercised and the need to sustain a viable system of democracy'. The Local Government Commission for England in 1992 had to have regard

to the need 'to reflect the identities and interest of local committees' and 'to secure effective and convenient local government'.

Issues about structure constitute a continuing theme in which
the balance between the roles of local authorities has been continuously explored.

## The financing of local government

As structure has been a recurrent theme so has the issue of financial resources. Broadly there have been two issues: the extent
and nature of local taxation and the grant system. The Layfield
Committee on Local Government Finance related these to the
role of local government, arguing that the 'financial system should
reflect the roles of the government and local authorities' (Layfield, 1976, p. 83). They contended that a choice had to be made
as to whether 'the main responsibility for local expenditure and
taxation is expressly placed either upon the government or upon
local authorities' (ibid, p. 298), and that, if the latter, local authorities should be given a local income tax in addition to the rates.

This choice is linked to the role of local government. If a local
authority is regarded as an agency for the delivery of a series of
national services, then the case for local authorities having the
main responsibility for local government expenditure and taxation is much weaker, whereas if local authorities are seen as political institutions for local choice, then greater responsibility for
local expenditure and taxation is justified.

With the growth in the duties imposed upon local government,
grants had grown in importance. At the time of the Layfield
report, local authorities depended upon central government
grant for 66.4 per cent of relevant expenditure (i.e. revenue
expenditure less income from rents, fees and charges). Many of
those grants had been specific grants tied to particular services. In
some cases they were percentage grants designed to encourage
expenditure, reflecting the wish of the relevant central government departments to see growth in services.

In the 1950s many specific grants were merged in a general
grant, partly because of the Treasury wished to eliminate percentage grants. It also gave local authorities greater freedom in the
allocation of income, enhancing their capacity for local choice.
Times have changed. Grant, from being a stimulus to expenditure,

became under the 1979–97 Conservative government an instrument for expenditure constraint.


## Conclusion

The roles emphasised in any period reflect choices made both nationally and locally. In reality the choice is never completely made between a political institution for local government and an agency for service delivery. The choice is on emphasis given, and the emphasis has been different at different periods. Yet the choice remains and the themes highlighted never disappear, becoming hidden rivers surfacing at different periods. In the final resort, as Wilson has written:

> The relation of the political to the administrative will be settled by the strength of the perception in the minds of citizens that the political considerations have primacy, that the administrative considerations fit into not over the political. If men are clear that what they hope to get out of local government is not only sweeter drains, roomier buses, greener parks, but an exercise of their own adult civic responsibility and political education then the foundation of local government is sound, and soundly understood. (Wilson, 1948, p. 21)

# 4 The Inherited World of Local Government

## Introduction

Within local authorities assumptions developed about their way of working. These assumptions belonged in part to the national world of local government, being shared by councillors and officers in all authorities, although there are also assumptions particular to individual authorities. The former are forces for uniformity, while the latter can sustain diversity. The assumptions were built up over the history of local government and are part of its inheritance. Between them they constituted a model of how local government should or does behave, influenced by and influencing the role of local government. They constituted the inherited world of local government.

This chapter will outline the conditions formed by dominant assumptions. Those conditions are under challenge, along with the assumptions underlying them, but they have a continuing influence in response to the challenge. Those challenges will be outlined in Chapter 7, and later chapters will record their impact on the workings of local government. To understand that impact it is necessary to understand the inherited world of local government which faced those challenges.

## The committee habit

Committees have been part of the working of local authorities since the origin of elected local government, and before. At one time in the nineteenth century Manchester conducted its business through 18 committees. Historically, local authorities were required to have certain specific committees. Many of these requirements derived from the boards whose powers came to local authorities.

Gradually such requirements were removed, many at the time of the 1974 and 1975 local government reorganisations. The requirement for a local authority to have education committees was removed as part of the Conservative government changes in education. Only the requirement for a social services committee remains as a curious anachronism in England (although no longer in Scotland). Yet the committee habit continues.

The committee system is a dominant condition of local government. It is assumed almost without question that councils conduct their business through an elaborate set of committees. The committee system moulds the working of local authorities, effectively defining the role of councillors. The committee cycle marks out the rhythm of their work. Positions of authority and status are established as chairs or vice-chairs of committees. The committee gives identity to the councillor within the authority. Councillors are likely to describe their committee role as 'I am the chair of housing' or 'I am on the social services and transportation committees'.

In the United Kingdom the council is responsible not merely for policy and the budget, but for all that happens within the council. There is no separate executive as in many other local government systems, or as there is in central government. It would be impractical for the council to conduct its business directly. It would be overwhelmed by the combination of the number of councillors and the amount of business. The council has to delegate, which it does to committees since it cannot delegate to individual councillors, although the law was uncertain until the 1986 Hillingdon ruling (*R* v. *Secretary for the Environment ex parte London Borough of Hillingdon*).

Committee working is the ingrained habit of local government. The committee system used to be seen as one of the strengths of British local government. Redlich stressed 'the extraordinary adaptability of the system to towns of the most diverse size and needs'. 'Its wonderful flexibility', 'its equally wonderful simplicity', its use of 'the special knowledge and talents of individual members', and yet 'there is not stagnation, for recruits bring fresh blood each year and prevent experience from generating into mere routine'. 'It is one of the pillars on which the self-government of English towns rests' (Redlich, 1903, vol. 1, pp. 324–5).

Thirty years later, Laski was to write: 'the committee system has proven itself. It stands with the cabinet and the modern civil service as one of the fundamental English contributions to the difficult art of self government. Its achievements become the more remarkable the more closely they are scrutinised' (Laski, 1935, p. 97).

For Finer, the committee tempered the 'occupational disease of the expert, the incapacity to see his own enthusiasm in due proportion to all the other enthusiasms and interests which constitute the total character of government and humanity. It is the committee's business to introduce and impose the sense of proportion after hearing what science has to say' (Finer, 1933, p. 223). Twenty years later, Smellie wrote, 'There is no better schooling in the art of joint discussion for the purpose of responsible decisions than the committee system of local government' (Smellie, 1957, p. 102).

Such views are rarely heard today amongst commentators on local government. From being a strength the committee system has come to be regarded as a weakness. In the past, and still the norm in the present, the tendency has been for committees to match departments, building a strong alliance of chair and chief officer. The basis of the alliance is that the chair needs chief officer advice and action and the chief officer needs the chair to give legitimacy and to win political support. In that alliance, the role of local authorities as providers of a series of separate services is reinforced. The committee system focuses the attention of councillors on particular services. It enables them to build up specialisms and expertise. That is its strength, but also its weakness. It can narrow councillors' concerns so that they become advocates for the services rather than for the local community.

Committees have a tendency to proliferate. In some authorities there have been over one hundred committees and sub-committees. Authorities have carried out reviews that result in reductions, but over time numbers creep up. In Edinburgh in the late 1920s there was a major review reducing the number of committees. Forty years later all trace of that reorganisation was lost and a new review then proposed a reduction on a similar scale, unaware of the previous review. Nevertheless, there has been a general tendency to reduce the number of committees since the Maud and the Bains reports.

Committees meet at regular intervals with agendas composed of items of current concern. The cycle can be described as undifferentiated, as opposed to one in which meetings are distinguished according to their purpose. In the undifferentiated cycle strategy and performance review can be items on a long agenda. It is hardly surprising that they are rarely discussed, as the chair seeks to fulfil what often comes to be his or her primary task – completing the agenda in a reasonable period of time. The formality of committees is necessary for authoritative decision-making. 'A good chair' is someone who controls the agenda and gets through the business.

The nature of the cycle has an impact on the overall workings of the authority. The cycle set out in members' diaries marks out fixed points throughout the year. While in a majority-controlled authority few decisions are actually made in committees but are made in group or in meetings between chair and chief officer, the time-table of such meetings is determined by the committee cycle. Thus, the main group meeting is likely to be held on the evening before or on the morning of the council meeting, which is the culmination of the committee cycle. The committee cycle determines the rhythm of councillors' work.

The committee cycle sets out the rhythm not merely for the councillors but for senior officers. Preparing for the committee meeting and implementing its findings are important parts of their work. Time-tabled in diaries will be not merely committees, and in some cases sub-committee meetings, but also pre-agenda and briefing meetings with the chairs and sometimes the deputy chair. Reports have to be prepared by specific dates, and by time-tabling, and in some cases this gives a misleading priority to the officers' work. 'We will need that report in time for the next committee meeting' sets a pattern of work.

Committee cycles vary in their frequency, from monthly, particularly in urban areas, to quarterly in some counties. The intensity of the pressures brought about by the committee cycle will also vary with the number of committees, which can be from four to twenty. Meetings are held in the daytime or in the evening. Evening meetings can make it easier for working councillors, but put more pressure on officers and may be resisted by retired councillors.

## The professional necessities

The workings of local authorities have long been based upon the professional principle. Traditionally each department was dominated by a particular profession. Certain professions carried high status: lawyers who had a virtual monopoly of the position of clerk, accountants and engineers. These benefited from history: 'undoubtedly the fact that the engineers were the first "technical" profession in local government was an important advantage for them over other later professions' (Laffin, 1986, p. 62). The maintenance of the district engineer's role in the post-reorganisation district shows the importance of status and professional history. Laffin shows that with the loss of engineering functions, engineers found it difficult to justify their continued presence at that level (Laffin, 1986, p. 63), and therefore extended their role.

Some professions play an important role in local government, but have never gained the same status: environmental health; trading standards; and perhaps housing managers. Within some departments there are groups of staff who do not belong to the dominant group and form 'semi-professions': careers officers; educational welfare officers; building control officers. New roles create new aspirations to professional status.

The professional model expresses continuity, emphasising training at the start of the career for periods that can last three or more years. That training teaches skills and knowledge that define the profession and inculcates the attitudes that distinguish it. Once successfully completed, no further training was required until recently even for administrative tasks, with the result that 'hardly anything in the nature of systematic effort had been made by local authorities either singularly or collectively to secure a high general level of efficiency, administrative ability and trained mental capacity in their effort' (Robson, 1931, p. 295).

Professionalism is a source of stability assuming unchanged or little changed knowledge and skill. Accepted knowledge can develop but only along accepted professional lines. Laffin concluded that 'although in general policy terms, the professions, once established, tend to be forces for conservatism and policy maintenance; in narrower terms they also act as forces for change' (Laffin, 1986, p. 224), and those narrower terms are terms acceptable to the profession.

The profession is for many the centre of loyalty. The professional association carries prestige, and many aspire to a position within it as they aspire to a chief officer position. The professional annual conference is a major occasion, particularly for those professions which focus on local government. The professional normally follows a career that leads from authority to authority as the ladder of advancement is climbed. In this way loyalty to the profession can have greater meaning for the professional than loyalty to an authority.

Professions differ in their culture. Their values differ, as do their ways of working. Each has its own language. The culture of local government is, in part, a set of cultures, each drawing upon its own professional basis, as much distinguished by what separates them as by what they have in common.

In the 1930s the contribution of the professionals was seen as one of the strengths of local government. The literature paid tribute to that contribution. The professionals brought expertise, certified and endorsed by professional qualifications. They brought standards accredited and safeguards enforced by membership of professional associations. Writers critical of the calibre of councillors (for it is no new phenomena to find such criticism) saw in the professional the guarantee of the quality of local government service:

> The fact that the work of local authorities is on the whole so well done, when so few of the ratepayers' elected representatives display either the power or the inclination to undertake any effective supervision of the Council departments, is in itself eloquent testimony, not only to the grip which the responsible officers have of the work to be done, but also of the grip which the work has on the responsible officers. (Hasluck, 1936, p. 82)

The strengths can be a weakness. Professionalism presumes an expertise accredited to be applied in all situations rather than expertise particular to a local authority. Professionalism is therefore a force for uniformity that can challenge the potential for diversity that lies within local government. The tendency to uniformity is reinforced by the career patterns that lead through different authorities. Professionalism can assume an authority that may not always be justified. It can challenge political control, posing professional standards against political choice. There is an 'inescapable tension between the lay councillor's political commitment and sensitivity on the one hand, and the expert knowledge of the professional on the other' (Young, 1988, p. 65).

As a source of continuity professionalism can inhibit change. Professions' accepted skills and knowledge, and professional standards can constitute resistance against the need for change. Professional boundaries can lead to rigidity when flexibility is required. It is not that professions resist all change. Change is part of professionalism, but it is change within accepted limits. Within those limits there can be professional innovators. Indeed the authority given by professionalism can legitimate innovation. The professional chief officer with political support can then be a source of difference and a force for change. The names of Henry Morris in Cambridgeshire (although whether education officers constitute a profession must be uncertain), of Sir Donald Gibson, architect-planner of Coventry, or of Sir Herbert Manzoni, city engineer of Birmingham, had significance in their authorities and beyond, both during their careers and after.

### The bureaucratic habit

Departments are an expression of professionalism but also of the bureaucratic habit. Local authorities are large-scale organisations carrying out a prescribed range of tasks in the provision of services. The bureaucratic habit is a response to that set of duties. Local authorities have been organised for direct control of services, enforced by organisational hierarchies, seeking uniformity of policy and practice. Uniformity of policy and practice was so deeply ingrained that almost the first response of new authorities in 1974 was to seek both, despite the possibility that differences in the predecessor authorities reflected differing needs and aspirations.

The bureaucratic habit is linked in an uneasy alliance with the professional necessities. Professionalism and bureaucracy are structured on different principles. The emphasis of professionalism is on the individual professional whose authority is certified by qualifications. The emphasis of bureaucracy is on the organisation and the rules by which it conducts its business. Professionals working in a bureaucratic organisation resent over-hierarchical or rule-bound control. There is a tension between professional and bureaucratic authority, but also an alliance which serves to enclose the organisation, so that it looks inward rather than outward to the public served. That alliance, expressed as bureaucratic professionalism, came under challenge in the 1980s and 1990s from politicians of the left and the right.

There is a necessity for bureaucracy in the working of complex organisations. In the Arden Report on Hackney, it is recognised that local authorities need sound rules and practice, most notably in financial control. It gives an account of an authority which 'had lost sight of the objectives of bureaucratic controls: accountability, scrutiny, the need to sustain public confidence' and therefore laid itself open to criticism that there was 'chronic waste, an absence of administrative standards, an apparent absence of awareness of the bare essentials of public administration' (Arden, 1987, p. 73). Recently a concern for equal opportunities in recruitment has been enforced by procedural uniformity through bureaucratic rules. The strength of bureaucracy is its weakness just as its weakness is its strength. Impartial application of rules can be lack of responsiveness. Rules can be a necessity but also a hindrance to action.

### The departmental base

Local authorities are divided up into departments, as organisational building blocks for the officer structure. There are departments concerned with services provided to the public and departments concerned with the central organisation of the authority. The boundaries between departments reflect the boundaries between professions responsible for particular services.

Departments based on a series of separate services both express and support the role of local authorities as agents for the provision of services, with central departments concerned with ensuring financial control and legal propriety. Departmentalism can be entrenched by the role, by the professional base and by the committee system. Role, profession, department and committee buttress each other.

The department which most emphasises its separatism is education. The phrase 'local education authority' carries its own meaning, emphasising a separate status. It has a history dating back to 1902 before which there were elected education authorities in England and Wales. The original bill made the local education authority almost independent of the authority, and although changed in the course of legislation, the separate nature of education remained. Prior to the 1974 reorganisation the education committee was not normally serviced by the clerk of the council like other committees, but by the education department. The Association of Education Committees set up after the 1939–45 war played a separate and independent role until effectively killed by the local authority associations after reorganisation.

The balance between bureaucracy and professionalism varies between departments, depending upon the degree of routinisation. In most departments there are routines that have to be carried out, often by administrative and clerical staff. Their work patterns can be different from those of the professional. Contrast the role in an education department of processing student grant applications in the office, with the work of education advisers visiting schools.

There can be tension in departments between the dominant profession destined for positions of power and status, and other staff. Other professions in the department may feel their contribution goes unrecognised. Administrative staff long experienced in the work of departments often resent the upwardly-mobile professional who moves from one authority to another. The massive building blocks that constitute departments have their own divisions within.

Departments are structured for the direct provision of services. Local government had for many years been built on the basis of the assumption of self-sufficiency. It was assumed that a local authority would itself provide the services for which it was responsible and itself employ all the staff required to do it. Given a new responsibility, it was assumed that the local authority would discharge that responsibility itself. Other means of service delivery were not on the agenda.

The assumption of self-sufficiency reflects the role of local authorities as agencies for the delivery of services. From their services they get their identity. It leads to what Finer identified as authorities' 'unyielding local resistance to voluntary schemes of co-operation' (Finer, 1933, p. 157), and he saw as the main reason for this their 'sheer infatuation with the ideas of their own independence, and jealousy of their neighbours' (ibid). If the identity of an authority derives from the services provided, such resistance becomes almost inevitable.

The assumption of self-sufficiency underlay past discussion of local government reorganisation. Larger authorities were advocated because of the need for specialised staff which, it was argued, smaller authorities could not afford. It could almost be said that 'The size of education authorities would be determined by the number of music advisers', because only larger authorities could afford to employ the number required. The arguments were contested by opponents of large authorities, but on the grounds that smaller authorities could afford to employ the specialists required. The assumption of direct employment itself was not challenged, as it could have been by joint appointments, part-time employment or the use of consultants. The assumption of self-sufficiency meant the issues were not even posed.

Local authorities in the past have used outside suppliers for the provision of goods and have used outside specialists or consultants. But for the main provision of services employment by the authority has been the natural assumption. It follows from the bureaucratic habit and the emphasis on direct control. It has not always been so. Particularly, but not entirely, in the smaller authorities, it was customary before 1939 for local firms to undertake the legal and accountancy work of the local authority. The writers of the time argued against such practice and in favour of the direct employment of staff, believing that the practice could lead to 'a clash of interest between public and private affairs' (Finer, 1933, p. 258), building up the case for self-sufficiency.

## Chief officers

At the head of each department is a chief officer. Until the 1974 re-organisation that position was often held for many years up to 65 and even beyond. The long-serving chief officer built status over time. He (for normally it was he) represented the department to the council and often to the outside world.

Within the traditional working of the authority the chief officer was the senior professional and saw the role as professional rather than administrative or management. He spoke with authority and his advice to council or committee was professional advice, which he expected to be accepted. The department spoke through the chief officer, and council and committee were not – and often still are not – expected to hear different views from others in the department.

In most authorities all reports went to committees in the name of the chief officer, and in many authorities all letters went out in his name. The chief officer was the department and the department belonged to the chief officer. If the chief officers' departments were their empires they had little need for contact with other service departments. One welfare chief officer in a large shire county before the 1974 reorganisation told me that he first met the director of education at a conference in London, two years after appointment.

Councillors would treat or were expected to treat chief officers with respect. They would be expected to make appointments if they wished to see them. Relations were conducted on a formal basis. Staff were generally discouraged from speaking to councillors, except when required to do so by the chief officer. In any views expressed, they were expected to be loyal to the chief officer and support his views.

The traditional model of the department was built around the chief officer, who certainly in the large authority was treated as a 'great man'. 'At one time the county surveyor's words were those of a god' said one county surveyor (Laffin, 1986, p. 151). There remains an image of 'what people imagine to be the practices of yesterday, represented perhaps by the austere figures of some of the great education officers and town clerks, of the past who gave strong advice, deflected the authorities from imprudent courses of action and maintained a clear distance from the world of party politics' (Young, 1988, p. 29).

The chief officer would be addressed as Sir by most staff. For many he would be a remote figure rarely seen. One junior solicitor in a clerk's department in a large city, recalled a visit to his section by the town clerk as a major occasion, marred by the clerk not knowing his name. Officers sought to gain experience of well-reputed departments for their curriculum vitae. The chief officers of such authorities would be prominent on the national stage – hence their reputation – and much of the running of their department would fall to the deputy chief officer.

Even if the image has a degree of exaggeration and not all could aspire to the role of the 'great' chief officer, it had a continuing influence on the working of local authorities. The position of clerk had a special importance. The clerk was normally the chief legal officer of the authority. In many authorities in the past the role was played by a local solicitors' firm, and at least one county clerk, although employed by the authority, was paid on the basis of fees for conveyances. The clerk was 'primus inter pares'. Authority came from the law and the reality that a local authority could act only when a legal power could be found. The clerk's role could be constraining, limiting action, or it could be entrepreneurial, seeking out policy space within the complexity of legislation.

The more outward-looking clerk could and did build upon the role so that it was in effect what was to become the role of chief executive. Great figures stand out, dominating the authority, to an extent indeed which few chief executives could do today. Sir Joseph Heron, who was clerk of Manchester for nearly fifty years, spoke out at council meetings and had been known to say to a councillor 'Sit down, you have nothing to say.' On being challenged on his right to speak, as to which ward he represented, Sir Joseph said 'A larger ward than yours, Sir.' 'I represent the entire city' (Simon, 1938, p. 408). Not many clerks went that far but on their position they could build a leadership role, where conditions were favourable. The role became more difficult to maintain as more departments were established and the position and status of other chief officers grew, although some clerks maintained the leadership role because of their personality or a recognised need for co-ordination. Headrick concluded in 1962 that 'the office of Town Clerk is an admixture, for in the office, the traditional functions, the special statutory duties and the response to the need for co-ordination are merged' (Headrick, 1962, p. 30).

### The search for co-ordination

Running through the workings of local government is a tension between the necessity of division and pressure for integration. While local authorities have for long been marked out by their departmental and committee structure, it has also long been recognised there was a need for co-ordination.

Finer highlighted 'a tendency towards the disintegration of the work of local authorities' as a result of the extension of functions.

It is as though a small part-time council of management had been suddenly called upon to run the equivalent of ten or fifteen large businesses with thousands of consumers and scores of employees. Now the instinctive reaction to this is to establish new Departments and division of Departments and to set up for each of the divisions a special committee of management. That is the first reaction. The second may sometimes be the attempt to co-ordinate the policy of all these Departments, divisions and committees into some nationally comprehensive scheme. There is ample evidence that outside a few of the more progressive large boroughs like Manchester, Birmingham and Liverpool, there is not a sufficient apprehension of disintegration. (Finer, 1933, pp. 224–5)

Finer saw the need for an agency in the authority capable of not merely 'planning all activities for today, but of co-ordinating all the relevant factors for a considerable way into the future . . . The necessary features of such an agency are, that it shall be in *permanent* operation, and so placed as to survey all the activities of the Council and the coming years, while preserving detachment from the special interests of each individual branch' (Finer, 1933, p. 233).

Leadership of the council could be provided by the chair of the council, and that role developed particularly in county and district. Chairs could serve for many years. Oxfordshire between 1889 and 1974 had the Earl of Macclesfield and his daughter Viscountess Parker as chairs for all but one period. Sir Offley Wakeman served as chair of Shropshire for over 20 years, appointing a young and dynamic clerk – Geoffrey Godber – and together they brought about major changes in council policies.

In the cities a mayor or lord mayor could play a leadership role, often serving for several years. Over time, the role of the mayor or lord mayor became wholly a ceremonial role, although in London after the First World War both Attlee in Stepney and Morrison in Hackney, appointed from outside the council, gave leadership in that role. The role of leader of the majority party became important and was given ever-increasing recognition, although not till after the 1974 reorganisation was the title of leader of the council widely adopted.

In nineteenth-century Manchester the council was 'broken up into a series of badly co-ordinated committees' (Simon, 1938, pp. 400–1). Conflicts had to be decided at council, where, however, the finance committee's views normally prevailed. Committees resented the finance committee's attempts at supervision. A general and parliamentary committee was suggested as an alternative co-ordinating mechanism because of that suspicion.

Co-ordination focused mainly on the finance committee, but at first it often had limited powers. In Wolverhampton the finance committee was relatively 'feeble' at the turn of the century. It lacked senior members, and 'those who wanted to restrict the freedom of the spending committees turned to the General Purposes Committee' (Jones, 1969, p. 232) containing the most senior members of the council. Even this mechanism proved ineffective and it was not until an embezzlement case in 1917 that the finance committee began to establish overall control.

In the working of authorities a key role in co-ordination came to be played by the budget and by the treasurer, for the finance committee was his committee and one in which the clerk had no clear role. The clerk's role was normally played out in the general purposes committee which contained the leading figures in the authority.

Budgetary processes concentrated on change, which more often in the post-war history of local government meant allocating the increment of growth. The issue was sharing that increment between different departments and between different activities in departments. Budgets specified not merely expenditure on activities, but on different categories of expenditure, such as staff. Once made, the budget was strongly controlled with all but limited virement between budget heads, requiring approval by the treasurer and the finance committee.

In the long years of growth the budget carried an expectation of further growth. Hopes unrealised one year were expected to be realised next year. There was no requirement to challenge existing expenditure. Allocations are easier to agree where all will benefit, and there is the hope of doing better next year. Fundamental change in the balance of resources can be brought about gradually (but by jointed incrementalism rather than by disjointed incrementalism as is assumed to be the traditional budgetary process), and without any department or activity necessarily losing out – what one had, one held.

## Councillor–officer relations

It was argued by researchers for the Widdicombe Committee that there was a model of correct practice in the relationships between councillors and officers.

(a) It is the officer's right to draw up the agenda (although the chairman may request to have items included) and to have sole responsibility for the drafting of committee reports and the recommendations contained therein.

(b) Officers should be provided with facilities for briefing of a committee chairman (and vice-chairman) shortly before a committee meeting. At the meeting the officers would normally take the chairman through the agenda advising him or her how best to deal with each item. At committee, officers would expect to chair the discussion.

(c) Appointment of officers should be on the basis of professional expertise, ability and experience. Officers would expect to be present at appointment panels and for the advice they gave to be a major consideration in the appointment. They would expect to make all appointments below a certain level.

(d) Members should channel their information requests through the chief officer, and/or, by agreement with him, through specified deputies (for specified types of information). Junior officers would have no access to members.

(e) Members should not become involved in the management of the department: that is the responsibility of the chief officer.

(f) Members should concentrate on making policy and leave the implementation of administration of the policy to officers.

(g) Officers should not be expected to have any involvement in the drafting of political manifestos;

(h) nor should they be expected to attend party group meetings (except perhaps in exceptional circumstances).

(Widdicombe, 1986b, pp. 125–6)

The practice has probably always varied. In the nineteenth century, before the development of an officer structure, the chairmen of committees could themselves be engaged in administration. It was probably never as simple as Redlich said:

The respect paid to the higher officials of a municipality and the confidence reposed in them by the committees, the Council, and the citizens at large, are due not to their official position but to their character, their ability, and the importance of their work. It follows that relations between the Council, its committees, and their staff are untinged by bureaucracy, and are characterised by those mutual feelings of loyalty and courtesy which mark the whole of English public life. (Redlich, 1903, vol. I, pp. 352–3)

Nevertheless that model represented to a considerable extent the assumed pattern of correct behaviour. The London Labour Party in the 1930s issued a memorandum to Labour members of London councils saying

The relationship of members of the Council (including Chief Officers), staff, and employees, in connection with the Council's business should be one of mutual respect but not of personal intimacy. Every municipal officer has his defined executive responsibilities; members of the Council have theirs, and they are *collectively* (not individually) supreme in the control of the council. For these respective responsibilities there should be mutual respect, but the relationship should be on a strictly business footing. (Laski, 1935, p. 110)

The model had its impact but there were also tactics to be used in what Lord Snell described as 'dependent-independence' (Snell, 1938, p. 68). 'Since, however, some councillors are liable to be annoyed by advice proffered by officials, officials have been obliged to work out more or less consciously the tactics of winning the confidence and support of committees. They can involve "deliberate diffidence" "a timely and merciful hint" "tactful soundings"' (Finer, 1933, p. 222). The official 'has to win the reality of power without seeming to secure it' and 'to achieve a modus vivendi with his chairman'. But there are councillors 'who enjoy teaching the officials their proper place' (Laski *et al.*, 1935, p. 93).

Councillor–officer relations as embodied in the model of good practice are guided by the principle that an officer's responsibility was to the whole council. It is a claim that the chief officer can still make when there is disagreement on the nature of reports to committees. Where a chair objects to a report, the chief officer can insist on his duty to the council. Normally that would not be lightly done, and most chairs in the final resort accept it, although some who see themselves as 'ministers' might seek to challenge it.

There are assumptions about the relationships between councillors and officers. 'The councils decide policy and the officers implement it' is a convenient assertion. It expresses a formal truth – that in the end only councillors can authoritatively make policy and that in practice implementation can only be carried out by officers. But it conceals the reality that policy is often made in implementation, that implementation influences the making of policy and that officer advice necessarily influences policy. Officers must carry the main burden of implementation but that does not mean that implementation is of no concern to councillors. The reality is a little different from the adage. The distinction between policy and implementation was never and is not clear cut. Myth and reality intertwine in the working of the authority.

## The rituals of local government

Local government has its ceremonies and rituals which are part of its ways of working. The mayor or lord mayor and to a less extent the chairs of councils are often the centre of those rituals. The annual general meeting of the council is the setting for the mayor-making ceremony. The council meeting has its preordained pattern and its combination of tradition and the rituals of political debate. In some councils the councillors are robed. The mayor or lord mayor enters with the mace. Politics have their own rituals which can mark the debate with an intensity all the more remarkable, because it is seen by few and is but little reported.

The rituals and ceremonies have their basis in history. Where there is a perceived continuity over reorganisation and sometimes where there is not, the council agendas of today are not all that different from those of the past. While there can be continuity there is also variation. Council meetings vary in length. In some councils meetings and speeches are time limited, while in others there are no limits. Some councils still have to approve the minutes of all committees, while others take only reports – and in some on a rota basis. In some councils party resolutions are common, while in others there are none.

While in many authorities the council meeting is only a ritual to be observed, in some independent-controlled authorities, council meetings matter, since decisions are made there by councillors. The council meeting can become important when an authority becomes hung. Suddenly the council can make a difference and it is even possible speeches are listened to.

## General uniformities and actual diversity

This chapter has described the inheritance of local government. That inheritance reflects the shared experience and the common discourse of the national world of local government, reinforced by the career paths of local government officers and the folkways by which the national world reproduced itself. The inheritance is to that extent an inheritance of uniformity.

However, what has been described are *tendencies* to uniformity rather than total uniformity. There was in practice considerable variation within shared general patterns. Thus departmentalism is often assumed to have reached its greatest dominance in the post-war period. There are myths about the past that have built up and influence the present. The period from 1945 to 1970 is seen as the golden age of the professional. It was, within this mythology, the period in which councillors accepted professional advice. It was never as simple as that. Local government contained the capacity for diversity within.

The researchers for the Maud Committee found certain general trends, but also diversity:

> There is much contrast between the authorities in the extent to which chairmen are involved in policy initiation and development. Factors such as their interests, their abilities, the time they devote to council work, the length of time they stay in office and the extent to which they are answerable to a party group which takes a strong line on policy issues all vary from case to case. (Maud, 1967, p. 157)

In the number of committees they identified broad trends. Most of the county boroughs over 200,000 in population had over twenty committees, while the non-county boroughs had 'on aver-

age about half as many committees as counties and county boroughs'. But although they presented a general picture, they said
'there is a considerable variation in the numbers of committees
in authorities of the same type and population range', and there
'appear to be a large number of anomalies', by which they meant
small districts having more committees than a large county borough (ibid, p. 6). They found that while many councillors favoured
the devolution of business to officers, many other members
regarded 'detailed control over administrative matters...as a
self-evident ideal' (ibid, p. 288) leading to varying practices.

Some clerks provided leadership which overcame departmentalism. 'In some authorities the influence of the clerk appears to
permeate the whole administration' (ibid, p. 236), but, as Headrick found,

> the office of Town Clerk in each of the 431 boroughs is moulded
> by three factors: organisation or structure, circumstances and
> personality in the broad sense. Where the position has been
> enhanced by the addition of co-ordinating functions, personal-
> ity and circumstances play lesser roles. But this kind of enhance-
> ment is not general, so that whether a Town Clerk is influential
> depends greatly upon himself and the particular circumstances
> in which he is placed. But all three play important parts in shap-
> ing the role of a Town Clerk. (Headrick, 1962, p. 209)

Amongst the 'circumstances' he mentions are the conception the
clerk has of the role, the council's expectations, length of service,
relations with the leader, size of the authority as well as aspects of
personality.

Norton, writing about the post-war period, points out that 'the
styles of County Clerks varied widely', and contrasts Walter
Lane's style of teamwork in Lindsey with Sir Andrew Wheatley as
the 'powerful mandarin' in Hampshire and Sir Edgar Stephens in
Warwickshire whose 'indisputable efficiency bordered on auto-
cracy' (Norton, 1989, p. 68).

In the 1960s the researchers for the Maud Committee found
variation in the extent to which chief officers met together. 'Of
those authorities from which we received information a little less
than half had no regular meetings of chief officers' (Maud, 1967,
p. 232). 'It is significant that, even in our small sample of authorities,

a variety of views were expressed about chief officers' meetings and that when meetings were held they took . . . different forms' (ibid, p. 235). Some included all chief officers, others only a selected group.

Examples of diversity were highlighted by Finer in the 1930s: 'the size, finances and functions of the local authorities, even in the same general category, vary so much and vary in such subtle degrees, that the character of a job even of principal officers, bearing the same designation in two continuous authorities is different' (Finer, 1933, p. 258).

The argument can be pushed too far. There was, and is, diversity, but diversity within defined limits. All authorities had committee systems which shared characteristics, had clerks, had professionally-based departments and faced problems of co-ordination. There was diversity, but within uniformities.

# PART II

# THE INSTITUTIONAL SETTING

# 5 The Institutional Framework

The structure of local government involves both the institutional framework of local government and the internal organisation of local authorities. The former involves boundaries, tiers and functions and is determined by legislation, while the latter involves the means by which the authority carries out its business and is to a large extent under the authority's own control although influenced by the inherited world. The institutional framework determines the rules by which the game of local government is played, and the nature of the internal organisation influences the way that game is played.

## The area of the authority

A local authority is constituted for a particular area. It is only or mainly in that area that the local authority has duties and powers, as it is only for that area that its councillors are elected. The area distinguishes one authority from another and is a major factor in determining its character.

### Scale and population

One element in determining that character is size. Authorities differ substantially in size, both in area and in population. Both have deep effects upon the workings of local authorities, as does the interrelationship between them, expressed in relative density or sparsity.

In Britain, there has been a presumption in favour of large authorities. One distinguishing feature of British local government, when compared with most other countries, is the size of authorities measured by their population. The average size of a

British local authority is about ten times the average size of local authorities in the rest of Europe. While many, although not all, countries have reorganised their local authorities, few have carried it as far as Britain. There is an implicit sizism underlying the attitude to local authorities, an attitude which underlay the reorganisation of 1974 in England and Wales and 1975 in Scotland and also the general approach to unitary authorities in England.

The classic writers on local government encouraged the view that size was associated with efficiency. Small authorities were seen as the problem. Robson attacked 'the large number of small authorities who lack either the means or the will to carry out the functions with which they have been entrusted' (Robson, 1931, p. 92). He went on to argue that:

> Even though the local councillors in these areas were able to combine within their persons the wisdom of a Solon, the inventiveness of a Bentham, and the administrative capacity of a Chadwick, it would still be impossible in most cases for them to accomplish anything of importance without drastic change in the present division of areas and the existing distribution of resources. The shortcomings of the small areas are due to inherent defects in the municipal structure itself. (Ibid, p. 103)

He believed in the need for larger authorities, as a general organisational requirement. 'The nature of local government has changed very considerably during the past twenty years, and just as the technique of industrial and commercial administration now requires far larger units of authority than formerly, so does the technique of efficient municipal administration now demand more extensive units of local government' (ibid).

Assumed minimums or norms of size have dominated discussions of local government for many years. The creation of county boroughs in the period between the creation of the county councils in 1889 and the local government reorganisations of the 1960s onwards were affected by different propositions about minimum sizes. Evidence to the Redcliffe-Maud Commission put forward propositions about the size required to run particular services. The Local Government Commission under Sir John Banham regarded 150,000 to 250,000 population as the normal size required for unitary authorities.

These views have been advanced but with no real evidence in their support. The arguments put forward focus on the administration of services reflected the concept of local government as an agency for the delivery of services. There is little evidence within the range of present authorities of the benefits of size in services provision. As Travers and his colleagues argued, 'Having examined evidence from Britain and overseas, it does not appear possible to argue a conclusive case for a strong and one-directional link between population size and efficiency or effectiveness... there is no one size-range which performs better than others across the range of services. It is not possible to say large authorities perform on the whole better than smaller, or small authorities perform better than larger, even in one specified service' (Travers *et al.*, 1993, p. 4).

Beliefs about size were sustained by the assumptions of the self-sufficient authority and by scepticism about joint working between authorities. One might have thought that the supposed necessities of size were challenged by contracting, but the Local Government Commission revived the arguments in favour of larger authorities by contending that size would enable authorities to achieve more favourable terms in contracts.

Sizism has brought an apparent uniformity to local government, eliminating the smaller authorities found in many other countries. Yet above a certain level (25,000 in Teesdale in England) there is diversity of size (up to over a million in counties and just over a million in Birmingham).

The size of the population influences for any given set of functions the level of expenditure and the number of staff, although that will also depend on the extent to which the authority provides services directly itself. The scale of the organisation has a deep impact on the workings of an authority. Too often local authorities are spoken about as though the issues are the same, irrespective of the size of the authority. Yet 'what is a matter of policy in Bideford may be a matter of execution in Birmingham' (Headrick, 1967, p. 73).

The task of a chief executive in an authority which employs only 300 staff is very different from that of a chief executive in an authority which employs 30,000 staff. It is possible for the chief executive to speak to all staff individually in the small authority. One chief executive in an authority with about 800 employees

used to meet small mixed groups of staff for discussions once each
week, so that over a year he met all staff. Such an approach is
impossible in the larger authority.

Small numbers of staff make it easier to establish a shared culture. Although East Cambridgeshire devolved responsibilities
to a series of cost centres, the chief executive saw no difficulty in
retaining a sense of common purpose. With only a hundred and
sixty employees, 'they are all within a shout'. Ease of communication makes more possible a shared culture. One chief executive in
Warwickshire argued that approaches he had adopted there,
would have been impossible in Nottinghamshire, his previous
authority, because of the effect of scale.

The debate about the effect of scale has a long history often cast
in arguments about efficiency; economies of scale are claimed, but
there are also diseconomies. Joseph Chamberlain believed that
once a certain point was reached (for him it was half a million) 'the
administration disadvantages involved in an increase in population are greater than the advantages' (Redlich, 1903, vol. I,
p. 243). Sizism has tended to dominate. Foster and his colleagues
concluded that although 'it would seem as if all the best arguments were for smallness in elective local authorities . . . all movement almost everywhere has been inexorably towards larger
authorities' (Foster *et al.*, 1980, p. 582). As scale grows so may the
complexity of the tasks faced. The large authority is likely to have
a greater range of problems and issues, although that will also
depend on the homogeneity of the area. Services have to be
organised on a larger scale, which is likely to increase problems of
control. As the scale of the authority grows, so do the problems of
communication, whether it is communication with the population
or with staff. Departments grow in size creating problems within.
In one large city it was said 'the housing department is too big to
be managed'. It was said in one large education department that
'the only way to solve the problems of a large department is not to
have a large department'.

On the other hand, greater scale is likely to mean that the local
authority has greater resources to bear upon the issues it faces.
That can mean the authority can employ specialisms which would
not be available to smaller authorities or undertake major initiatives
by concentrating resources. Much of the debate about scale has
been based on the self-sufficient authority. Contracting out has

undermined the self-sufficient authority. A local authority does not have to employ all staff. Small authorities can draw in specialised skills as required.

On visits to authorities, I have found it impossible to categorise large authorities as always efficient and effective, or small authorities as limited in innovation and outward-looking approaches. Stevenage, Eastleigh, Harlow and South Somerset are amongst the many innovating smaller authorities. In a small authority, assuming the will is there, it is easier to bring about change.

Other factors are involved in the impact of scale. As population increases so does the number of councillors although not proportionately. In England the range of population in district councils and unitary authorities is from 25,000 to one million, but the range in the size of councils is from 20 to 117. The ratio of councillors to population varies from one to a thousand in small authorities to nearly one to ten thousand in the largest authorities. This variation has an impact on the extent of contact between councillors and citizens and on the workload of councillors.

The interplay between the scale of the authority and its ways of working is more complex than much analysis has suggested, and the interplay concerns not merely the efficiency and effectiveness of services but the whole way of working. Some propositions can be put forward:

- There are economies of scale in larger authorities: for example, the management superstructure can be proportionately less than in smaller authorities.
- There are diseconomies of scale in larger authorities: for example, the problems of communication and co-ordination can be greater than in the smaller authorities.
- Innovation can be more easily and more quickly undertaken in the smaller authorities, provided that innovation can be achieved with existing resources.
- Innovation that calls for an investment of significant resources can be more readily achieved in a larger authority.
- Departmentalism can be more entrenched in larger authorities as bigger departments can be relatively self-contained.
- Councillors are likely to represent fewer electors in smaller authorities and can therefore make contact with a larger proportion of them.

- Councillors in smaller authorities can be more involved in detail, with the possibility, however, of weakening management responsibility.
- Councillors in larger authorities are likely to spend a greater proportion of their time on council affairs, with the possibility of more full-time councillors.

These propositions indicate tendencies, rather than necessities. They show the complexity of the interrelationship between scale and the way of working.

*Scale and area*

There is another measure of scale: the area of the authority which, far from increasing with population, may be inversely related. The authorities with the smallest population are often those with the largest area. They include authorities such as Craven, Teesdale, Eden, Cumbria and North Yorkshire, where it is common to find councillors who say 'I represent more sheep than people'. To meet a councillor in Cumbria whose electoral district includes Scafell, Scafell Pike and Great Gable gives one a sense both of area and height!

Inevitably, area and the related factors of density and sparsity have an important impact on the working of the authority. Time taken in travelling becomes an important factor. In Craven it takes some councillors over an hour to travel by car to council offices. In North Yorkshire it can be a day's journey to visit a school from Northallerton, the county town.

The greater area in rural authorities is likely to mean that councillors spend less time in the council offices than in urban authorities. Group meetings are likely to be less frequent. Where councillors live further away they meet their colleagues less frequently. This point may be countered in far-flung authorities such as the Highlands or the Western Isles in Scotland, where some councillors have to stay overnight to attend meetings. Both the cohesion and conflicts in the political groups can be affected by geography. It will be more difficult for councillors to appreciate the problems of areas separated by many miles, than for councillors in an authority based on a single town or city. It is probable that in sparsely populated authorities a higher proportion of councillors live in the area they represent. The politics of geography can be important in rural areas – an effect all the greater if Independents are to be found in any number, and they are found in greater numbers in such areas.

For officers, the problems of knowing their areas is greater in larger areas. There is a choice between time spent travelling and isolation in the council offices. Decentralisation to local offices is one option, but the limited population base and lack of resources may make that difficult. Most communication with out-stationed staff may be more dependent on the written word, e-mail or the telephone.

The authority with a smaller area normally centring upon a town or city, will have opposite features. It is easier for councillors to attend meetings. There are likely to be evening meetings and more group meetings. More frequent contacts may lead to cohesion, but can equally lead to conflict. Councillors are not so likely to live in the areas they represent. The politics of geography are likely to be less intense. In principle, if not in practice, it should be easier for chief officers and senior management to know their area, and to communicate with staff.

Not all these effects are necessarily realised. There are countervailing forces, since area and population are inversely related. Some of the benefits of limited areas – if benefits they are – are cancelled out by the greater size of population. The interaction between scale of area and of population is important in understanding the diversity of local authorities.

### The character of the area

The boundaries set for an authority define an area and give it an identity which can gain meaning over time. 'Boundaries which were the result of historical accident have created loyalties, influenced trade and communications and created offices and expectations' (Smellie, 1957, p. 146).

The area will have its own distinctive problems and opportunities. As John Ransford, the secretary of the Association of Directors of Social Services said in his evidence to the Hunt Committee, 'Their needs differ, and certainly the way in which they want to receive services culturally will differ. It will differ from, say, a former mining community to a suburban community. People will have different expectations' (Hunt, 1996b, p. 34). The extent of deprivation, the nature of the physical infrastructure and the economic health of areas vary. These differences derive from the social, economic and environmental geography of the country, but the boundaries determine the particular combination within a local authority's area.

There is a critical choice in drawing boundaries as to the extent to which areas should be relatively homogeneous or whether they should be heterogeneous. A particular choice is whether suburban areas should be included in the same authority as the inner city. In the United States it is commonplace to draw boundaries between the two. In Britain many towns include suburban areas, although because urban boundaries have been maintained unchanged over time, even after unitary status, there are now significant suburban areas beyond the urban boundaries. In the recent reorganisation only York extended its boundaries amongst the unitary authorities, although there were some amalgamations of adjacent authorities. In London, there are inner-city authorities such as Hackney, Tower Hamlets or Southwark and suburban authorities such as Sutton, Bexley or Harrow, while in others such as Brent there is a mixture of areas.

A particular choice is whether town and country should be combined in the same authority. The Boundary Commissioners charged with implementing the Municipal Corporations Act of 1835 were clear on their choice. 'We also thought it important in settling the limits of each borough to include within it only a town population having the same views and the same interests, whereas, whenever a rural district is part of a borough, dissensions easily arise from a real or even a supposed diversity of interests, which are likely to increase with the increasing wealth of the borough' (Redlich, 1903, vol. I, p. 231). The Redcliffe-Maud Commission made a different choice, arguing that there was a 'growing interdependence of town and country' (Redcliffe-Maud, 1969, paragraph 243). Although the recommendation of the Redcliffe-Maud Commission for unitary authorities outside the metropolitan areas was rejected by the Conservative government, their views on combining urban and rural areas were given expression in the boundaries of both county and district. Humberside was a storm-tossed amalgamation of the incompatible rural East Riding and the politics of Hull, tied in turn to North Lincolnshire with its own mixture of town and country, by the thin thread of the Humber Bridge.

The Redcliffe-Maud Report recommended a similar approach in the three metropolitan counties that it proposed since their proposed boundaries extended beyond the built-up area. This proposal was largely rejected by the Conservative government for those areas. There was, however, a contrast between West Yorkshire and South Yorkshire areas (where metropolitan counties were introduced, although not recommended by the Redcliffe-Maud Report) and the other metropolitan areas. As a result of the abolition of the West Riding County Council the boundaries of Bradford and Leeds extend far beyond the core cities, including rural areas and moorland.

Another choice is the extent to which distinct towns or areas are brought together in the same authority. The prosperous and affluent area of Solihull also includes the former Birmingham overspill housing estate of Chelmsley Wood. Sefton includes the different areas of Southport and Bootle and the area between, with the consequence that

> the council is geographically unstable. There are different aspirations and some antipathy between residents of the different settlements, especially between Bootle and Southport, and this is reflected in councillors' attitudes (or in public perception of their attitudes) in decision-making. These geographical differences tend to be reflected in the pattern of political representation, which sometimes leaves a major party unrepresented across the whole of a major settlement. The geography has more than less often proved a stronger force than local politics. (Local Government Commission, 1997, p. 16)

Lancaster District Council brought together Morecambe, the old seaside resort, with Lancaster, the historic and university town. Many shire districts are combinations of small towns which in nearly any other country in Europe would be local authorities in their own right. Tendring brings together Harwich and Clacton, Wychavon brings together Droitwich, Pershore and Evesham. Identity is hidden by the names, since the council dared not take the name of any one town. The same is true of some metropolitan districts. Kirklees contains Huddersfield and Dewsbury as well as other small towns.

The artificiality of these authorities has often had the perverse effect of the authority being over-concerned to establish its identity. They have been reluctant through decentralisation and in policy to recognise that identity may be best based not on the authority, but on the areas and communities within.

Whether an area should be homogenous or heterogeneous is a disputed question. If the local authority is seen as the means by which individuals can choose the distinctive mix of services that suits them, then that is most likely to be achieved in homogenous areas. Homogeneity can also be an argument for smaller authorities: 'The smaller the population the better local authorities can reflect the wishes of their inhabitants' (Foster *et al.*, 1980, p. 560). If the role of the local authority is seen as reconciling and balancing differing interests, then the case for heterogeneity is stronger.

Heterogeneity or homogeneity will affect the range of problems and the ways they are handled. The planning issues are different for an authority whose area includes the town and the area around it, from one restricted to the built-up area. The way such issues are handled will vary with the relative weight of particular areas within the authority.

The politics of authorities reflect the area. The greater the heterogeneity the greater the likelihood of political change. In Sutton the spring line where the chalk hills turn into clay, marks not merely geology, but social (from stockbroker land to professional and public service) and political composition (from solid Conservative to Liberal Democrat with two Labour islands in ex-GLC estates). There are by contrast inner-London boroughs where the Conservatives have rarely, if ever, gained more than a handful of seats and outer London boroughs where the same is true of Labour. If there is to be opposition it must come from the Liberal Democrats, as it did to the extent of gaining power in Tower Hamlets and in Richmond. Hung authorities grew in number because of the combination in the counties and in some shire districts of rural areas where the Liberal Democrats were the main opposition to the Conservatives, with urban areas of Labour strength – becoming less likely in some counties with the creation of unitary authorities. In the urban areas outside London as well as within it there are authorities whose area, at least in normal times, ensures permanent one-party control.

The character of a local authority reflects the nature of the area. Local government is necessarily linked to geography, but the impact of geography is determined by the way the institutional framework defines the area which shapes politics and pressures as well as problems and opportunities.

## The tiered structure

In much of the country there has always been a tiered system of local government. Indeed the legislation creating county councils originally envisaged only a limited number of county boroughs as all-purpose authorities. The number grew as legislation was discussed in Parliament. In the rest of the country there was a tiered system of counties with urban districts, rural districts (and parishes) or non-county boroughs in the shires and the London County Council and the metropolitan boroughs.

The tiered system was extended by the 1974 and 1975 local government reorganisations. Indeed it became universal except in the Island authorities in Scotland. In England, there was a difference in the division of functions between the tiers. The main responsibilities of local government, at least as measured by expenditure (in particular education and social services), were placed at the county level in the shire area and at the metropolitan district or London borough level in the metropolitan areas and in outer London (with, in inner London, education the responsibility of the Inner London Education Authority and social services being the responsibility of the London boroughs).

The relationship between the tiers of local government is not hierarchical, although there were tendencies to such a relationship in the pre-1974 counties. Yet the differing scale of authority and the distribution of functions had an impact on the relationship between tiers. In the shire area the county was not merely a larger authority but had the greater share of the functions of local government. County councils saw themselves as the major authority. In addition in most cases after the 1974 reorganisation the county councils saw themselves as continuing authorities as opposed to many of the shire districts which were amalgamations of previous authorities. Resentment was naturally greatest in the former county boroughs which were former most-purpose authorities with a strong sense of history as well as of a scale which they felt could and should encompass a wide range of functions. There was in many other districts a resentment against what was seen as the counties' presumption of superiority.

In the metropolitan areas the balance was different. Whereas the county had a larger scale in both area and population, it lacked education and social services, so that the greatest share of expenditure was at metropolitan district level. Most of the metropolitan districts were former county boroughs representing distinctive areas with a long history, as opposed to the metropolitan county with no history or shared sense of identity. The districts could and did continue to see themselves as the major authorities.

The Greater London Council covered an area recognisable as London and inherited the traditions and the buildings of the London County Council. The lower tier of London boroughs were all small in relation to the scale of resources of the Greater London Council. There were 32 London boroughs and the City of London, marking a contrast with the number of metropolitan districts in the metropolitan counties, which was as few as four in South Yorkshire, and no more than ten in Greater Manchester. In London, the Greater London Council saw itself as the major authority and was a focus of attention in a way that did not apply to the metropolitan counties.

The London boroughs were mostly newly created amalgamations of smaller metropolitan boroughs with limited functions. Many of them lacked and lack a distinctive area with an identifiable centre so that one cannot tell other than by road signs whether one is in Hackney, Camden or Islington. They have been described as 'constituted as largely arbitary slabs and slices of the built environment without clear geographical boundaries on identities, only very weakly capturing the loyalties of local social or economic elites or of local "communities"' (Dunleavy *et al.*, 1995).

In the 1980s and 1990s the institutional framework changed with the abolition of the metropolitan counties, the Greater London Council and later the Inner London Education Authority. This change was followed by the creation of unitary authorities in Scotland and Wales and in parts of England in the reorganisations of the 1990s. The Labour government has introduced legislation to create a new Greater London Authority with a strategic role, leaving the London boroughs with their main functions.

The abolition of the metropolitan authorities and the Greater London Council did not mean the transfer of all their functions to the metropolitan districts and to the London boroughs. Most of the expenditure remained at the metropolitan level where these functions were exercised by joint boards responsible for police (since made the responsibility of a separate police authority), public transport, waste disposal, and fire and civil defence. Joint boards were also created in London, although on a lesser scale because of the responsibilities exercised by central government.

Joint boards were composed of councillors, appointed by the constituent councils. The working of joint boards is affected by their separate status, leading to members seeing their responsibility to the board rather than to the authority that appointed them. Joint boards are indirectly elected single-purpose authorities. They became part of the new complex structure of community government but with a distinctive institutional link to local authorities.

In the newer unitaries, joint committees and joint boards have been created, but on an *ad hoc* basis varying from area to area, in some cases by voluntary agreement and in others by statutory orders. In England (except where the county has been abolished) the joint arrangements are between county and unitary authorities, with the county normally having a majority of the votes.

## The functions of the authority

### The unitary authority

The search for the 'the unitary authority' dominated the recent process of local government reorganisation, leading to unitary authorities in Scotland and Wales and adding 46 unitary authorities to those already existing in Greater London and in the metropolitan areas. To an extent the phrase 'unitary authorities' is an illusion, focusing as it does only on the functions of local government at a particular time. It represents the belief that all those functions should be carried out by a single tier of local government, but ignores the extent to which functions previously carried out by local authorities are carried out by special-purpose boards.

The aspiration to unitary status was most marked in those authorities which saw themselves deprived of status in the reorganisations of 1974 and 1975. Proud cities saw themselves reduced to shire districts and never accepted their reduced role. The belief in unitary authorities, particularly in urban areas, drawing upon a long history, was deep. It seemed common-sense that it was the right way to run local authorities. It had been the main recommendation of the Redcliffe-Maud Commission for most of the country. The Commission based its recommendations on its view that 'where a county borough under strong leadership has co-ordinated its services and set out to achieve objectives through the use of all its powers, it has been the most effective local government unit we have known' (Redcliffe-Maud, 1969, paragraph 252). In these views the Commission reflected a consensus of writers who drew upon nineteenth-century opposition to *ad hocery*, which led Mill to argue that 'there should be but one elective body for all local business, not different bodies for different parts of it' (Mill, 1904, p. 271). There was admiration for city government in the

> general realisation that city government is in practice more democratic and popular than county government, notwithstanding that the franchise is legally the same in both cases. This is due partly to the long distances to be travelled and the time and expenses involved in attending meetings of the county council and its committees at the county town; partly, no doubt to the discontent and apathy of the local population caused in certain cases by the failure of the county councils to provide satisfactory services, coupled with the impossibility of obtaining sufficient representation on the council to secure redress. (Robson, 1931, p. 133)

The unitary authority came to be accepted as the ideal form of local government, so that counter-arguments were not even considered until the Banham Commission began to encounter problems in its search for unitary authorities in England. Because of sizism the Commission assumed that unitary local authorities normally had to be over 150,000 in population. A tiered system makes possible smaller authorities, closer to their electorate for functions that do not require larger areas, even though that advantage has not been fully realised in this country.

In practice the outcome of the process of reorganisation has meant that while there are unitary authorities mainly in the urban areas and in Wales and Scotland, much of England remains with a tiered system.

### The multi-function authority

However, whether the local authority is a so-called unitary authority, a shire district or a county council, it is a 'multi-function authority'. A multi-function organisation faces what Vickers has called the 'multi-valued choice' (Vickers, 1972). It has to choose between conflicting purposes or values. There is no overriding purpose that can determine the choice – it must rest upon political judgement as to the *relative* value to be placed on different purposes. The budgetary process of local authorities is governed either explicitly or implicitly by the choice on the balance to be placed on differing purposes. It is not an *absolute* choice between one purpose and another, for no authority can abandon expenditure on roads or care of the elderly. The budgetary process although carried out in different ways is moulded by the choice or the balance between different purposes, even when that choice is not made explicitly. The choice between different purposes is not limited to the budgetary process. In one district council, set in an area of outstanding natural beauty, the council was committed to conservation, but also, because of unemployment, to economic development. In many cases coming before the planning committee, these concerns were in conflict. Councillors and officers sought to achieve the 'right' balance between these concerns, and in the end that had to be a matter of judgement.

From the multi-functional nature come a number of characteristics, the response to which can vary from authority to authority:

- The necessity of the multi-valued choice and the degree to which it is favoured.
- The search for balance, and the extent to which it is appreciated.
- The capacity for synergy and the extent to which it is realised, for services can complement each other.

*The range and mix of functions*

The range of functions seems more dependent on historical accident than on any worked-out approach to the government of
local communities. Certain functions seem inherently to belong to
local government – and are so found in most countries. They are
related to locality and grounded in the physical infrastructure.
Refuse collection, parks, street cleansing, local roads, are almost
necessary functions for local government, but beyond that there is
variation between countries and over time.

The nature of a local authority and its working are in part a
reflection of its perceived role, but roles perceived are in part
a reflection of functions. Roles changed from the nineteenth-
century focus on the physical infrastructure to concern for the
social condition because of growing responsibilities for education
and social services, although there was a post-war emphasis on
town-centre redevelopment and large-scale clearance schemes.
The removal of public utilities had an impact not merely on role
but on ways of working. The presence in most urban authorities
of major trading functions had its influence on the nature of the
authorities. It tended to sustain departmentalism, as each public
utility had its own committee and its own department with separate accounts. For Page in the 1930s the issues of co-ordination
included whether one meter-reader could cover both electricity
and gas (Page, 1936). The culture of local authorities is in part a
product of their functions. The disappearance of many health
functions in local authorities removed the powerful medical profession from the officer structure, and meant its impact on the
culture was lost.

The way functions are divided between authorities in a two-tier
system also influences the way of working. The relative status of
professions can be affected by the particular mix of professions.
The nature of political weight given to a service may depend on
the other services in that authority. Thus in the metropolitan
county, trading standards gained importance as one of the few
direct services for the public. In metropolitan districts and the
new unitary authorities, trading standards has much less political
significance, and hence, less status. The relative status of particular chairs, committees and chief officers is a product of the functions of an authority. The presence or absence of education and

social services has an impact on the status and political weight of other services.

Depending on the mix of services, the budgetary issues faced by local authorities also vary. Whether education is or is not a function of the local authority has an important effect on the budgetary equation. When education was added to inner London boroughs following the abolition of the Inner London Education Authority, social services was no longer the 'big spender' but found it had a rival for political attention. The shire districts which became unitary authorities have found that far from having more resources for existing services, education and social services have greater political claims, putting pressure on resources for services that had hoped to gain from unitary status.

### The financing of local government

The financial basis is part of the institutional framework. It was subject to major change over the lifetime of the Conservative government aimed at central control over local government expenditure. That has not always been the approach of central government. As the Audit Commission has argued, it 'would be wrong to characterise the history of local government as one of central government always attempting to restrain local government expenditure and activity. In the latter half of the last century and in the period after 1945 central government used local authorities to expand services and encouraged capital expenditure' (Audit Commission, 1997c, p. 9).

The basis of local taxation was changed from the rates to the community charge and then to the council tax. Local authorities' taxation powers were subject to capping. Grant systems were changed and changed again as the government sought to use them to control local expenditure. Controls over capital expenditure have been changed almost continuously. Instability in the financial structure has been a condition of local government.

The changes are influences for uniformity:

> In particular, strong national media, the spending expectations created by service-based SSAs, the visibility of nationwide performance indicators, the Treasury's desire to control overall

public expenditure and high-profile central measures to deter 'irresponsible' local authority behaviour have all contributed to a presumption that if a local authority makes decisions that deviate from the national norm, there must be something wrong. (Hunt, 1996b, p. 71)

The financial framework has an impact on the relationship of the authority to its public. The council-tax demand, like the rates and the poll tax before it, has a visibility that marks it out as different from most national taxes which are normally paid automatically, as VAT is paid when goods and services are purchased or as income tax is paid through PAYE. The council tax does not automatically increase its yield with either income or expenditure. It has to be raised each year. The payment of the tax can be the public's main visible relationship with the authority, since services are not automatically identified by the public with the authority, but with the school, the library or the staff providing the service.

A local tax can be argued to be a condition of local choice. In the institutional framework that choice has been restricted both by capping and by the dependence of local authorities upon central-government grant leading to the gearing effect (or a relatively small percentage increase in expenditure leading to percentage increase in taxation three or four times greater). Such features limit local accountability since local authorities (and probably increasingly the public) see their financial position as more dependant on the decisions of central government than on their own expenditure decisions.

The Labour government has argued that it will replace 'crude and universal capping' (DETR, 1986), and has taken powers under the Local Government Act 1999 to add to the factors to be taken into account in determining whether to cap an authority. It remains to be seen how these provisions will be applied in practice. The dependence upon central government grant will remain largely unchanged.

### Electoral arrangements

Elections are determined, and have been determined since the present structure of local authorities was built up, on the first-past-the-post system, although in the past-elections to other local bodies were determined in different ways. In the nineteenth century, elections to school boards enabled minorities to be represented with multiple voting for the number of places, allowing all one's votes to be cast for one candidate. The first-past-the post system inevitably means that there is a greater likelihood of majority control, although in recent years the strength of the Alliance and later the Liberal Democrats has made hung authorities more common.

Electoral arrangements are not uniform. In counties, London boroughs and the new Welsh unitaries, elections are held every four years. In the metropolitan districts, elections of a third of the council are held every year except the fourth year in which the metropolitan county councils used to be elected. Shire districts and unitary authorities in England have the right to choose between all-out elections and elections by thirds. In the new Scottish unitaries, elections are held every three years. Changes are proposed by the Labour government, which involve an extension of annual elections and the introduction of biennial elections in counties and shire districts.

The practice in a particular type of authority is accepted as the norm by officers and councillers in such authorities. In London boroughs the Labour government's proposal to hold annual elections is seen as creating major problems, whereas metropolitan districts cannot see what the problem is. The differences have an important influence. There can be a more sudden turnover with four-year elections as opposed to the gradual changes in the composition of the council brought about with elections by a third. The political cycles can have an effect on the financial cycle, with balances likely to be more heavily drawn upon in election years where there are four-year elections. There is an impact on strategy with the four-year term, setting a political horizon which may not exist with annual elections. Political attention may focus more on electoral matters in election years, while in other years they may centre more on elections in the political group!

Other factors in electoral arrangements are the number of councillors in electoral districts, which can vary from one to three, even in authorities which have elections by thirds. The number of councillors per ward affects, other things being equal, the number of electors represented and arrangements for sharing constituency work.

The size of the council is partly determined by population and by functions, but there can be variations. The size of the council has an impact on the size of groups. A majority Labour group of 87 in Birmingham in 1996 was different from a group of 29 in Redditch , although the latter was seen as a large group in the experience of that authority. The ratio between chairs and vice-chairs and backbenchers and the nature of group working are all affected by the size of the council, and the political arithmetic. In the Portsmouth unitary authority the Labour group had 21 members out of 39 in 1996, which meant that virtually every member held a chair or vice-chair position.

The size of councils in Scotland has been and is different from England and Wales where virtually all councils have at least 30 councillors (although Rutland has only twenty councillors, even though a unitary authority). A number of the former Scottish district councils had 12 or less councillors and five of the new unitary authorities have 20 or fewer.

If the council has even numbers the council can be tied, requiring the casting vote of provost, chair or mayor. Who holds that position can give a particular group a majority. The election of the provost, chair or mayor is then crucial. The tie is resolved in England and Wales by the casting vote of the previous mayor or chair, and in Scotland by lot. Chance or chance by the accident of who was mayor or chair before determines the outcome of who controls the council. It would be much simpler if all councils had odd numbers, so the need for a casting vote did not arise!

## The framework of accountability

Local authorities are subject to electoral accountability but the institutional framework also contains provisions which enhance or sustain accountability. The Local Government (Access of Information) Act gave the public greater access to the meetings of the council, its committees and sub-committees and to the information on which their business is based than any other institution of government. It has direct effects both in opening up the formal working of the authority and in driving deeper underground the informal discussions which underlie that working.

Local authorities are subject to external scrutiny by the courts and there has been an increase in litigation (Loughlin, 1996; Bridges *et al*., 1987). The ombudsman considers cases of alleged maladministration leading to injustice. The auditors appointed by the Audit Commission have responsibility for probity as well as reporting on economy, efficiency and effectiveness. The responsibilities of auditors will be extended in a 'best value' regime. Surcharge with disqualification can be imposed by the courts on councillors and officers on the basis of a finding by the auditor, although the Nolan Committee recommended the abolition of these processes in favour of other mechanisms, and the Labour government proposes Standard Boards to enforce codes of conduct.

Local authorities have to appoint a monitoring officer with a duty to submit a report, which must be considered by the council within 21 days, on any contravention of any enactment, rule of law or code of practice or on any example of maladministration. Equally the chief finance officer has to submit a report on any decision to incur or likely to cause illegal expenditure. External and internal scrutiny reinforce public accountability. It leads to a proper caution, but if carried too far can maintain excessive adherence to rule and documented procedures.

While these institutions sustain a necessary uniformity of proper practice, they can extend their influence beyond that necessity. It is possible for both the external and the internal institutions to move beyond their specified remits to consider issues of policy and local choice. Recommendations on best practice by the Audit Commission may be an influence limiting diversity. The ombudsman may gradually be led from questioning the administration of policy to questioning the policy itself.

One monitoring officer submitted twenty reports in a year to his council, many of which were complaints that the council had not paid attention to his previous reports objecting to the council's insistence that the treasurer be part of the management team. Such examples are however rare. Care is exercised by monitoring officers not to abuse their position. Many have been reluctant to use their formal powers. That does not mean they have no influence. A monitoring office may tell the leadership 'If that happened I am afraid I would have to report on it as a monitoring officer.' The treasurer will say 'The Auditor would not stand for it', and may even have had a word with the auditor to ensure it. Or it

will be said, 'That will make a case for the ombudsman.' In the discourse of local government these institutions have their impact.


## The structure of community governance

Local authorities are set in a network of institutions, including:

- other local authorities in tiered systems, including parish and
  town councils
- adjacent authorities
- joint boards
- joint committees
- partnerships or trusts constituted by local authorities
- urban development corporations, city challenge boards and
  housing action trusts
- health authorities and health trusts
- training and enterprise councils
- the governing boards of educational institutions
- police authorities
- national park authorities
- regional development agencies
- regional and national bodies operating a local level
- central government departments and agencies operating at
  local level.

In addition, one could include, as a part of the network, private or
voluntary bodies charged with governmental functions.

  This complex system impacts on local authorities directly.
Many local authority services are closely related to services provided by these bodies. The work of social services is related to the
health services, and the formal legislation requires co-operation
as symbolised, although not necessarily achieved, by the creation
of joint committees. The work of local authorities in economic
development is closely related to the work of training and enterprise councils, and to regional development agencies.

  There is interaction between the role of local authorities and
the relationship to the system of government. If the role is seen as
mainly the provision of services, then the interrelationship will
be limited. If the local authority role is community leadership

concerned with the overall economic, social and environmental well-being of its area as proposed by the government, then it will be concerned with many aspects of the bodies discussed. Depending on the role, different patterns of relationship will develop, as discussed in Chapter 13.

## Internal structure

The institutional framework influences the internal structure of the council. It constitutes the council as the source of authority for all actions taken in the name of the authority. That distinguishes the position of the council in the United Kingdom from systems in which there is a political executive in the form of an elected mayor, appointed mayor or a cabinet. Such systems seperate the representative or quasi-legislative role of the council from the executive role. In the United Kingdom all roles have had the same basis in the authority of the council. This can mean the legal form does not represent the actual form. As Caulcott has written, 'the legal form of a local authority pays no regard to the reality of power . . . a local government officer is the servant of the whole council . . . The reality is that if one party has a majority on the council, then that party acts as the government of that council and officers have to answer to them' (Caulcott, 1996, p. 81).

The Labour government has legislated a directly elected mayor for the new Greater London Authority. It proposes legislation to encourage local authorities to adopt structures based on a separate executive. For the time being the internal structure remains based on the overall authority of the council. The council can and does delegate its authority to committees, which can delegate to sub-committees or to officers. The council's authority cannot be delegated to an individual councillor, which means the chairs of committee do not have formal authority in their own right, but the practical authority that comes from their ability to command a majority on the committee, although this may not apply in a hung authority.

Under the Local Government and Housing Act 1989 it is not possible to constitute a committee composed of representatives of only one party. One-party committees or sub-committees had developed in at least a third of authorities, not normally as decision-making bodies, but as settings for discussions between the political leadership and the chief executive and other chief officers. In Coventry a one-party Policy Advisory Committee existed from 1938. The practice was growing because it enabled the official structure of the authority to reflect the political reality of majority control. The system was evolving in some authorities towards a semi-cabinet system. The legislation limited the gradual evolution of the system towards new models. It is ironic that the Conservative government which introduced this legislation was later to issue a consultation paper on internal management which proposed amongst other models a cabinet system for local government (Department of the Environment, 1991), proposals now adopted by the Labour government.

## Conclusion

The institutional structure is both a source of uniformity and a source of diversity. It defines a common framework for local authorities, although within that framework there can be significant variations in the type of authority, both in function and electoral basis. It defines the areas of authorities, and it is the differences between areas which is the main basis for diversity in local government. The institutional structure is a basis for continuity, yet change is possible and has taken place. Tiers, functions and finance have been subject to considerable change and this is likely to continue.

# 6 The Conditions of Central–Local Relations

Central government has an influence on the workings of local authorities as a force for uniformity – or at least intended uniformity. Central government initiates the legislation which constitutes the institutional framework within which local authorities act. Its policies implemented through legislation, regulations and controls constrain the workings of local authorities. Central government, both directly and more recently through the next step agencies, acts directly in the process of community governance.

## The metaphors

Various metaphors have been used to describe central–local relations. Rhodes has argued that, in the past, debates took place between those who saw the relationship as one of 'partners' and those who saw it as one of 'agency' (R. Rhodes, 1981). Neither word captured the complexity of the relationship. Partnership suggests joining together in the pursuit of shared aims, which only partly describes the relationship, since there are occasions on which a local authority and central government will be in disagreement on both aims and means. Agency implies a principal–agent relationship in which the local authority carries out the wishes of central government, making no allowance for independent action by local authorities.

Rhodes used the language of 'networks' and 'resource-exchange', as metaphors which capture the aspect of the central–local relationship in which central government and local authorities seek to influence each other (R. Rhodes, 1988). Its weakness, as Rhodes recognised, is the superior resources deployed by central government. It ignores the element of 'hierarchy' in the relationship, itself a metaphor which reflects the ability of central government to instruct a local authority through legislation or powers given by legislation.

Other metaphors have been put forward. Bulpitt used 'dual polity' to describe the relationship over much of the century, distinguishing the national concerns that occupied central government from those issues it was content for local government to deal with. Rather than partnership or agency, he posited separation (Bulpitt, 1983). Saunders too separated the concerns of central government from those of local government in his metaphor of the 'dual state'. This metaphor distinguished between the social investment and social consumption functions of the state. He argued that the former are carried out mainly at national level and the latter at local level, but that tensions can arise between them (Saunders, 1982).

The reality is that no simple metaphor can describe the relationship. 'Partner', 'agency', 'networks', 'hierarchy', the 'dual state' and the 'dual polity' all capture aspects of the relationship which can gain greater or lesser prominence at different points in time. Sometimes and in some places, the relationship can be one of 'conflict' or one of 'co-operation'. At times, central government will be acting as 'judge' between different bids or as 'arbitrator' between different local authorities or between local authorities and other bodies; and central government and local authorities can have a 'learning' relationship when central government learns from the initiative of local authorities and local authorities draw upon the expertise of central government. The relationship can take many forms (Griffith, 1966) and can use many instruments (Chester, 1951). Rather than capture the relationship in a single metaphor this chapter sets out the conditions of the relationship, within which different patterns can develop and different metaphors be justified.

## The conditions of the relationship

*The place of local authorities in the system of government*

Because there is no written constitution, local authorities derive their position solely from legislation. They have been set up by statute and could be abolished by statute, although the Labour government's action in ratifying the European Charter of Local Self-Government accepts that 'the principle of local self government shall be recognised in domestic legislation, and where practicable in the constitution' (Council of Europe, 1985, Article 2).

Standing over local authorities is parliamentary sovereignty and the oft-repeated statement that the United Kingdom is a unitary state. Because there is no written constitution, there is no constitutional foundation for local authorities, even though local authorities could be argued to be part of the constitution. These conditions support an assumption of hierarchy in the relationship.

### The basis in elections

Both central and local government are based on elections. They give each an elected basis of authority that can and has led local authorities, particularly in periods of high conflict, to oppose policies of central government, normally within the law.

Both central government and most local authorities are controlled by representatives of political parties. Where they are controlled by the same party, councillors will use political contacts to influence central government and central government may appeal to party loyalties. Where they are controlled by opposing parties, as they tend to be increasingly over the life of a Parliament, councillors will be less able to use political contacts, although they may be helped by councillors of the government party, where there is agreement, as there often is, about the welfare of the area.

### The divided worlds

There are deep divides between the worlds of local government and central government, so that one can almost describe them as two worlds acting in isolation and in ignorance of each other. It has long been so. Finer wrote:

> Between the higher civil servants of Whitehall and local councillors and officials there yawns a wide black gulf. The former are recruited mainly from two or three universities, from a highly selected group and without experience of business, industry or the rest of the country. The latter live out their

lives, and therefore seek to live them out on the best terms possible, in Durham and Cornwall, Stockton and Devon, Manchester and Methyr, London and Lincoln. There is necessarily a gulf of *interest* as well as of knowledge...It is vitally important to secure that the affairs of a locality are cared for continuously by people whose capital joy is to be involved therein. But once this occurs their *interest* diverges from that of the central authority.

Nor is that all: the truth as gleaned from life in a locally restricted area differs from that gathered from the facts of a whole nation. (Finer, 1933, pp. 6–7)

Now, as then, there is the world of the locality with its politics and the world of the centre with its politics. Each has its own administrative structure with its own traditions. While the world of local government has been based on the dominance of the professional, the world of the civil service has been built upon the dominance of the administrative class. The two worlds have their own cultures and their own ways of working. There is a different type of knowledge at each level. Many decisions at national level are necessarily separated from direct experience. At local level, far more issues will be appreciated through direct experience. The life of the councillor, even the chair of a major committee, is in and about the locality in a way that is not possible for a minister.

The relations between the two worlds are grounded in misunderstandings, for each knows little of the other. Careers but rarely cross the divide, although recently a number of civil servants have sought and obtained senior appointments in local government, and in the past two senior civil servants have obtained posts as clerk of the London County Council or director-general of the Greater London Council. The appointment of Michael Bichard, the former chief executive of Brent and Gloucestershire, first as chief executive of the Benefits Agency and then permanent secretary of the Department of Education and Employment marks a significant if rare development. Occasional secondments are made. But the normal pattern is separate recruitment, separate training and separate careers. Nor until recently, with the possibilities opened up by new regional offices, has experience outside Whitehall brought understanding of the world of locality into the

workings of the civil service, and even now those appointed to
regional offices fear the accusation that they 'have gone native'.
There has been no equivalent to the French prefect with control
over but also understanding of local affairs.

Hasluck, no great friend of local government, drew attention to
the lack of understanding:

> A good deal of the misunderstanding and ill-feeling which
> exists in places arises from the fact that there is little human
> contact between the two forces. Whitehall seems very remote
> from the Town Hall, and the civil servants who keep sending
> these orders and hints and circulars and advice are thought of
> by many local councillors, and even by some of the local offi-
> cials, as a body of fussy, meddlesome armchair critics, dabbling
> in high-faluting theories and prescribing impossible standards
> for hard-headed local experts who have all the real knowledge.
> (Hasluck, 1936, pp. 128–9)

Local politics is separated from national politics. Local political
leaders, even of great cities, carry little prominence in national
politics. Indeed advocates of directly elected mayors put forward
that lack of national prominence as one reason for their proposals,
neglecting perhaps the reality that the explanation lies in the
structure of our politics, which a change in institutional form may
not be sufficient to alter. Local political leaders and politicians are
given little recognition in the national parties. The election of
David Blunkett, when leader of Sheffield to the National Executive Committee of the Labour Party, makes the point because it
was exceptional. Experience as a local political leader carries no
weight in national politics. If a leader is elected to Parliament,
he or she normally resigns as leader and leaves the council. The
ex-leaders have then to work their way up from the bottom of the
parliamentary ladder.

In other countries it need not be like that. In France the dual
mandate means that a majority of the Chamber of Deputies are
'maires' or in effect leaders of their local authorities. In the United
States the Governor of a state no bigger in relative size than an
English county can become President of the United States. In other
countries and in different ways there is interaction between
national and local politics.

The separation between national and local government has long been present in our system, although at one time it seemed possible to bridge the divide with the example of the Chamberlains basing their national careers on Birmingham Council. It may be that the existence of administration by municipal corporations and by local justices of the peace created a separation (or dual polity) between local and central government in contrast with centrally appointed local administration in other countries.

Separation leads to misunderstanding, or perhaps lack of understanding. That matters less if the dual polity is maintained. If, however, central government seeks to intervene in local matters, than lack of understanding adds to difficulties and increases conflict. Intervention based on misunderstanding can lead to confusion rather than effectiveness. It leads to the strange phenomenon that there is at local level a perception of increasing central control and at national level a perception of lack of control. Perhaps what is least appreciated at the centre is the diversity of local government.

The separation in practice has been matched by a separation of views. The classical writers were divided between those who celebrated local government and those who believed in the innate superiority of the centre where expertise was deemed to lie. It was the clash between Toulmin Smith and Chadwick. Mill, however, saw the need to bridge the divide:

> The authority which is most conversant with principles should be supreme over principles, while that which is most competent in details should have the details left to it. The principal business of the central authority should be to give instruction, of the local authority to apply it. Power may be localised, but knowledge to be most useful, must be centralised; there must be somewhere a focus at which all its scattered rays are collected, that the broken and coloured lights which exist elsewhere may find there what is necessary to complete and purify them. To every branch of local administration which affects the general interest, there should be a corresponding central organ, either minister, or some specially appointed functionary under him; even if that functionary does no more than collect information from all quarters, and bring the experience acquired in one locality to the knowledge of another where it is wanted. But there is also

something more than this for the central authority to do. It ought to keep open a perpetual communication with the localities; informing itself by their experience, and them by its own; giving advice freely when asked, volunteering it when seen to be required; compelling publicity and recordation of proceedings, and enforcing obedience to every general law which the legislature has laid down on the subject of local management. That some such laws ought to be laid down few are likely to deny. (Mill, 1904, p. 281)

### The assumptions of centralism

In isolation beliefs are built up about local government. Those beliefs or assumptions come to be accepted in the folkways of central government – the village of Whitehall. They reinforce each other and determine the attitudes of the centre.

The 'calibre' of councillors and officers – an undefined concept – is assumed to be low and becoming lower – as opposed to some mythical past age. Local authorities are often described as 'small', as in such statements as 'How can one give substantial powers to small local authorities?', although some local authorities in the United Kingdom are larger than some states in federal countries. It is assumed that local authority expenditure should be controlled by central government. 'Over-spending local authorities' are condemned, although all the phrase means is that the view of a local authority on the need for expenditure in an area differs from that of central government, which is hardly surprising since most would assume that local authorities had been given their own taxation powers so that they would make their own decisions on both expenditure and taxation.

It is assumed that local authorities are unpopular, although survey evidence suggests they are more widely trusted than 'Parliament and Government to do what is right' (Dickson *et al.*, 1995, p. 15). It is often argued that more people with problems seek help from MPs rather than from councillors, although the evidence is to the contrary. It is widely believed that national elections are determined by national trends. As discussed in Chapter 8, while there is a national swing which affects local election results, there are local factors operating at both the authority and the ward level.

Around these and other interlocking beliefs an image is built up
of local authorities which can become an elite contempt.

> A gap of understanding exists between central and local gov-
> ernment, much of which appears to be based on simple ignor-
> ance (or worse still, mistaken, stereotyped views). Civil servants
> appear, in some cases, to have little understanding of what local
> elected members and officers actually do ...

> ... a number of ministers and civil servants appear to believe
> that quality of local government members is not as good as it
> used to be, and not good enough by any standards. The mun-
> dane nature of many local government services appears to
> encourage (at least some) civil servants to believe that they pos-
> sess 'Rolls Royce minds, while local government officers have
> motor cyclists' minds'. (Jones and Travers, 1996, pp. 100–1).

This elite contempt is no new feature and was reflected by some
writers on local government.

> Social ideals of the whole community as interpreted by Parlia-
> ment were far in advance of any enterprise shown by local
> authorities; the exceptions are almost negligible. Even where
> Parliament has made statutes giving permission for certain
> things to be done by local authorities, hundreds of opportunities
> have been neglected by the local authorities. (Finer, 1933, p. 182)

Some officers look wistfully back to perhaps mythical days when
county or town clerks would take up residence in grand London
hotels and summon permanent secretaries to them, but that was
only true of a few. The general attitude of civil servants to local
authorities has a long history.

*The public expenditure process*

In the public expenditure process local government expenditure
financed from its own tax has normally been treated as part of the
public expenditure total. This Treasury convention has conditioned the relationship, building a continuing concern by central
government with the level of local government expenditure. For

a brief period, with the introduction of the community charge local authority self-financed expenditure (LASFE) was omitted from the control totals. That did not last long and the Treasury evidence for the Select Committee of the House of Lords on Central–Local Relations produced arguments which the Committee clearly found less than convincing (Hunt, 1996a). However, the Labour government has proposed a seperation of LASFE from the three-year projections, recognising that it does not have direct control over it (Treasury, 1998).

The practice had a distorting effect on the resource allocation process in central government. Faced with a choice between cutting expenditure which is directly under one's responsibility, and expenditure which is the responsibility of local authorities, ministers must be tempted to cut the latter. It is easier to believe that local government expenditure contains waste than to acknowledge it in one's own ministry.

Ministers equally will be concerned that when they have gained resources for a local authority service, it should be spent on that service. It leads to pressure for specific grants tied to the service. Failing that, pressure will be put on local authorities, as has been done by both the Major and the Blair governments, to spend additional resources on that service. At that point the confusion implicit in the public expenditure system becomes important. While both governments in their public expenditure plans allocated additional resources for education compared with previous plans, many local authorities were already spending more than allowed for in the revised plans. If local authorities had conformed to government plans, they would have had to reduce local government expenditure on the service, even though an increase was announced. The public expenditure process sets conditions for confusion and recrimination in the relationship.

### The myth of equalisation

One belief dominant in local government finance is in equalisation – that as far as possible all local authorities should have the same level of resources in relation to their needs although there can be and is dispute and disagreement over need, since judgement of need necessarily contains a subjective element. As Peter Wilkinson, the director of local government studies of the Audit

Commission argued in his oral evidence to the House of Lords Select Committee, the UK goes further than most countries in aiming to equalise resources in relation to needs (Hunt, 1996b, p. 69). Equalisation was not a dominant concept in local government finance until the post-war period and then it was equalisation up to a point. The principle was extended in the 1970s and maintained in its full rigour by the Conservative government. Indeed a whole grant distribution industry has been built around it.

## Regional offices

Except for Scotland, Wales and Northern Ireland, ministries have not been structured on a geographical basis and there has been no equivalent of the French prefect representing the state at local level. Recently government regional offices were established by the Major government, but they run counter to the main organisation of central government and their status remains uncertain. The impact of the Labour government's regional policy has yet to be established.

## The diversity of central government

One should not assume that central government speaks with one voice or that different departments act in the same way as other departments. One of the main findings of Griffith's classic study of central–local relations in the 1960s was of different patterns of relationships in different departments, and differences remain. Thus the Hunt Committee received evidence showing the 'wholly positive relationship' between social services and the Department of Health (Hunt, 1996a, p. 14) which they contrasted with other departments.

The Local Government Commission in their evidence to the Hunt Committee said:

> Central government is not monolithic; agencies and departments view local government in different ways. Counties deliver services in which the national interest is strong, overseen by a wide range of Departments of State which value the opportunity of dealing with a relatively small number of local councils. District services are largely under the oversight of the

Department of the Environment, which absorbs some of their strong sense of local place. (Hunt, 1996b, p. 353)

## The hunting of local authorities

In recent years there has been a growing tendency for national politicians to attack particular authorities controlled by the opposition. Conservative Secretaries of State singled out particular Labour-controlled local authorities for condemnation only to be replied to by shadow ministers singling out Conservative-controlled authorities. Lambeth and Westminster rivalled each other in the attention paid, but the roll-call of abuse extended far beyond those authorities, although after the 1993 and 1994 local elections it became increasingly difficult for Labour spokespersons to find authorities to condemn as the number of Conservative authorities declined to a handful.

This development is new. While from time to time the problems of particular authorities such as Poplar in the 1920s demanded attention on the national scene, 'the dual polity' ensured the separation of local and national politics. There was no mileage to be gained in attacking particular local authorities. The institution of local government was to be respected. Enoch Powell said in an Oxford seminar that if he had made such an attack when he was a junior minister in the Ministry of Housing and Local Government, he would have been summoned the next day to meet the minister to be rebuked.

The attacks are often based on inadequate knowledge. Indeed it could be argued that national politicians are not in a position to make informed judgements about local affairs, particularly when that judgement may not be shared by local people. The danger is that such attacks, which are not normally associated with statements in praise of other local authorities, serve to create a hostile attitude in much of the national media, which has joined in the hunting.

## The move to selectivity

The policies of central government have normally been directed towards all authorities rather than to particular authorities, although there have been programmes for capital approvals involving detailed negotiations between departments in central government and local authorities. There has been an emphasis on legislation for all authorities. Grants have been distributed according to a formula applicable to all, and although there have been accusations that ministers have 'tweaked' the formula to help their favourite authority, there are limits to the extent to which that has been possible. While legislation limiting the discretion of local government has often been justified by the alleged failures of particular authorities, that legislation has been general in impact.

There are, however, indications of selectivity, with central government discriminating between authorities. The urban programme in its various forms led to certain authorities being identified as recipients and involved ministers in the response. Government programmes, as in City Challenge or the Single Regeneration Budget, involved competition between authorities leading to judgements on their bids, an approach which was being extended by the Conservative government as in the capital programme. The regional offices played a major role in the process of selection.

The Labour government has given indications of supporting selectivity in dealing with authorities. It has maintained, although modified, the competitive regimes. It has introduced pilot projects such as the 'best value' pilots established through a bidding procedure. At the same time it has taken powers to intervene in particular authorities, as with the powers taken in education which give the Secretary of State power to direct that specified functions of a local education authority be undertaken by an officer nominated by him. Similar powers to intervene have been taken for failing authorities under a 'best value' regime, while 'beacon councils – the very best performing councils' will be given 'additional powers and freedoms' (DETR, 1998b, p. 21).

These powers of intervention are reinforced by the development of inspection. Inspectorates have always played a role in central–local relations, but the emphasis has been on inspection of services (Rhodes, 1981), whereas recent developments have extended inspection to the organisation and management of local authorities or their departments. Thus OFSTED's remit has been extended from the inspection of schools to education authorities. The social services inspectorate with the Audit Commission has undertaken investigations into particular social services departments. The Audit Commission has been given a role in monitoring local authorities in the 'best value' regime.

## Patterns of central–local relations

From these conditions develop patterns of central–local relations. The actual nature of the relationship has varied and will vary over time. It will vary from authority to authority depending, for example, on the extent to which the authorities' policies cohere with or differ from those of central government. It can differ according to which key actors within local authorities – whether politicians or officers – are known within central government. The relationship varies from central government department to department.

However, the relationship between individual local authorities and central government has been, for many local authorities, curiously passive. For local authorities it is not a relationship in the sense of interaction between themselves and central government. There are routines to be carried out which involve correspondence and contact between departments of the local authority and equivalent departments of central government. These routines are carried out within a defined framework. For local authorities that has the appearance of an imposed framework. Discussions may go on at the Association level, but for an individual local authority the outcomes are not seen as the product of discussion but as decisions made.

Legislation is passed, regulations are promulgated, and decisions are made on standard spending assessments and revenue support grant covering both levels and formula. There are rituals that are carried out by some authorities. The delegation to the department to challenge the grant settlement was one such ritual. It had become for some a regular event in the financial year although it has been indicated by the government that they will be discontinued in the year 2000 – at least for a time. The leader, backed by the treasurer and chief executive and sometimes other councillors, went to London and was met by a minister of state or junior minister backed by an array of civil servants. In a few rare and selected cases they would be met by the secretary of state. Meetings lasted between half an hour and an hour. Such meetings were unlikely to change the nature of an authority's standard spending assessment or grant settlement. They were a ritual. The authority had to be seen to be making a case and the department had to be seen to be listening.

For most authorities personal contacts with central government will be limited. I was at a lunch where a senior civil servant whose work dealt largely with local government met a particular major city chief executive for the first time. There has always been more contact with certain authorities than with others. Some local politicians have strong links with ministers. Some chief executives and chief officers have been identified in central government as an elite with a contribution to make. A few chief executives and chief officers have cultivated a wide range of contacts in central government. Generally, however, for many authorities, central government is known more by its actions than in interaction.

It may be that the development of selective regimes will lead to more interaction between individual local authorities and central government. The development of regional offices allows that possibility. There have so far been only limited steps in that direction. The role of the regional officers in judging bids has previously prevented much interaction in preparing them, although that is now growing. Inspections by OFSTED have not been seen as involving interaction but external judgement. Competitive bidding as an expression of selectivity can reinforce the passive position of the local authority.

The passive position of most, although not all, local authorities in the relationship questions the relevance of some of the metaphors that have been used to describe the central–local relationship. Metaphors that imply interaction, such as 'partnership' or 'resource-exchange', seem far away from the reality of central–local relationships as experienced in many authorities. Many of these metaphors were developed in and for the national world of local government where they may have more relevance.

## The national world of central–local relations

At national level, the local government associations, and now in England, the Local Government Association, relate to central government and its departments. There is close contact between the Association and central government. Even at times of hostility between the associations and the Conservative government, the routines of discussion carried on. Consultation is a way of life for the officers of the Association and the civil servants with whom they deal. That consultation has its own rituals, some of which are laid down by statute.

The Consultative Council on Local Government Finance as a formal meeting between ministers and the leaders of the Association was created by the 1974–9 Labour government as the means by which the leaders of local government would be persuaded of the need for expenditure constraint, as the leaders of the trade unions were persuaded to accept wage constraint. The Conservatives early abandoned the road of persuasion, operating instead through legislation and statutory controls. That meant the Consultative Council had no longer a role and became instead a ritual stage to be gone through. The new Labour government elected in 1997 has used the language of partnership and has created regular Central – Local Partnership Meetings.

In many ways the 1974–9 Labour government's approach (and perhaps that of the 1997 Labour government) was based upon an illusion that local government leaders could deliver local authorities in the same way as trade union leaders were able to deliver their members – at least for a time. There are in that sense no national leaders of local government. The world of the Association is for many councillors and officers a remote body far from the realities of their local world. They do not see themselves or their authorities as first and foremost a member of the Association, as active trade unionists see themselves as members of a trade union. For a few, the active few, much of whose life as a councillor revolves around the Association, it can be different and it must be different for an official of the Association whose whole working life is concerned with representing local government.

There are dangers in the role of local government associations. A national association of local government is almost a contradiction in terms. Local government is based on local authorities with a capacity for diversity. The danger faced by a local authority association is that it will reduce diversity to the enforced uniformity of an association view. The more the association is expected to speak for local government, the more the danger grows.

The Association to be successful has to move in and about the village of Whitehall and to be accepted there. Much of the work involves contact with the civil service. Gradually and almost imperceptibly the main actors in the Association can come to accept the assumptions of the village. The danger is greatest for officials whose career rarely involves a return to local government and whose visits to local authorities are much less frequent than their journeys in and about Westminster and Whitehall.

There is a danger too that the routines of consultation over an endless process of legislation and regulation come so to dominate the work of the Association that it becomes a reactive body. The treadmill of consultation can so absorb that in the end the Association is working to the government's agenda. The position was well illustrated in those days when the working routine of the associations began each day with the opening of the mail, but the dangers remain, even if processes have become more sophisticated or at least more complicated.

These are dangers that the Association can overcome only if aware of them. It requires attention paid to learning from the diversity of local authorities and to the development of strategies that can influence the agenda of discussions with the government. The Association is set at the point where the pressures for uniformity and the pressures for diversity meet. The resulting tensions are suggested by the competing metaphors of central–local relations, but cannot ever be completely captured by any single metaphor.

# PART III

# CHANGE AND THE WORKINGS OF LOCAL GOVERNMENT

# 7 The Challenge for Change

## Introduction

In any period there will be challenges to be faced by local authorities, opportunities to be seized and changes to be made. Within the workings of local authorities can be found both continuity and change. Local authorities are structured for continuity in their committees and departments but have to sustain a capacity for change. The 1974 reorganisation illustrates both continuity and change. It led to a reconsideration of the ways of working in most local authorities based on the recommendations of the Bains Report and the need for a corporate approach expressing the role of local authorities in community governance:

> Local government is not, in our view limited to the narrow provision of a series of services to the local community, though we do not intend in any way to suggest that these services are not important. It has within its preview the overall economic, cultural and physical well-being of that community, and for this reason its decisions impinge with increasing frequency upon the individual lives of its citizens.
>
> Because of this overall responsibility and because of the interrelationship of problems in the environment within which it is set, the traditional departmental attitude within much of local government must give way to a wider-ranging corporate outlook. (Bains, 1972, p. 6)

The recommendations of the Bains Report had a major impact on the structure of the new authorities. It led to structural developments designed to give expression to the corporate approach. A policy and resources committee was generally established 'to guide the Council in the formulation of its corporate plans and objectives' (ibid, p. 164).

In most authorities the position of clerk was replaced by the position of chief executive, as in the words of the Bains Report's job description: 'the head of the paid service ... with authority over all other officers so far as this is necessary for the efficient management and execution of the Council's function', and the 'Council's principal adviser on matters of general policy' (ibid, p. 165). The chief executive was to be the leader of the management team of chief officers, which was to be of 'an entirely different nature' from previous chief officer meetings in most authorities. It was 'to have a corporate identity and a positive role to play in the corporate management of the authority' (ibid, p. 48). The Bains Report also made recommendations on departmental and committee structures. It had a widespread impact on the structure of the new authorities.

These changes in structure were, however, changes within the inheritance. They were adjustments within an established way of working rather than a new way of working. The building blocks of committees with their regular cycle of meetings and the pressure of the agenda remained, although they were arranged in a different formation. The professionally-based department remained the main building block of the officer structure, despite some tentative moves towards multi-professional directorates.

It is with the period since the 1974 reorganisation and in particular since the election of the Conservative government in 1979 that the remainder of this book is mainly concerned. That period brought new challenges to local government. These challenges have had an impact on ways of working. Yet despite those challenges the inheritance has retained its influence. There has been both continuity and change, and uniformity and diversity, as will be seen in the discussion in later chapters on current ways of working.

It is normal to describe the challenges as deriving from the policies of the Conservative government, and certainly they have been an important and at times a dominant force in bringing about changes in the workings of local authorities. Yet those changes in legislation should themselves be seen as a response to changes in society and in the economy that have had their own impact and their own dynamic.

## Societal change and the government of certainty

With the dominant model of local government in the post-war era of the welfare state having been that of an agency for the delivery of a series of established national services, local authorities in their organisation and ways of working gave expression to the government of certainty. The tasks to be carried out were clear. Given that certainty, the tasks could be simply defined. 'Roofs over heads' became the dominant issue in education, as schools had to be built to cope with rising school numbers. With the facilities and the resources, it was assumed the teaching profession would deliver. Three hundred thousand houses a year was a slogan of a Conservative government and confidence was placed in architects to find the means, with all the problems that high flats and systems buildings have left behind. It was a period in which party politics had little part to play, beyond what Bulpitt in the characteristic text of that era showed to be largely (although not entirely) a politics of patronage (Bulpitt, 1967). In the development of town centres, in the clearance of 'non-conforming uses' from the inner city, or in the 'spaghetti junctions' wished upon great cities, professional certainty prevailed over what was often a subterranean political instinct, unhappy at what was felt to be the destruction of communities. The voices that gave expression to that instinct were normally minority voices. The onward march of the dominant ideas, far from being challenged, often gained support from leading councillors of all parties, who accepted the certainties of the time and trusted in the judgement of the professionals.

The task for local authorities can be seen as having moved from the government of perceived certainty to the government of acknowledged uncertainty, as the nature of society and economy have changed. Many towns and cities have lost their past roles. The industries, or in some cases, the industry on which they depended and which defined their roles, have been lost. Towns and cities can be the source of dynamism in the economy and in society, but a new role has to be found which some seek in the growth of the service sector while others seek in the growth of industries based on new technologies. Economic change brings social costs and those costs are felt unevenly in what can easily become a divided society.

Society is changing in many dimensions, including demographic change with more vulnerable elderly and single-parent families and including the development of a multi-cultural society. Social problems grow in intensity. Conflicting demands of different groups in urban areas have to be reconciled. Many towns and cities have a physical infrastructure that requires renewal if environmental conditions are to support a new role. It is a society marked less by the large factory and its familiar working patterns than by smaller working units and new forms of telecommunications.

Rural areas are part of the transformation, whether in the small towns that attract new growth, which itself may overwhelm the very environment that attracts it, or in villages where conflicts can grow between the demands of incomers and the needs of families long a part of the local community. The demands of recreation bring new pressures.

It is not so much the rapidity of change that creates uncertainty but its multi-faceted nature. In the transformations of community life, new problems emerge often imperfectly understood. As change interacts with change, trend projection becomes inadequate. If there is uncertainty about the problems, there is also uncertainty about the solutions. Today, while there are ideas about the inner city, there is less certainty that there is a right solution. If this doubt is true of the inner city, it is true too of many of the problems facing local authorities and other agencies: urban transport; isolation of rural life; the challenge of education; the care of the elderly.

The government of uncertainty confronts the growing awareness of the 'wicked issues', which are multi-faceted issues which defy simple solutions, and cannot be solved in traditional ways (Clarke and Stewart, 1997). They include environmental issues, crime and disorder, racial discrimination and drug abuse. They are called wicked issues because they have not been 'tamed' (Rittel and Webber, 1973). They cannot be handled as traditionally local authorities have handled problems. They cannot be set within any one organisation structured for the certainty of both problem and solution.

The environmental issue cannot be resolved by any one level of government – it requires action at international, national, regional and local levels. Even at local level many agencies and organisations are involved. Yet traditionally inter-organisational working has not been easy to achieve within our system of government. Within a local authority there are issues as to where the environmental focus fits within the departmental structure. If placed within existing departments, it will be interpreted as a planning or an environmental health problem, confining the issue within the boundaries set by particular professions. If a new department is created it proclaims to other departments that environmental issues are not their concern.

The emphasis in the workings of government has often been upon linear thinking in which activities are related to specific objectives. Linear thinking ignores the interaction between objectives, which can complement or conflict. The environmental issue arises from interaction between objectives. Activities launched in pursuit of economic development or transportation objectives can themselves create environmental issues. Linear thinking cannot encompass the environmental issue – for that, holistic thinking is required.

The full impact of the environmental issue lies in a time-span beyond much organisational concern. Absolutes are at stake whereas much organisational behaviour deals in increments. Above all, the environment is an issue as yet imperfectly understood. We know some of the problems, but not necessarily all and not with any certainty their causes.

Many of these characteristics – but above all, imperfect understanding, the need for holistic thinking, the danger of confining the issue within departmental boundaries and the imperative of inter-organisational working – are found in other 'wicked issues'. Thus growing crime and disorder has created an awareness that safer communities cannot be built by the police alone, but that the policies of other organisations may have partly created the conditions for growth of crime and that new policies by those organisations can assist in overcoming those conditions.

Local authorities face directly the challenges of a changing society. In that response there have been broad trends, but also variation. There are general trends reflecting both societal change and ideas about the response to such change. Those ideas develop and are spread through professional channels. As local education authorities came to realise – in some cases tardily, for mind-sets are not easily changed – that their task was no longer 'roofs over heads' for expanding school populations, but rather the management of 'declining rolls', then conferences and professional journals began to focus on the issue.

New issues can come on to the agenda of local authorities which can involve not one profession, but many. They will be brought by the general pressures of society, as economic development became of concern to many authorities in the early 1980s and community safety in the 1980s and 1990s.

Thus a series of factors brought the environmental issue on to the agenda of local authorities. Local circumstances are important. In Stroud the furore around trees threatened by a hypermarket was coupled with the election of a number of Green Party councillors, focusing the attention of other parties on the issue. International incidents – Chernobyl, and the dying of the seals – resonate. National hazards compel attention, as with BSE. Agenda 21 and the Rio conference focused attention. There is a complex pattern of influences at work. There is the direct effect in and on the locality but also national and international influences, some because of central government action and some despite it.

Faced with the government of uncertainty, there has been a challenge to the processes that expressed the government of certainty. While generally the achievements of the welfare state remain highly prized, the forms in which it has been expressed have been challenged. There has been on both the left and the right a challenge to what has been called bureaucratic professionalism. Traditional ways of working have been variously seen as inefficient, unresponsive and producer-driven.

### Changed and challenging publics

This reaction is in part a response to the perceived failures of past policy, as seen in the alienated housing estates, controversy over educational standards and the inadequacies of newly-developed town centres. The political reaction echoes the public reaction. Public attitudes change subtly and in many ways. It is no longer accepted, if it ever was, that government knows best. Means of protest grow in intensity – from the use of ombudsmen to active protest. More assertive consumers have rising expectations. The public, or at least articulate elements in the public, seeks choice, which means diversity, where previously there was uniformity of provision.

Nor can the public be regarded as homogenous – an undifferentiated public for whom uniformity of service is a natural condition. There are many publics of a local authority. Local authorities are set in a multi-cultural society, with differing needs. A meals-on-wheels service that provides the same meals for old people from Asian communities as for other people is not meeting needs. A local authority's area includes many communities. While there are communities of place which may seek to maintain the distinctiveness of their area, there are also communities of interest, of background and of concern. Each presses its views upon the authority.

Increasingly then it is realised that bureaucratic professionalism had paid too little account to the views, concerns and experience of the publics it professed to serve. The results have been described by Wainwright in characterising not merely local government but an enclosed system of government.

> The consequences are visible in the often well-intentioned legacy that post-war social democratic governments left to those who grew up during the post-war boom and since, a legacy for which these latter generations have appeared at times rudely ungrateful: university campuses on bleak parklands, miles away from city life, designed with little practical knowledge of students' needs and desires, medical training and hospital organisations developed with little knowledge of the particular concerns of women, transport systems worked out as if children did not exist, employment legislation passed as if the passing was enough and the implementation could be left to the courts, without thought that the knowledge of the workers affected should be built in, investment grants made to keep jobs in a poor region, without consideration given to the inside knowledge needed to monitor their use. The list is endless. (Wainwright, 1994, pp. 279–80)

Gradually it came to be realised that an enclosed system of government would require to change or be changed. The challenges posed by a changing society could not be met by such a system. The weaknesses had become exposed as the solutions accepted with such confidence in the 1940s to the 1970s became perceived as the problems of the 1980s and beyond. The change of attitude is symbolised in the housing developments of the previous periods, many of which had become areas of both physical and social decay by the 1980s. Many prized developments of the earlier period were demolished in the latter period.

## The Conservative government's legislation

The legislation of the Conservative government, particularly from 1987 onwards, can be seen as a response to the perceived failure of bureaucratic professionalism. The response was guided by the neo-liberal ideology of the new right. If the inherited structure and processes of government reflected the assumption that both the problems and the solutions were clear, then the emerging challenge led to a rhetoric that the market would provide the solutions.

The rhetoric was not matched by reality. As Le Grand and his colleagues have shown, what was introduced for most local government services subject to legislation was not the market of market theory which, under the conditions of perfect competition, will deliver the efficient solution defined by that theory. Rather than introduce markets, particular market mechanisms were introduced, creating quasi-markets whose outcomes will be a product of the way they are structured (Le Grand and Bartlett, 1993).

Parental choice was introduced into education, but it was a restricted choice. Parents could, given the constraints of geography and space, choose the school to which they sent their children, but could not choose the curriculum which they were taught. Nor did parents face a market choice, since payment continued to be made through taxation. The introduction of compulsory competitive tendering did not introduce consumer choice, but choice by the local authority.

Rather than see the changes brought about by the Conservative government as the triumph of the market over action by government, they should rather be seen as a set of particular market mechanisms within frameworks set by government. One of the lessons of this period must be the limitations on the practical possibilities of replacing action by government by action through markets. Even such apparently clear cases as the privatisation of nationalised industries have been associated with the growth of the regulation by OFGAS, OFTEL, OFWAT and other regulatory bodies.

Although the legislative programme of the Conservative government cannot realistically be seen as the replacement of action by government by the market it still had a major impact on local authorities. Quasi-markets presented challenges to past ways of working based on professional bureaucracy, and to assumptions about direct delivery of services.

### The changing financial framework

The workings of local authorities in the post-war period were based on the assumption of growth. The Labour governments of 1974 to 1979 marked the end of the era of assumed growth and introduced an era of restraint for local authorities which was achieved by persuasion reinforced by grant reduction. The Conservative government turned to legislation, culminating in the introduction and the withdrawal of the poll tax and the general application of local tax capping. The government set the criteria for local government expenditure, above which the cap will be applied. Most authorities capped themselves. The effect in authorities spending at the cap was that they no longer made a decision on the balance between expenditure and taxation – it was made for them.

The cumulative effect of the Conservative government's policies was to impose constraint and reductions on local authority expenditure, at a time of growing demands for services and rising expectations. The budgetary procedures established in the immediate post-war era were based on the assumption of growth, financed by growing government grant. The procedures focused, therefore, on the increment of growth and on the allocation of resources between competing services, meaning that there was no necessity to examine existing levels of expenditure. They were the base from which discussions started. The effect of the Conservative government's policies was that discussion often focused on existing levels of expenditure with the choice concentrated on where cuts were to be made, transforming the climate of decision-making.

*The changing management of services*

Legislation was directed at changing the management of local authority services and the form of service delivery. Compulsory competitive tendering, originally applied to construction, building maintenance and highways under the 1980 Local Government Planning and Land Act, was extended by the Local Government Act 1988 to a wider range of blue-collar operations and to leisure management. The process was extended to professional work by the 1992 Local Government Act. Compulsory competitive tendering required local authorities to put out specified activities to competitive tendering and to allocate the contract on commercial grounds. The secretary of state had sanctions if the authority is judged to be acting 'anti-competitively'. The provisions varied depending on the act concerned and varied over time as new regulations and guidance were issued.

The legislation challenged the assumption that a local authority has to provide a service directly. It showed the possibility of other forms of service delivery, although in practice it focused attention on one particular possibility – the delivery of a service through an external contractor chosen through competitive tendering.

Even where the local authority won the contract for its own direct services organisation, there would be a significant change in the way of working. Provision of the service was separated from specification of the service, and rather than control being exercised through hierarchy, it was exercised through a contract. This separation of processes tended to be reinforced by an organisational separation of client from contractor.

The reality of competition introduced powerful drives to reduce costs which advocates saw as stimulating efficiency, but opponents saw as endangering quality and reducing pay levels and conditions of service. The motivations of direct services organisation changed. A commercial culture was encouraged. The DSO looked critically at its relations with the authority and rather than pay overheads for the support services it received sought its own semi-contractual relationship, specifying the services it required and the costs. Compulsory competitive tendering had impacts beyond the services affected, encouraging a separation of client and contractor and the introduction of trading arrangements between units within the authority. Some but not all of these impacts will continue under the best value regime introduced by the Labour government, described later in this chapter.

In community care the assessment of need has been separated from the provision of services. In addition the financial arrangements instituted by central government were designed to encourage 'a mixed economy of care', with increasing use made of private contractors and the voluntary sector. Although social services have not been subject to a formal requirement for competitive tendering, there is the same separation of provision from the determination of requirements and the development of other forms of service delivery.

In education the emphasis has been placed on the local management of schools. Schools are given their own budgets, according to a formula which makes a large part of their budget dependent on the number of pupils, introducing an element of competition for the exercise of parental choice. These changes have brought about a major change in the role of the education authority, with the management of influence becoming even more significant and with what were previously support services provided directly to schools becoming trading units dependent on the readiness of schools to purchase their services. The devolution of management responsibility to schools has been a factor in encouraging a more general management devolution within authorities.

## The growth of local governance by appointment

Over the lifetime of the Conservative government activities were removed from the control or influence of local authorities and given to appointed boards. Local authorities no longer made direct appointments to health authorities. Health service trusts were created to run hospitals and community health services. Training and enterprise councils exercised substantial responsibilities in training and economic development. Grant-maintained schools, sixth-form colleges and colleges of further education were removed from local authorities' responsibilities to be governed by appointed boards which received their funding from nationally appointed bodies. Housing associations increasingly took over the social housing functions previously exercised by local authorities. Police authorities were set up separated from local authorities. Urban development corporations and housing action trusts took over major responsibilities for redevelopment in certain urban areas.

These changes had a direct effect upon the functions carried out by local authorities, but they were also a major change in the system of community governance, or the processes through which local areas are governed. It led to fragmentation at a time when many of the issues confronting local communities demand a capacity to work across organisations. The phrase 'fragmentation' is used not because there was differentiation between or within organisations. Any organisation or system of government has to be differentiated to carry out its tasks. Equally any organisation or system of government has to have a capacity for integration. A system of government is fragmented if it is differentiated without the requisite capacity for integration.

### The overall legislative challenge and response

It would be impossible to describe in this chapter all the changes brought about by the programme of the Conservative government of 1979–97. That has been done in other works (e.g. Stewart and Stoker, 1995). The legislation had a powerful impact on local authorities, posing challenges that local authorities have had to face. It should not be assumed that their response to the challenge was uniform. The legislation had to be met, but it could be accepted with reluctance or greeted with enthusiasm. Thus in response to compulsory competitive tendering (CCT), some authorities did everything possible to ensure that services remain in-house. Others maintained neutrality between in-house providers and external contractors, while yet others favoured external contractors, not necessarily submitting in-house bids. Some authorities of differing political stances developed voluntary contracting out, either because they favoured the use of private contractors or to evade the rigours of CCT. Despite the uniformities imposed by legislation, a choice had still to be faced over the response, both to the particular legislation and to its overall impact on the working of the authority. Research by Lamb and Geddes concluded that 'the scope for choice does ... appear to have been significantly reduced' in the three policy areas they examined – community care, schools management and local economic development – 'although it differs significantly from one policy area to another'. They found, however, that the authorities studied had 'not been slow to maximise the scope for choice offered even in areas where local discretion is peripheral' (Lamb and Geddes, 1995, pp. 55–6).

While it is recognised that CCT required separation of the client from the contractor in making the contract, there could be and were considerable differences in how far that separation was carried. Where there was an external contractor, there was an inevitable separation, but the relationship could be one of conflict or co-operation. Where the contractor was a direct services organisation of the authority, there could be considerable variation both in the extent of separation and in the relationship. Client and contractor could be in separate departments or the same department. The emphasis could be placed on their separate interests or on their shared interests.

However, despite the variations, in all authorities the government legislation has had an impact. Loughlin has identified the change in legislation from that of earlier periods:

> Much of the new legislation affecting local government has been more directive in nature. Extensive powers have been vested in Ministers to oversee conduct in local government. Precise duties have been imposed on local authorities to undertake particular tasks. A broad range of powers to hold local authorities to account for their activities has been conferred on a wide range of agencies or interest groups. These trends do not, however, signal the abandonment of framework legislation. If for no other reason, the pace of change has required the Government to rely, so far as practicable, on delegated powers. Nor have these changes generally produced a more direct and accessible legislative style; the complexity of the system and lack of clarity about the Government's objectives have invariably combined to frustrate simplicity in the drafting of statutes. Ambiguity, complexity and the vesting of broad powers in Ministers have always been facets of local government legislation. The most important features of this new style of local government legislation, then, are that these new powers are intended to be extensively used and the new legislation is designed to define the precise boundaries of the central–local relationship.

In order to appreciate the significance of the change in style of local government legislation, it is thus essential to consider not only the actual style of drafting but also to acknowledge the fact that the function of these statutes in the regulatory framework has fundamentally altered. It is this basic functional change which ultimately determines the distinctiveness of this legislation. The powers acquired by Ministers were intended to be used as drafted, the duties imposed on local authorities were designed to be fully enforced, and the legal framework established was devised to govern. (Loughlin, 1996, p. 390).

The legislation was designed to have maximum impact.

## The challenges to come

There are new challenges. The Labour government elected in 1997 has introduced a series of measures affecting local authorities. The legislation on a Scottish Parliament and a Welsh Assembly will have an impact on local government. In London there will be an assembly and a directly elected mayor from the year 2000; regional development agencies in England have been appointed. In services such as education and social services, the role of local authorities is being redefined. Local authorities are being given new roles in community safety and public health to be exercised in partnership with other public bodies. Government policies on social exclusion challenge local authorities. All these and other measures will have their own impact on local authorities.

The main challenge comes from the overall policies for local government. The prime minister has written:

We need a new – a different – local government to continue the task of modernising Britain. A new role for a new millennium. A role that challenges the sense of inevitable decline that has hung over local government for the past 20 years and provides local people and their representatives with new opportunities.

At the heart of local government's new role is leadership – leadership that gives vision, partnership and quality of life to cities, towns and villages all over Britain. It will mean councils using their unique status and authority as directly elected bodies to:

Develop a vision for their locality . . .
Provide a focus for partnership . . .
Guarantee quality of services

but for these tasks local government requires a new legitimacy in a strong democratic base. 'Revitalising local democracy is a big task' (Blair, 1998, pp. 13–15). He concluded:

I want the message to local government to be loud and clear.

A changing role is part of your heritage. The people's needs require you to change again so that you can play your part in helping to modernise Britain and in partnership with others, deliver the policies for which this government was elected.

If you accept this challenge you will not find us wanting. You can look forward to an enhanced role and new powers. Your contribution will be recognised. Your status enhanced.

If you are unwilling or unable to work to the modern agenda then the government will have to look to other partners to take on your role. (Ibid, p. 22)

The government's detailed policies for local government are set out in *Modern Local Government: In Touch with the People* (DETR, 1998b) and it is intended that they are being carried forward with legislation in the 1998/99 and 1999/2000 parliamentary sessions. The White Paper sets out an agenda for 'modernising' local government. The government's programme contains three key elements. The first is community leadership represented by the proposal of the government to place a duty on local authorities 'to promote the economic, social and environment well-being of their areas' (DETR, 1998b, p. 80). This represents a recognition of the wider role of local government as more than an agency for the delivery of services; 'it will enshrine in law the role of the council as the elected leader of their community with a responsibility for the well-being and sustainable development of its area' (ibid). The government will place on local authorities a requirement to develop community planning as 'a comprehensive strategy for promoting the well-being of their area' (ibid, p. 81) which it had previously described as a process 'in which local stakeholders can be brought together to identify the needs and aspirations of local communities and improve service provision in response to those needs and aspirations' (DETR, 1998a, p. 36).

The role of the local authorities in community leadership is justified by their base in local democracy, but the White Paper highlights the low turnout in local elections as an indicator of the need for democratic renewal. The second element is therefore democratic renewal directed at enhancing electoral turnout and involving local communities through new initiatives for public participation. The government is considering measures to make it easier to vote. They propose more frequent elections and measures to encourage public participation. The government argues that the traditional committee systems do not provide the basis 'for modern, effective and responsive local government' or provide 'clear political leadership' (DETR, 1998b, p. 25). Legislation will enable local authorities to introduce new political structures based on a separate executive. These will include:

- A directly elected mayor with a cabinet
- A cabinet with a leader
- A directly elected mayor and council manager (DETR, 1998b, p. 27).

The new Greater London Authority will have a directly elected mayor. Elsewhere local authorities can be required to hold a referendum on a directly elected mayor by a petition signed by 5 per cent of the electorate or on an option set by the government if it considers an authority has not developed its own proposals for change. It is recognised that within options for executives there are choices to be made. An emphasis is placed by the government on the role of backbench councillors in scrutiny, but that word can be given different meanings (Stewart *et al.*, 1998). How these new structures will work in practice will depend on the choices made, for example, on the relative powers of the executive and council.

The third element is the replacement of compulsory competitive tendering by best value. Best value 'will be a duty to deliver services to clear standards – covering both cost and quality – by the most effective, economic and efficient means available' (DETR,

1998b, p. 64). The Local Government Act 1999 requires them to set performance and efficiency targets and to review services over a five-year period, considering alternative ways of delivering them. These reviews should 'embrace fair competition as a means of securing efficient and effective services' (DETR, 1998b, p. 70). The challenge to the assumption of self-sufficiency is maintained, but it is intended to avoid the rigidities of CCT.

These key policies, involving as they do the role of local government, relations with the public, political structures and alternative forms of service delivery, constitute a new challenge to change in the workings of local authorities. The White Paper contains a series of proposals designed to reinforce the challenge by a mixture of incentives and sanctions. 'Beacon councils – the very best performing councils' (ibid, p. 21) will be rewarded with a relaxation of controls and additional powers. At the same time audit will be extended and inspection grow. 'The Government will act whenever authorities fail to remedy clear performance failure either in respect of substance . . . or process' (ibid, p. 26).

The full impact of these challenges lies in the future, and that impact will be mediated by the inherited world of local government as past challenges have been. Their impact in practice remains to be seen.

## Conclusion

Local authorities have faced the challenges for change described in this chapter. In the next chapter the changing politics of local authorities is described, reflecting the impact of the challenges but bringing their own challenges. In the succeeding chapters the ways of working of local authorities will be discussed, showing the impact of those challenges as mediated by the inherited world of local government. While the challenges described can be seen as forces for uniformity, in the responses the impact of forces for diversity can also be found.

In the concluding chapter, the impact of the challenges to come will be discussed, showing that within the Labour government's programme there are forces both for uniformity and diversity, whose relative strength remains to be determined.

# 8  A Changing Politics

## The historical background

Local government is a political institution constituted by a political process – the local election. Normally that political process is based on political parties, but there are over 10 per cent of councillors who are Independents in shire districts and Scottish unitaries and almost 25 per cent in Welsh unitaries.

Party politics are not new to local government. Indeed in the early nineteenth century the first elections in municipal corporations with their open hustings were sharply contested, as Alexander's history of Reading shows: 'The early elections of the reformed corporation were highly competitive and partisan' (Alexander, 1985, p. 6). Parties did not necessarily reflect significant policy differences. Many issues were not decided on party lines, with divisions crossing parties between economisers and modernisers (Fraser, 1976). Although party machines became sophisticated in running elections, and caucuses could be significant in determining the election of aldermen, there was often no overall party control, with chairs being chosen not on party lines but according to perceived ability. Sitting councillors were often returned unopposed, with contests taking place only when a vacancy occurred. Within the council, the 'election over, party colour rapidly fades and absolutely disappears from the ordinary business of municipal administration' (Redlich, 1903, vol. 1, p. 276).

The first election in the counties was marked by more contests than was to be the practice in later elections. Game and Leach have shown that at least a third of those councils were 'unqualified party political councils, in which most or all members were elected on party labels, which were recognised too in the subsequent conduct of council business' (Game and Leach, 1989, p. 29). Other counties were classed by Game and Leach as largely or entirely non-party, with some being 'crypto-partisan' with party conflicts beneath the surface. After the first county elections, contests

124

became less frequent and most counties operated on a non-partisan basis. For the other authorities a varied pattern emerged with party politics strongest in urban areas.

The franchise was gradually extended, with an impact on council composition. The local franchise differed from the national franchise until 1945, with if anything the local franchise being more restrictive because it was linked to the payment of rates. In addition a limited business vote continued until 1969 determining the result in certain central wards in towns and cities.

Until 1974 (and a little later in London) all councils in England and Wales, except the urban and rural districts, had aldermen who were elected by the councillors (although at one time existing aldermen were assumed to be able to vote, it later became a convention and then a law that they should not) for six years, local elections being then for three years.

The aldermen were normally elected from senior councillors. They represented a long-serving group, who were not subject to the necessity of fighting elections. As a result many served for long periods. Twenty-eight aldermen were still serving in 1939, who were elected to their councils in 1889 (including Lloyd George on Caernarvonshire). Many of the aldermen saw themselves as concerned with the overall affairs of the area. They tended to be the older and often dominant group on councils, serving longer than if they had to stand for election. They were generally conservative (with a small c) in their approach to council business. They could be, even in party-controlled authorities, a little remote from party conflicts. On the abolition of the aldermen, many who sought to remain on the council had difficulties finding seats, being out of touch with party organisation.

The growth of the Labour party in the twentieth century following the extension of the franchise led to an intensification of party conflict, with a greater number of contested elections and a greater alignment of party and policy. The other parties, especially after the First World War and the relative decline of the Liberals, responded by forming anti-socialist alliances, in some authorities fighting elections under labels such as progressive or moderate, with slogans of keeping socialists or even politics out of local government.

Although elections were increasingly fought on party lines, party policies did not necessarily dominate the working of local authorities. There could be agreements between parties on how the aldermanic positions were allocated – although they could break down when the arithmetic of the council was finely balanced. Chairs could be shared, and even where this was not done, opposition parties might be given the position of vice-chairman. It was, for example, not until 1955 in Wolverhampton that the Labour group took all the chairs (Jones, 1969). In Nottingham a degree of consensus was embedded in a series of concordats between the parties 'designed to enhance inter-party co-operation and lessen friction over patronage placements' (Hayes, 1996, p. 23). The consensus was finally broken in 1959 by the Popkess affair when the Labour councillors voted to suspend the chief constable.

The party group, if it existed, would not be openly acknowledged and such positions as leader of the council were relatively unknown, although the London County Council recognised the position of its two leaders in the 1930s and resolved they should be called leader of the council and leader of the opposition (Laski, 1935). The Greater London Council, modelling itself to a degree on the House of Commons, represented strong party dominance and influenced the politics of the metropolitan boroughs. In many counties and districts the position of chair of the council was the effective position of power. In boroughs the position of lord mayor or mayor once had a significance beyond the ceremonial and the social, with individuals sometimes serving for several years.

The former position of the mayor is illustrated by the arguments used by the council in Birmingham in urging Joseph Camberlain not to resign as mayor following the death of his wife, when he felt the burden of ceremonial duties:

> In making this request the council desires to point out to his Worship that it regards his services, as Chairman of the Council and as a Member of its various Committees as the most important of the duties of the Mayoralty, and that it considers his counsel and directions, in his official capacity as Mayor, to be essential to the satisfactory conduct of the Parliamentary business to which this Borough now stands committed; and further, that the Members of the Council will readily do their part to relieve the Mayor from those merely ceremonial duties which he justly feels that he cannot now discharge. (Birmingham City Council, 1875).

In Independent authorities the position of chair still retains influence. In Berwick-on-Tweed, long after reorganisation the mayor chaired the policy and resources committee for his or her year of office.

In the post-war period it was difficult to see strong lines of division on policy in many authorities. There was a shared commitment to growing services, fuelled by growing government grant, to large-scale housing projects, and to town-centre redevelopment. Comprehensive education was supported by many Conservative authorities and there was a commitment to direct-service provision. Disagreements could be marked, but often, although not always, they centre on patronage as much as on policy, as party groups became more determined to obtain chairs and aldermanic places (Bulpitt, 1967).

While it is possible to write of the developments of politics in local government in general terms, the pattern varied considerably. It is not even possible to write in simple terms about contrasts between rural and urban areas. Each authority had its own political history and was influenced by its particular combination of personality, environment and events, which can mean that the pattern of politics at any given moment of time was likely to differ between what appear to be similar authorities. Bulpitt found significant differences in the policies and practices of authorities such as Salford and Manchester even though both had Labour majorities. Manchester 'had a tradition of tolerance where the distribution of patronage was concerned and the leaders were against highly disciplined party groups in local government'. 'The physical, social and economic environment, and occasionally of individual Council members or County and party politics' and the importance too of 'personal differences between members of the Council and the past political history of the authority . . . in determining the character of the party political debate, the state of inter-party relations, and the degree of political restraint exercised' (Bulpitt, 1967, pp. 118–20).

### Increased politicisation

Reorganisation in 1974 and 1975 had a major impact on the politics of local government, leading to increased politicisation, with an emphasis on party discipline, recognition of groups, the majority group holding the chairs and vice-chairs, recognition of leadership positions, and offices in the council building for groups, leaders and, in some cases, chairs. A number of factors combined to have this impact. The abolition of aldermen removed an influential group less involved in party activity. The introduction of payment of councillors with attendance allowances at a rate more generous than it later became (as it failed to keep pace with inflation) opened the way to full-time councillors. The merging of urban and rural politics in the counties and shire districts led to the more assertive politics of the urban areas dominating, often with leadership coming from the large town or city. National party influence encouraged the organisation of councils on political lines, with the strongest change being in the attitude of Conservative central office, which actively encouraged local branches to contest elections under the party label rather than to support Independents.

Party politics was sharply aligned on the new Nottinghamshire council in 1974 where the new Labour majority, with leading group members drawn from partisan Nottingham, asserted its control. The party manifesto had set out the requirements of party control supported by offices and services for the political leadership. Similar trends could be found in other counties. John (later Sir John) Grugeon, the Conservative leader in Kent, recognised that he spoke the same language as the Nottinghamshire leadership on control of the council, even though he did not support their politics.

Policy disagreements between the parties had begun to grow in the 1970s. In Birmingham under Francis (later Sir Francis) Griffin the Conservatives pursued a policy of disposing of council property, some of it acquired in the city centre as part of Joseph Chamberlain's municipal vision. The sale of council houses marked out party divides in many authorities. It was, however, in the 1980s that party groups worked out distinctive approaches. An assertive right and an assertive left arrived. Both rejected the dominance of bureaucratic professionalism: the one by asserting a market rhetoric and the other by asserting the need to respond to local communities. Both challenged 'provider dominance' and championed consumers.

Change was not uniform. In a few counties and in more districts, chairs were still allocated to all parties – at least for a time. In

Clwyd, allocation was proportionate to party strength. In 1974 in Cambridgeshire the chair of social services was given to Labour. In Northumberland, a tradition of cross-party working in the former authority, based on a wartime agreement to minimise conflict, continued into the 1980s, leading the council to share party representation on the Association of County Councils, after other counties had abandoned the practice. There were counties like Cornwall and several in Wales which had an Independent majority. Gradually most counties and districts became subject to stronger political control.

The intensification of the political process grew with change in national political attitudes. The Thatcher government had a major impact on local politics, both on the Conservatives and on opposition parties. It led to a sharpening of political conflict at local level. Changes in the Labour party had their own impact on local politics. Yet the response varied depending on the balance both within parties and between them. The Widdicombe research found 'the remarkable survival, in a surprising number of authorities, of some of the old bipartisan consensus which earlier prevailed over a wide range of policy and procedural issues' (Widdicombe 1986a, p. 205). As in so much else in local government there were broad trends but also diversity. The Widdicombe researchers conclude the 'overall picture is one of an underlying diversity which is mediating and channelling in different ways the impact of increasing uniformity'. They identified sources of diversity: different sets of functions, social, economic and demographic structure, the state of the local economy, local topography especially in rural areas, and recent political history (Widdicombe, 1986b, p. 205).

## Local elections

The local election is the foundation of the political process. Because of the relative homogeneity of many authorities, elections by the first-past-the-post system can have an even greater impact on local authorities than on Parliament. It can lead to one-party authorities. Thus in the unitary authority of Stoke-on-Trent, the local elections in 1996 returned 60 Labour councillors out of a council of 60, even though other parties won over a third of the votes. Councils can be almost permanently controlled by one party on the basis of what may be a minority of the votes. The system of voting can result in a party being the largest party even though it did not obtain the largest number of votes, as happened in Lambeth in 1982, when Labour gained 32 seats, with 33.2 per cent of the votes and the Conservatives gained only 27 seats with 39.0 per cent of the votes.

Chapter 5 discussed the differences in the basis of elections, which have a marked impact on the working of the council. There can be a sudden turnover of councillors with all-out elections. In Islington in 1968 the Conservatives gained control and not one of their councillors had previously been on the council. Whether that is seen as an advantage or a disadvantage is arguable. Where retirement is by thirds, control can change from year to year although this is unusual in practice.

Most elections are now contested in England, although in a few safe Labour areas such as Barnsley and Knowsley and in some rural areas, there are still uncontested elections. At the 1995 elections 8.3 per cent of wards were uncontested in the shire districts. Unopposed elections are more common in Wales and Scotland. Thus in the 1993 county elections in Wales 22 per cent of the seats were uncontested and even in the new unitary elections of 1995, 16.3 per cent of seats (Rallings and Thrasher, 1997).

In most of the United Kingdom elections are decided on a party basis, with, since the 1980s, at least three parties contesting elections. There are exceptions even in areas long dominated by party politics. In North Tyneside in 1996 the leader of the council, Brian Flood, was defeated by an Independent in reaction by local residents frustrated at the lack of government resources for regeneration. In successive county elections in the Sawley electoral district in Derbyshire, William Camm defeated all three main parties, who in 1993 obtained only 27 per cent of the votes between them. In Lancaster, the Morecambe Independence party held 13 seats in 1992, although they lost much of their rationale when they were persuaded to support the council's submission to be a unitary authority.

Local elections mean that the political composition of the local authorities varies. There are authorities that are normally controlled by Labour or by Conservatives, although exceptional political conditions, locally or nationally, can overturn normality. There are authorities in which one party can gain virtually every seat and regards itself as permanently in control. There are authorities in which there is an expectation of political change. In some authorities there is a greater likelihood of being hung. The social geography of an area is an important determinant of its composition, but each area has its own political history. The variation in the results of local elections is an important source of diversity in local government.

It is often assumed that local elections are determined by national politics, and this belief is inculcated by the media presenting local elections as though they were a form of opinion poll for general elections. There is inevitably a close relationship between voting in local and in national elections. A town with a safe Labour parliamentary seat will normally have a safe Labour authority. That does not mean that national voting patterns determine local voting patterns. It means that committed Labour voters tend to vote the same way in national and local elections. It would be as logical to argue that local voting patterns determine national voting patterns as to argue the reverse. The basic political disposition of the electorate reflects the reality that many of the electorate – even in these volatile times – have a normal disposition to vote for a particular political party in all elections. Around this disposition swings take place, which can be caused by both national and local factors.

The differential pattern of voting for the Liberal Democrats (or their predecessor parties) shows the influence of local factors. In Liverpool, Liberal strength at local level led to them becoming the largest party on the council, before they gained a parliamentary seat there. Liberal Democrat advance in Sheffield, where they now have a majority on the council, was based on local activity not on national politics. In London their strength in Richmond, Kingston, Sutton and Tower Hamlets has been based on local advance and has not been matched by equivalent strength in other London boroughs with the same social composition. In 1997 local success was translated into parliamentary success in several constituencies.

There is a national swing which reflects the national popularity of the parties. There are however local factors which are ignored by the media, as Bristow showed in Wolverhampton (Bristow, 1982). Labour suffered an unexpected defeat in Tameside in the 1970s over education, as did the Conservatives in the 1980s in

West Wiltshire over the sale of the council's software business. Around national swings there is considerable variation. In 1996 in some authorities the Labour share of the vote increased by over 20 per cent compared with 1992, but in some it increased by less than 10 per cent. Differences of that order are enough to determine both local and national elections. Research by Miller showed that while overall 83 per cent had local choices that were in accordance with their current parliamentary preferences, 17 per cent had not (Miller, 1988). Opinion polls show a readiness to vote in different ways in local and national elections. When elections were held on the same day in 1997 there was a marked difference in the votes cast for parties in the county elections, compared with the parliamentary elections.

Variation between authorities is not the only variation. There are variations within authorities, which may reflect differences in the swings between different areas, but may reflect the impact of the candidates. Where all-out elections are held in three member wards, as with the election of the new unitaries, elections held after a boundary review and in elections in London boroughs, it is common to find differences of over 10 per cent in the votes cast for different candidates of the same party.

Turnout in local elections is low at about 40 per cent (or 30 per cent below the voting at national elections) or less making the turnout much lower both in absolute and relative terms than in countries in Western Europe (Rallings *et al.*, 1994).

Low turnout is not the result of recent reductions in the power of local authorities, as is sometimes suggested. Similar or lower turnouts can be found in the 1930s, although then it was argued a little optimistically to be an indication of satisfaction. 'The widespread apathy is in great part due to the general excellence of local government administration, and to the probity and devotion to the public good of the great and honourable body of men and women whose labours have won the local government service of their country the admiration of the world' (Snell, 1933, pp. 78–9). Rather than satisfaction, low turnout may reflect the role of local authorities as agencies for the delivery of a series of assumedly national services, rather than as a political institution, constituted for local choice and local voice.

Elections vary in turnout between authorities. The authorities which have lower than average or higher than average turnout in one year will normally have had a lower or higher turnout in other years. Turnout is highest in Wales. Authorities with the lowest turnouts are usually Stoke-on-Trent and Hull. Turnout increases with the degree of competition, so Liberal Democrat strength increases turnout, as does marginality. Controversy increases turnout, as the difference of over 10 per cent in turnouts between Derbyshire and Staffordshire in 1989 shows. Amongst metropolitan districts Bury and Stockport have high turnouts and Wigan and Sandwell low turnouts. Richmond is normally amongst the highest in London, while Barking and Dagenham has low turnouts. While there are particular political factors in some of these authorities, such as the intensity of Liberal Democrat activity in Richmond, social composition has an impact on turnout. Rallings and his colleagues, examining the variations, concluded that 'the most important set of variables determining turnout are socio-economic', and 'the second most influential is probably the marginality or otherwise of the council/ward' (Rallings and Thrasher, 1994, p. 25). Not all differences can be explained in this way; why are Bury and Wolverhampton consistently high and Sandwell and Wigan consistently low? The researchers conclude that the explanation may well be 'unmeasurable aspects of the political culture', leaving unresolved whether that is the culture of the council or of the electorate.

The election of councillors for wards or electoral districts is an important influence on the workings of local authorities. Concern for 'the patch' is part of the working life of the councillor. There is variation within authorities and between them in constituency work. There are differences in the size of wards as there are in the number of councillors in each ward. There are differences for councillors because of different electoral pressures. A narrow majority is a powerful incentive to be concerned with the constituency. The advance of the Liberal Democrats in many areas was based on community politics. Success has its own imitators, with Liberal Democrat focus leaflets, outlining achievements in the area, being increasingly matched by other parties.

Territory matters, and is given expression in the surgery or advice bureau which is held in the councillor's ward or electoral district, although there will be areas where they are not held and councillors rely on other forms of contact. Where they are held, surgeries mark out fixed points in the diary. They are important to councillors. One leader being shadowed by people from industry found they were surprised that in a busy diary she found time to listen to people's problems about repairs. To her it was important, not merely because she had to be elected, but because it gave her direct contact with the public.

There is evidence that housing issues tend to dominate councillors' surgeries. The use of surgeries may be declining, because councils are developing other ways of dealing with people's problems. Neighbourhood offices and one-stop shops provide other channels. It is, however, not unknown for an officer to recommend a member of the public to go to a councillor. 'There is nothing more that I can do. All I can suggest is that you raise it with a councillor.'

This point highlights the issue of whether a councillor should press for special treatment for a constituent, and whether the officers should respond to such pressure. There is a distinction between a councillor putting the constituent's case, possibly more knowledgeably than the constituent, and pressing for special treatment because the case is put forward by a councillor. Councillors vary in their approach, even in the same authority, as do officers in their response.

Ward representation can affect the allocation of committee places. In one authority, there was a representative of each ward on every committee except policy and resources. Councillors are expected to speak on behalf of their constituents or in defence of their area. In some authorities they are given that right to speak on local issues and even to vote on a committee even if they are not a member of it. Councillors may be allowed to vote against or at least abstain on local issues, despite a party whip. Territory matters in the working of local authorities. It can matter even more where Independents constitute the majority. Territorial politics can then be as intensive as party politics.

## Nature of local politics

Although most councillors are elected on a party basis and most councils are controlled by a majority party or by a combination of parties, it should not be assumed that there is a uniform pattern. Even where different councils have the same party control, what a particular party label means can vary significantly.

There are strong geographical effects on the parties. London politics are not necessarily the same as the politics of other areas. The composition of London councils is markedly different from some other authorities. Young and Rao's survey showed that in 1993, 69 per cent of councillors were under 55, whereas in the counties the figure was only 34 per cent (Young and Rao, 1994). The London boroughs have generally seen some of the most radical politics both of the left and the right, although authorities such as Barking and Dagenham and Kensington and Chelsea represent a more traditional approach. It was not always so. Ken Livingstone has characterised Lambeth as 'a quiet backwater of local government where the leadership was never challenged. Like other inner-city councils, a strong authoritarian, quite conservative labour administration had been in power since the war, led by a handful of competent working-class men who ruled over a group of mediocre councillors who were treated as lobby fodder' (Livingstone, 1984, p. 15). As the social and economic structure of inner-city London changed so did the composition of its councils.

The politics of the urban North East has been dominated by the Labour Party with strong roots in mining and shipbuilding. Most authorities operate with traditional committee structures, and accepted group discipline. They have tended to resist management fashions. Style can change. Newcastle stood apart as a commercial centre, but also as an authority in which there was strong Conservative opposition that once could hope to come to power. The long leadership of Jeremy Beecham dominated the authority for many years, giving it a distinctive style. North Tyneside fell into the traditional North-Eastern style, except for the existence of a stronger Conservative party. It was subject to a sudden change, with the old leadership of the Labour group leaving the party after forming an alliance with the Conservatives. The access to power of a group of younger councillors challenged old assumptions and produced one of the most radical council reorganisations. North Tyneside stood then in contrast with other authorities in the North East.

In Wales it has been argued that 'Welsh politics appears to tolerate only stability and consensus' (Boyne *et al.*, 1991). Councillors are long-serving. Some chairs seem to have almost life tenure. The Labour-controlled councils of South Wales, many of them based on the former coalfields, have their own political culture with intense involvement of councillors in the details of committee work. The committees are many and large in membership. Education (and to a lesser extent social services) can consist of the whole council, for as one councillor said, 'What councillor in Wales would not be interested in education?' Councils in Mid-Wales and the North have shared many of the features of the South, although with a strong Independent membership.

Each authority has its own political history. The pattern of Liverpool politics has to be seen against its history. Leader dominance exemplified by the Braddock leadership was based on small party membership, making it vulnerable to a militant take-over. The sectarian politics of Liverpool and the intensity of industrial politics had their own impact. Parkinson set his analysis of the Militant Tendency in Liverpool against a background of economic decline, leading to 'alienation from the economic and political mainstream', encouraging 'a politics of frustration' (Parkinson, 1985, p. 175).

Some authorities have a history of one-party control. Permanent one-party control, associated with overwhelming majorities, can have its dangers. In the views of many, the difficulties of Doncaster and West Wiltshire were related to over-large majorities and the dangers that can come from apparent certainty of power. Large majorities can lead to divisions within the group, and the large majorities gained by Conservatives in the counties in 1977 almost eliminated opposition and led to votes against the group decisions in the council itself.

In some dominant-party-controlled authorities such as Gateshead and Newham, group discipline in committees is relaxed, with no group meetings beforehand, and any major difference only resolved at the whole group meeting before the council. The leader of Stoke-on-Trent, commenting on television, when his party had gained all the seats on the unitary authority, said jokingly, 'the chief executive will have to be the opposition'.

Large majorities and the permanence of power do not always have this effect, nor is power always as permanent as it sometimes seems. The Liberal Democrat gains in Tower Hamlets, Wear Valley and Sheffield in what were assumed to be safe Labour authorities showed the possibilities of challenge. The unpopularity of national government can challenge assumed certainty of control.

The Conservatives were reduced to controlling only 13 councils in 1996. Labour controlled only 4 London boroughs in 1968.

In some authorities change is anticipated. Even a party that has been in power for over ten years, as in Bolton or Birmingham, knows from past experience the possibility of swings in control. It can affect attitudes to the rights of the opposition, if the leadership of the majority party have themselves experienced opposition.

In some authorities Labour and Conservatives have a good relationship, working together on certain issues. In North Warwickshire, the Conservative leader seconded the Labour leader's proposal for an 18 per cent rate increase. In authorities where control changes fairly regularly, each party feels its time will come. Attitudes to Liberal Democrats can be different. They can seem intruders in an established game, creating new situations and even requiring new rules. In hung authorities a small Liberal Democrat group can be felt to have influence out of all proportion. At one seminar for county councillors in a recently hung authority, discussion of how it might be organised confronted the repeated question 'Why should five councillors have such influence?' Chief officers too can be puzzled by the growth of the third party. In one authority which had been controlled by both Labour and Conservatives since the 1974 reorganisation and now controlled by Liberal Democrats, it was said, 'We know what Labour and Conservative stand for, but we do not know the Liberal Democrat position' on, for example, competition.

Threat of loss of control can increase hostility between parties. In 1985 the previously safe Conservative majority in Hereford and Worcester saw its majority fall to two. They reinforced their control by increasing their majority on committees and allowing substitutes. It increased opposition frustration, which grew when it became a knife-edge authority (one without a majority) controlled by the casting vote of the chair, leading to long and bitter council meetings.

The political pattern is a product of history, of the personalities involved, of the composition of the party groups, itself related to the nature of the locality, and of the changing arithmetic of the council. Particular events can have a significant impact. In Birmingham the abstention of twenty Labour councillors in a council vote in 1987 over the proposal to close Martineau House – a seaside home – led to a period of internal division. In Kirklees in the

1980s an inquiry by the chief executive and director of finance into the behaviour of a chair of housing led to divisions in the Labour group which led to a period in which there was no clear leadership in the council. In Wiltshire in 1985 there were at least two Conservative groups, split on issues of school reorganisation. In 1997 in East Staffordshire there were two Conservative groups because of a dispute over the leadership, as also in Fareham. In Corby the Labour leadership were deselected, fought the 1996 election and were defeated. In Walsall the Labour group split, as a result of the leadership's pursuit of decentralisation in forms opposed by local trade unions, after the intervention of the national party.

Financial crisis can have its impact. In several London boroughs the financial problems that came to a head in the early 1990s forced a reconsideration of past policies. Thus Camden had been an authority which until the 1980s had almost known no financial problems because of its high rateable value. Councillors had to recognise not merely the necessity for cuts but the inadequacy of its financial procedures. Another London borough was described as caught in a 'web of illusion', with reality only triumphing when the council was faced with a counsel's opinion on the illegality of deficit financing. The impact of financial problems is not restricted to London. When Wigan became capped, sharing with Barnsley and Rotherham a combination of factors giving it a low standard spending assessment, it was a profound shock to the authority which had seen itself as different from 'high-spending' authorities.

Events occur which have a resonance long after their immediate effect has been felt. The high hopes held out for the student games in Sheffield and the reality of its financial problems disturbed relations between councillors and officers, as blame was passed from one to the other. In Knowsley, the proposal to merge the authority with Liverpool led to over 80,000 cards or letters to the Local Government Commission – admittedly in part the result of an effective local authority campaign. The extent of support surprised but gave a new confidence to the authority.

Events can have a resonance outside the authority. The replacement of Andrew McIntosh by Ken Livingstone on the day after the GLC election is still quoted in discussions of the leadership role in local government. It has become part of the mythology of local government – although based on a real incident it now has a life of its own. Not merely has it become a weapon in party politics. 'You may think you're voting for a party led by X, but how do you know who the leader will be after the election?' It has assumed a significance in discussions about directly elected mayors, the argument being that the electorate should know for whom they are voting as leader.

## Party styles

There are within each party distinctive choices on styles, and different balances between the styles exist in different authorities. Within the Conservative Party there was and still is in some authorities a strong paternalist quasi-feudal tradition, where party ideology has been played down (Widdicombe, 1986b, p. 206). That tradition supported education and social services. While resisting extravagance it was accepted that the authority should aim at a good standard of service provision. Councillors holding to that tradition tend to favour provision of services by 'our staff'. There has been, also, a strong commitment to economy. Where that viewpoint dominates, councillors leave the running of the authority to the officers, subject to tough budgetary constraint. They are proud to be low-spending authorities. More recently a 'Thatcherite' element amongst councillors has become important. These councillors are committed to reducing the role of the local authority by contracting out or other forms of externalisation, by the transfer of local authority housing to housing associations and by a strong drive on value for money. They favour the development of the internal market and charging policies. This stance is likely to be associated with detailed involvement in the work of the authority. Councillors will distrust officers, seen as associated with past provider-dominant ways of working. These types do not cover all the strands in Conservative approaches. In some rural authorities there will be strong sense of conservation, preserving the character of an area. Others by contrast will put an emphasis on encouraging commerce and industry in economic development.

Conservative approaches vary from authority to authority. It is not possible to set out a distinctive geography. Proximity to the centre might be held to be associated with the Thatcherite model,

and that would be confirmed by Brent, Wandsworth and Westminster, although not by Kensington and Chelsea. Kent, with its
new management approaches, had to be balanced by Surrey
which was more traditional in approach. The more rural authorities tend to have the paternalist approach, although there may be
a strong drive for economy which can lead to tension within the
group. Suburban Conservatism has a tendency to radical right
initiatives, but also a concern for services – particularly those
services seen as critical by the suburban residents. Thus in one
London suburban authority, public feeling was aroused by a suggestion that a pilot project for the Heritage Department meant
'privatising our libraries' and the proposal was quickly dropped.

A statement that united a number of Conservative leaders is
marked by the range of themes brought together. 'Good local
government epitomises everything Conservatives stand for: civic
pride; the need to deliver value for money; the importance of
local communities; the devolution of responsibility to the local
level; the need for choice, diversity and excellence in the provision
of services; the importance of encouraging self reliance and
responsibility: and the value of voluntary service.' It shows the differing and perhaps competing themes in present-day Conservativ-
ism in local government (Conservative Political Centre, 1996, p. 32).

Labour groups vary in politics and style. There is the traditional
Labour authority marked out by a commitment to trade union
values, but also by strong departmentalism and strong service
committees. It will not be a high-spending authority. It will have
a powerful leader whose views on the budget will prevail, but
who will not pursue many new initiatives. The group will tend
to accept and support the leadership. A new chief executive
described a Northern authority as having a culture 'reflected
in detailed job descriptions, lengthy negotiation with the trade
unions, little interest in quality of the job, a commitment to a routine and professional training but not management development
and with detailed controls especially over personnel'. In other
Labour authorities there is a commitment to growing services,
frustrated by constraint and cutbacks. They are authorities ready
to innovate and stress redevelopment, which could be the focus of
the leader's attention.

In the 1980s, new styles of 'left-wing' Labour politics emerged,
although a 'left' Labour group in one area would be regarded as

right-wing in another. There were many variants of 'left' Labour. The hard-left councils were typified by Liverpool in the early 1980s. They had a centralist approach, both in the running of the authority and in the operation of the political group. They were committed to housing expenditure and resisted cutbacks in expenditure generally to the limits of the law and beyond. Soft left councillors were a mixed group, often including what Laffin has described as 'educated radicals' (Laffin, 1989, p. 57), interested in a variety of initiatives – decentralisation, community involvement and equal opportunities. They are now increasingly interested in quality issues and involving the public in service provision or as citizens. They have come to accept working with the private sector and in partnerships generally. New Labour councillors place greater emphasis on management change, not merely accepting the necessity of competition, but pursuing internal trading, and even in some cases externalisation of local authority services, working closely with the private sector. They are likely to support proposals to replace committee systems with new models of political executive.

Attitudes are not fixed. There has been a greater readiness in many Labour groups to face up to trade union challenge, where it stands in the way of necessary cutback, service improvement and innovation. Value for money has come to be accepted not merely as a necessity, but as a principle. 'Waste of money is waste of the workers' money' might be a traditional Labour councillor's response today.

The Liberal Democrats vary greatly in approach. Although the Liberal Democrats were formed by an amalgamation of the Liberal party and the SDP, in local government it was the Liberal Party that was dominant and its traditions have most influence on Liberal Democrat groups. Many are deeply committed to community politics, defined in the 1970 Liberal Party conference resolution as 'Our role as political activists is to help organise people in communities to take and use power, to use our political skills to redress grievances, and to represent people at all levels in the political structure' (Horton, 1978, pp. 143–6). They place an emphasis on style of working, stressing open government, decentralisation to neighbourhood or area committees and developing other forms of community involvement. While it might be thought that decentralisation was a common approach for Liberal Democrats, the emphasis given to it and the form it takes varies from authority to authority. There are marked differences in policy and practice, as shown by Pinkney's comparison of three Liberal councils (Pinkney, 1983).

Generally, Independent authorities are characterised by an emphasis on the politics of geography, with planning issues being of particular importance. 'The one issue on which the public contacts us is planning.' In Wychavon, councillors had the right to attend and to vote in planning committees when issues about their area were on the agenda. Each councillor is seen as first and foremost a representative for an area, which he or she champions and is expected to champion. For this reason committees tend to be large. In South Herefordshire at the time of my visit each committee consisted of the whole council, making unnecessary routine council meetings. In Shetland each councillor sat on five committees of their choice, with the size of committee being determined by the choices made.

The Independent tradition makes the council reluctant to accept formal leadership positions. In Wales there was an informal leadership in some authorities, based upon the respect for a particular individual, often an older and experienced councillor whose wisdom was recognised. In Powys, Councillor Pritchard played this role, not by a dominant stance, but by a few words which were always listened to. In Gwynedd, Councillor George was seen as influential as an informal leader.

Sometimes within an independent authority informal groupings are believed to exist. In one authority there was said to be a farmers' caucus. Generally, however, there are no fixed groupings. Networks vary. The telephone plays an important role in preparing for meetings. A councillor will seek support on a local issue and will often gain it, where no more general concerns are nvolved. That apart, officer reports are very influential, although discussion at committee can be important and a good speaker gains respect. Some issues arouse deep concern, as in Gwynedd, where there was wide support for the bilingual policy and equally wide concern over threats to village life and over the nuclear issue.

Independents can be members of political parties who fight local elections as an Independent, as had been most common in the Conservative Party in England, and although it had become much less so after the 1974 reorganisation, there was an increase of the phenomenon in 1996, because of Conservative unpopularity nationally.

Residents' associations may promote candidates. Epsom and Ewell has been safely controlled by representatives of Residents' Associations since 1933 although surrounded by party-controlled authorities. The Residents' Associations have more than half the population in membership with street representatives in many areas. The objectives of Ewell Residents' Association are fairly typical: 'To safeguard and promote the interests of residents and to encourage them to take an active part in local affairs. To assist in just, efficient and economical local government and to nominate candidates for Borough and County Council elections and keep local government free from party politics.' Councillors represent their own residents' association. Although they meet together before the council there is no group discipline and it is not uncommon for views to be divided and for decisions 'to be left to be decided on the night' in the light of discussions. Councillors attend monthly meetings of their own residents' association and hold two public meetings a year. Associations advertise for candidates when required. Councillors have been deselected who have not been seen as working actively for their areas.

Authorities controlled by Independents or run on independent lines are always liable to be overtaken by the growth of party politics (except apparently Epsom and Ewell; and in Powys in 1974 Brecon councillors who had been elected on a political basis in the previous authority agreed to conform to the independent style). The growing strength of the Liberal Democrats has led other parties to organise. In South Lakeland, Conservatives started to hold group meetings after the Liberals began to hold theirs. In West Dorset, although the largest number of councillors remained Independent, an increasing number, particularly from the towns, had been elected on party labels. The authority was not organised on party lines. Groups may have met but were not formally constituted. The Liberal Democrat group became increasingly discontented about its allocation of places on committees and formally constituted itself as a group in 1996. This led to protests about bringing party politics into West Dorset, but set off a train reaction. Conservatives followed and then Independents constituted themselves as the West Dorset group which was joined by four Labour councillors. The remaining Labour councillor refused to join and raised the issue nationally so there is now a Labour group.


## Conclusion

This chapter has explored changing local politics. It has shown general trends to politicisation, but also considerable variations. There are uniformities derived from shared electoral processes and the influence of national parties. Yet those electoral processes have produced both in the past and in the present a diversity of local politics, and national party labels can hide the diversity within parties. Local elections and local politics are a major source of diversity in local government.

# 9 Political Structure Processes and Culture

This chapter explores the political processes, structures and cultures in and about the local authority, showing the variety on which the diversity of local government is based.

## Party groups

Councillors are organised into political groups. Such groups have had a statutory base since the Local Government and Housing Act 1989 established them for the procedures allocating committee places between parties, leading even Independents to form themselves into groups for the purpose of the Act. A group will consist of all councillors belonging to a political party, although other party members may attend from the party organisation. Groups are an essential part of the workings of local authorities. They are the means for the determination of leadership positions and of positions on the council, and of the stances to be taken by councillors on issues coming before the council, and committees. They impose a whip to ensure party members adhere to group decisions although the extent of group discipline can and does vary.

Groups are no new phenomenon. The 'caucus' developed early in local government. Thus in the nineteenth century in Leeds there were frequent complaints about the Liberal caucus. 'Quite early on a Tory councillor complained: If gentlemen were to come there with measures cut and dried it is all a farce coming there to discuss them; and the Tory press urged Independent members not to stand for the dominance of a caucus' (Fraser, 1976, p. 126).

Although groups have long played an important part in the working of many authorities, only recently have they been given recognition in the workings of the authority. Sometimes even now phrases like 'we will consider that in another place' indicate the existence of the group without naming it. Although critical to the workings of local authorities, groups remain largely outside the formal structure. There have been exceptions. In Berkshire, at reorganisation, groups were given formal recognition as committees of the council, serviced by the committee secretariat. That has normally no longer been possible since the 1989 Act requiring membership of committees to be proportionate to party strength. This rule has not been applied in a few authorities, with unanimous agreement not to do so as allowed by the Act. In Barnsley, the provisions of the Act were not applied by agreement, and the Labour group machinery was reflected in the formal committee structures. Key decisions were processed through the leader's policy advisory committee which consisted of the Labour group executive. They then went to policy sub-committee A, which was the whole Labour group. Once policy sub-committee A considered the issue, it then went to policy sub-committee B which contained the opposition and then through the leader's policy advisory committee to the appropriate committee. The authoritative decisions made under this system, which had operated for about twenty years, were recorded in a library of 1,700 files.

Groups vary in the frequency of meetings. For some groups the pre-council meeting will be the only regular meeting even if it meets only once a quarter as in some county areas. In other cases the group will meet not merely before the council meeting but in mid-cycle to discuss issues of policy. In Coventry the Labour group meets weekly. In many authorities groups meet before committee meetings.

Groups can vary in size from small opposition groups of fewer than five to majority groups of eighty or more. Majority groups can be as small as sixteen in England and seven in Scotland. The style of meeting will vary with the size of the group, but there is a general tendency for groups to be constrained by the necessities of the agenda, particularly when meeting before the council. Alexander has pointed out the difficulties of large groups. 'Full group especially in authorities where the controlling party is heavily dominant may be an ineffective decision-making body. Effectiveness is influenced by size, by the length and complexity of agendas and by limitation on the duration of meetings' (Alexander, 1986).

One response has been the use of away-days and discussion groups. In 1990 in Manchester an all-day group meeting was held to deal with the difficult budget, leading to an agreed process which covered the organisational, financial and political requirements for dealing with the problem. It led to the involvement of the previous leadership who had been excluded from any position following the election of Graham Stringer and his supporters to group leadership, as they themselves had previously been excluded.

There are lines of division within groups. These can divide the group into two blocks, as in Walsall, where the Tribune group in the 1980s ceased to attend group meetings when the 'right' gained control. In other cases there are a variety of factions, which mean that group decisions can vary from issue to issue. In one Conservative-controlled county there were factions with labels such as 'the landed estate' or the 'ex-military' and it was difficult to tell how the group would vote on any issue. In a county, newly-elected councillors coming from different areas may not know each other. There were thirty-three new Liberal Democrat councillors in Somerset in 1993. In such circumstances it takes time to establish group attitudes.

Where a group is sharply but narrowly divided, a small number of councillors can change the control of the group. In Sandwell a faction called Solidarity controlled the group. Their policy was based on low expenditure building up balances for a 'rainy day'. In 1987 the group leadership was defeated by the Realignment composed of the previous 'left' allied with some Solidarity supporters, who said, 'We wanted something to happen. We were tired of waiting for a rainy day.'

Groups are not necessarily attended only by councillors. The model standing orders of the Labour Party require the attendance in a non-voting capacity of representatives of the outside party. In Harlow the Labour group is open to the public in the same way as committees. In the Conservative Party the party agent may attend. Myths are built up by officers about the influence of party representatives, forgetting that normally councillors will see themselves as rightly dominant in the group: 'We are elected, they are not.'

Groups carry beliefs. 'The group must decide' is the challenge to over-dominant leadership. 'That must go to the group', 'Why was the group not consulted?' are the accusations that can be used against group leadership. Leaders backed by their group can use a similar terminology. In Barnsley, 'the group is Caesar' was an often-used phrase. The belief in group decision-making can be seen as a challenge to perceived officer domination or to a leadership that over-reaches itself, but it can support a leadership that carries the group with it.

Group discipline can be seen as crucial, even to the extent of eliminating any real decision-making or any purpose in discussion at committees. 'Labour and Conservative party groups both operate extensive whipping systems which have increased in scope and effectiveness in recent years. Liberal Democrats operate in a more informal way, but they too, as they have come to control or share power in increasing numbers of authorities, place growing emphasis nowadays on party cohesion and public displays of party unity' (Game and Leach, 1995, p. 39). Some chairs even take pride in saying 'I got through the business in a quarter of an hour. It was all cut and dried beforehand.' Yet I have heard councillors say, 'The opposition made a good point, but we had already decided, so all we could do was ignore it.' Some groups can be more relaxed, allowing for more open discussion in committee and even freedom in voting on many issues.

There is variation in the extent to which the group accepts leadership. There is at least one Labour-controlled metropolitan district where the leader chose the chairs without challenge. That has been common in Conservative authorities whereas in many Labour-controlled authorities there is often an insistence that the group must decide, although it may approve the leadership's recommendation. In some, the leadership will make no recommendation, leaving it to the group.

Oxford Labour group was an example of a group opposed to a dominant leadership. There was a three-year rule for chairs. The title 'leader of the council' was eschewed. The group resisted the creation of a policy and resources committee and the leader of the group did not chair a committee.

Even where leadership is accepted there are certain beliefs that govern the workings of the authority. The spirit of 'All councillors are equal', 'We are all elected representatives' is a powerful force which has led some authorities to resist the introduction of special responsibility allowances. It has a special significance in authorities where Independents are dominant or where the independent tradition governs inter-party relations. In Berwick-on-Tweed the Liberal Democrat leader proposed the appointment of a leader of the council and was defeated, with members of his group voting against.

Local authorities can make appointments of assistants to political groups, taking account of the political affiliation of the candidates in ways that are not permitted for other appointments. The Local Government and Housing Act 1989 prescribes that there can be only one such appointment for each group. Many local authorities – including highly political ones – have not made use of this provision, although there can be staff appointed as assistants for leaders or for chairs. Where political assistants are  appointed their role varies. In some they are assistants to the leader. Not all leaders seek them. One leader in a London borough defeated attempts by some in the group to have a political adviser appointed by arguing 'the borough party are my advisers'. In some authorities, advisers are mainly concerned with the group. Their roles can involve research, links with the party or ensuring communication. Where a good relationship exists with officers they can be a useful channel of contact. On the other hand they can be resented by officers as assuming an authority they do not formally have. Even in the same authority their role can vary between parties. Leach and his colleagues found in one authority differences between the low-key research assistant, the aggressive gatherer of political ammunition and the translator between the political and officer structures (Leach *et al.*, 1997). In one London Labour-controlled authority, the administrator/ adviser of the group was seen by the officers as important. She restructured meetings and instituted action notes for the chief executive and chief officers, bringing order to the administration of the group.

## Group leadership

The leadership of the majority party is critical. Increasingly local authorities are regarded as having an 'administration' – at least where there is a majority party. The party that has a majority on the council will choose the chairs and vice-chairs, and the leader of the party will become leader of the council. The phrase 'the administration' has become part of the terminology of the council.

Leadership is formed by the party groups. Party groups elect councillors to a number of positions in the group, which may but does not necessarily mean they hold a position in the council: normally including the leader, a deputy or deputy leaders, group secretary and whips. The leader may chair the group, although the Labour Party requires election of a separate chair. In addition to the named officers there may be other elected members of a group executive, whose numbers depend on the size of the group.

The group executive's importance depends in part on the leader and in part on the group. There may be a process of creeping commitment as the leader carries the group officers, whose recommendations then carry the group, as described by Green in Newcastle (Green, 1981). This process depends upon collective responsibility ensuring the leader a block of votes as a starting point for building a majority in each setting.

The key role is group leader. The leader is usually elected by the group, although in a few Labour authorities such as Harlow the local party is involved through an electoral college. Once elected, group leaders will usually be re-elected at the next annual general meeting, although contests are common and leaders can be defeated when the composition of the group has changed or when leaders have outstayed their welcome. A defeated leader can come back, as Peter Soulsby came back in Leicester. Long periods in leadership can be found. Councillor Hall, the Labour leader of Stevenage, has been leader for over twenty years. David Williams has been leader of Richmond since the authority became Liberal in 1982 and was leader of his group before then. Some Labour authorities such as Norwich (as a reaction against the long-term leadership of Arthur South) have time limits. On the other hand, Labour in Brighton abandoned time limits to retain Steve Bassam as leader. In Harrow under the Conservatives there was a convention that the leader served for four years. Contests are particularly frequent in London, where defeats or narrow majorities are common.

There is or was a *cursus honorem* in some Conservative-controlled authorities. In one East Anglian district one went from deputy leader, to leader, to deputy chairman, to chairman of the council, spending two years in each position. In Hereford and Worcester there was a similar progression with longer in each position. A combination of electoral defeat and retirement of the leader meant the deputy leader was leap-frogged into the chair of the council. 'If events had followed their natural course I would have waited until I was 82!' In such councils the position of chair of the council retained its importance, so that in one county the leader was described as 'not so much a prime minister as a combination of leader of the House and chief whip'. In Gloucestershire in the early 1980s the chairman of the county council and of policy and resources was an Independent, although a member of the Conservative group. The chairman of the Conservative group was not called leader. The chief executive supposed, 'he was group leader, but certainly not leader of the council'.

The leader of the majority group will normally be called leader of the council. That title will be widely used in the council and may even occur in standing orders. In Independent-style authorities the title will be resisted. Sometimes hung authorities agree to abandon the title, although joint leaders have been appointed where a coalition has been formed. The leader of the council is likely to chair the policy and resources committee or its equivalent, but a few leaders choose to take no chair, relying on the position of leader, or take a chair in which they have special interest. Thus the Redditch leader held the position of chair of housing. One Doncaster leader in the former county borough took the position of chair of the race (course) committee as a safeguard against corruption. In Surrey the Conservative leader held no position except chair of the reorganisation committee because of time pressures. In Craven the position of leader of the council was separate from leader of the group and there was a separate chair of policy and resources committee – a deliberate spreading of power in a Liberal Democrat council. In Sunderland the deputy leader chaired the main management committee, with the leader as vice-chair. In some county councils the Leader of the majority party used to be chair of the council, including at one time Louise Ellman, the Labour leader in Lancashire.

The position of leader of the council carries weight inside and outside the council. While the leader does not have the full ceremonial and social duties that attach to the mayor or chair of the council, the importance of the position is increasingly recognised by the local media and by organisations in the area. It is often remarked that local government's leaders rarely have national prominence – David Blunkett and Ken Livingstone being exceptions in the Labour Party, while Lady Young, Lord Bellwin and Lady Blatch attained ministerial positions in the House of Lords from a basis in local government leadership in Oxfordshire, Leeds and Cambridgeshire respectively. The lack of national prominence does not lessen the growing reality of local prominence, especially in major towns and cities, where leaders receive considerable media attention.

A leader's role involves the maintenance of a set of relationships. A leader's position depends on the group and a leader has to devote attention to the relationship with the group and individuals within it. The leader's relationship with the deputy is important and is sensitive if the deputy is a potential rival. In one authority the former deputy leader was described as 'the sort of deputy who is not a challenge to the leader'. The leader came to rely on him. When the deputy leader was defeated, he was given an official role as 'assistant to the leader'. There may be more than one deputy. In Sevenoaks the leader had two deputies each responsible for a group of services. In the new unitary Brighton and Hove there were five (later four) deputy leaders with responsibility for particular themes.

The critical relationship with the officers is with the chief executive, although the leader also needs a close relationship with the treasurer. The relationship with other chief officers may well depend on the relationship with the chairs. It may reflect the interests of the leader. One Conservative county leader interested in conservation was said to have had twenty meetings with the planning officer for every one he had with the director of social services.

The relationship between the leader and party outside the council can be close and co-operative, but can also be marked by conflict. Some leaders ignore the party organisation, while others build upon it. Increasingly the leader plays an important role with organisations and agencies in the community. As local authorities come to accept a role in community leadership, they recognise the importance of external relations and many organisations making contact with the authority expect to deal with the leader.

The development, maintenance and balancing of these different relationships mark out a leadership style. It can be absorbing in time. In a large authority it will come close to a full-time job and more. Leaders may work up to a twelve hours a day although they will vary in the time they can spend and how they allocate that time. They vary in the extent of direct support in office facilities. Variations in the level of payments are emerging, with some councils making no special responsibility payments, while Scottish authorities and some in England such as Barnsley, Camden and Leicester paying the leader over £20,000 per annum, still a low payment in relation to MPs who have less responsibility.

Leaders have different styles. The model of the city boss has become more difficult to sustain, although such figures stand out in the past. For many leaders today the relationship with the group is critical. There can be differences in the extent to which the leader sees the role as giving a lead and expecting it to be fol-lowed, or as one of building agreement. Equally there are differ-ences in the extent to which the leader seeks to guide the chairs or to accept their separate responsibilities.

In particular authorities certain styles of leadership have become the norm and may constrain new leaders, until they have established their own style. Leaders can vary in the extent to which they seek involvement in management or rely on their chief officers. They can vary in the extent of their involvement in com-munity leadership. Variation in leadership is not an independent variable but it will be related to the traditions of the authority and present circumstances.

Leach and Stewart argue that the nature of leadership is in part a product of personality, but is also influenced by the circumstances in which leadership is exercised (Leach and Stewart, 1990). They identify the political party involved, the party arithmetic on the council, the political culture of the authority and the external pres-sures on the authority. Majority group leadership obviously differs from leadership in opposition. Different writers identify different styles of leadership. Leach and Stewart distinguish between leadership from the front, consensus-building and non-directive leadership. Gyford and his colleagues identify leadership styles varying from low-key to assertive or even authoritarian (Gyford *et al.*, 1989). In their research for the Widdicombe Committee while identifying wide variation they saw a broad trend 'in the direction of more open and more consultative leadership under which discussions in the group become a crucial, perhaps *the* crucial element in the final decisions' (Widdicombe, 1986a, p. 90), a trend they found stronger in the Labour and Liberal parties.

The variety of political leadership both in style and way of operating was a dominant impression of my visits. Some names stood out, even after the leader had left that position. A leader in a county was marked for his pursuit of financial constraint and cutback. He was a dominant figure long after his formal positions had been given up. It was said even after he had left the council that 'he is alive and well in the council'. The chairman of one county council was looked back on by the Labour leader as a 'man amongst mice'. His approach was the traditional paternalistic conservatism of the shires that eschewed party politics. There had been a leader of the Conservative group but few officers could recall his name. In one county the chair of finance was a dominant figure. It was said 'Many do not believe he has left and they are waiting for him to return and tell them to stop doing what they are doing.' His position was balanced by the leader who played a key role in holding the group together and whose authority was decisive when he exercised it because of his support in the group.

Limitations on time can be a key factor in the role, particularly in the relationship with officers. One Labour leader was a full-time director of a housing association, and the chief executive felt that time pressure meant they could never talk long. A Conservative leader in a London borough was a bank manager who came into the authority after 5.00 pm, seeing the chief executive once a week. He worked through the papers at the weekend, writing letters or memos by hand, having refused secretarial help. A Conservative leader was impossible to contact at work, having a secretary who protected him from interruptions. He was seen as making hasty decisions and being difficult to have a discussion with. Contact was largely over the phone in the evening. Time can be important in relationship to the group. When Mrs Terry became leader of Hertfordshire she talked to each member of the group, as later over reorganisation of the council structure. Not all leaders would find that possible because of time commitments.

*Leadership and innovation*

Some leaders play a key role in initiating ideas. In one authority the Conservative leader was seen as 'endlessly thinking of ideas', which he put in papers for the group, often without waiting for officer comments. Such leaders resent the necessity of persuasion through meetings. 'I would have enjoyed it more if there were no group meetings, no committee meetings and no council meetings.' One Labour leader endlessly raised issues. A chief executive said of him, 'I've had twenty memos since Friday, and that is apart from the talks.' On the day of my visit the leader in a shire district had just said to the chief executive as they passed in the corridor, 'when are we going to do an audit of the county's education service?' It was a typical idea of his, coming suddenly out of the blue. Leaders have different focuses. Some are concerned with policy issues. Others are seen as 'having no political objectives, only managerial ones'.

Dick (later Sir Richard) Knowles was associated with the redevelopment of the city centre in Birmingham and the creation of the International Convention Centre which had all-party support and was begun in the period of Conservative leadership under Neville Bosworth. In Bradford, Councillor Pickles developed a concept of Bradford plc, later challenged by his Labour successor's concept of Bradford community council.

David Blunkett's leadership in Sheffield represented a change of style of in the authority and in its role, especially in economic development. John Harmon in Kirklees led major organisational changes and built the authority's role on environmental issues. Councillor Hart in Kent drove through major management change, working with Paul Sabin, as chief executive. A new Conservative leader in Rossendale introduced a 'business approach', building an organisation around two chief officer posts of borough director and director of operations. David Wiltshire carried out similar changes in Wansdyke, based on a general manager.

Leaders can be a major source of innovations and therefore of variation in local government. It would be misleading to argue that these innovations and initiatives reflect only the leadership. A leader does not act alone. He or she responds as well as proposes, listening as well as telling. Party, group, management team, chief executive, chairs are all part of the complex network of interaction.

A leader's ideas may run ahead of the group. Shortly after the 1992 election, John Harmon, the leader of Kirklees, circulated a paper to the group on the future of local government, based on community leadership. It was neither rejected nor accepted.

Indeed it was not really discussed, probably because the group was not ready for it. Gradually the ideas have come to be accepted.

Leaders have to recognise that change does not come easily where ways of working are ingrained. One leader said, only half-jokingly, 'My greatest triumph was to replace the previous committee cycle that seemed to operate according to the phases of the moon.' One Labour leader in an inner London borough argued that the authority had been successful in dealing with government in seeking funds for regeneration, because 'we compromised'. The issue for the group was posed by him as 'Do we want to do something?' and 'What will we accept as conditions to achieve it?'

Not all leaders see their role as being to bring in ideas, but rather to react to ideas or deal with issues as they arise. One Liberal Democrat leader avoids firm positions, 'changing his stance with bewildering frequency, stirring the water to see what is revealed'. Some leaders try to secure that all business comes to them. 'Everything of importance came into this room' – a self-defeating effort to avoid mistakes in an authority in which Labour had a narrow hold on power. Some leaders seek control through dominance. One leader was said to frighten his backbenchers through his verbal, almost physical, dominance. The leader's room can be seen as the 'centre of power' to which the leading members summon officers to deal with issues on their political agenda. A long-standing leader pointed out that he had appointed different chief executives at different periods for different tasks. There are varying conceptions of the role depending on the emphasis given to the political or management agenda. One conservative county leader, committed to maintaining services, saw his role as chairman of the board, with the chief executive as managing director.

*Change in leadership*

While some leaders continue for long periods, leaders can be defeated. In a shire district used to light leadership, a Conservative leader and former headmaster 'tried to run it as he had run his school' and was unseated within two months. In a mining area there was an informal but dominant miners' group within the council which selected the leader. It removed a leader who showed too much independence. In one London borough a

Conservative leader who had been effective in opposition was seen as failing to consult in power and was defeated. In Southampton the leader of the Labour group lost a vote of no confidence in the council over a proposal to remove the chief executive, because with a majority of one, a disaffected Labour member resigned the whip. The Labour group sought to remain as a minority administration. This arrangement was agreed but the opposition insisted the leader resigned. It was said a Labour leader in Strathclyde was defeated because he had neglected his home base through work in Europe and with COSLA. A leader has been known to resign and been persuaded to continue. On the day I visited Lambeth in the 1980s the leader had resigned because the group had rejected her proposal to remove the chief executive. She later withdrew it – 'a typical day in the life of Lambeth' it was said. Sometimes, rather than defeat the leader, a warning shot is fired and a deputy leader close to the leader is defeated.

Continuity in leadership requires sensitivity to the group. The Conservative leader in one county was committed to cutbacks, but saw the need to make concessions. Ninety-nine times out of a hundred the group supported him, often with reluctance. One wealthy council councillor after voting for a reduction in home helps came to the director of social services with a proposition that he would pay for those in his area himself – he saw it as a duty. The leader 'sniffs the air' sensing group attitudes. He delights in dealing with people. He is on the watch lest cuts go too far. At one group meeting which had agreed to cancel bus subsidies, the leader ended the meeting with a joke: 'We had better stop there, if you are to catch the last bus home.' It was greeted in deadly silence. He knew he had gone too far.

Much more common than defeats are resignations by leaders, often by leaving or being about to leave the council. One former deputy leader gave up the position when he realised 'I had been overtaken by power. I took a hard look myself and I did not like what I had become.' He had just approved a £1 million contract without thinking about it. He was taking power for granted. He later became leader of a different authority, but believed he had learnt from his experience.

One of the most remarkable careers on a council was that of Basil Jeuda, who was made leader of his group in 1981 (it had expanded from 9 to 35) when he first joined the Cheshire County Council and gave it up when he left the council in 1985. He was a leader who believed in major change. He was succeeded by John Collins, who had the approach of one trained in thermodynamics 'to believe in the small reversible change'. It was said in Sheffield that while 'David Blunkett inspired, Clive Betts listens'. David Blunkett was concerned with ends, while Clive Betts was more pragmatic, concerned with needs.

When a group has to select a leader it may seek one different from the previous one. When David Bookbinder resigned the leadership of the Labour group in Derbyshire, there were signs that he was losing support, although none would challenge him. The new leader, Councillor Doughty, who was not his chosen successor, reversed some of his policies, rejoining the Association of County Councils, seeking to alter the perceived isolation of Derbyshire. In Hull, Sir Leo Schultz dominated the group and the council, settling the budget himself, controlling the education committee by being chair of its finance sub-committee. He ignored and did not attend the city party. He was both respected and resented. The memory of his period as leader is still powerful. The new now long-established leader is a consensus leader not seeking to impose views, involving the group and working with the city party.

The Conservative leader in a London Borough was a charismatic figure committed to changing the council. His vision was of a council that would 'deliver services at a price which residents are prepared to pay'. There was a hectic three weeks following the election. In week 1, a statement of the council vision was produced. In week 2, the manifesto was turned into policies for the council and committees. In week 3, the outline of a new organisation was prepared. The speed of response was built on past work. The leader believed the council should set policy and cash-limited budgets, leaving to heads of services the responsibility for managing their operations. This approach led to delegation by committees, not welcomed by the more traditional members. The number of committees and their membership were reduced, so most councillors had only one committee and some not even a main committee. Discontent was caused too by the promotion of newly-elected councillors including the chair of social services. Threats to vote against or resign grew. The leader resigned because he became a parliamentary candidate. The new leader had the same approach to management, but was more a networker, believing in political management by walking about. The change was necessary for group stability.

In both Coventry and Wakefield the election of a new Labour leader led to the rehabilitation of councillors previously seen as rebels in an attempt to create a more united group. The reverse can happen. When Lady Porter was elected leader in Westminster, chairs were removed to establish a younger and more assertive group.

The leadership in Arun had supported the management revolution brought about by the chief executive. Challenge grew, and a new leader, deputy leader and new chairs were elected. The immediate issue was concern for the environment which reflected strong feelings in the town and villages. The previous leadership sought change in an area on the South coast popular with the retired or soon-to-be-retired who wanted little change and the conservation of the area. Because of the views of the leadership and chief executive it became a pioneering authority for the introduction of business principles driven through by strong central direction. Now the emphasis is on consultation with staff, with parishes and with interested groups.

Until the mid-1980s one North West authority had a dominant and experienced leader and a Labour group which accepted that leadership and whose members saw their role as dealing with routine committee work and pursuing individual complaints. Over the years redevelopment and building projects expressed their political achievement. The Labour group began to change. While many of the experienced councillors remained wedded to traditional ways of working and were supported by a chief executive who eschewed management fashions, there was a growing number of younger councillors who wanted to challenge those ways, rejected the paternalism of past attitudes and sought to involve the public. On the death of the leader, a new leader was elected who brought a new style of leadership, consulting and seeking to build a consensus. He moved gradually, keeping the more traditional members on board. At the heart of the changes is the community strategy based on the three core values: consultation and participation; customer care and quality services; and corporate working and partnership. Some councillors accepted the change reluctantly, saying 'not the community strategy again' whenever it is mentioned.

Leadership is grounded in local circumstance, often formed by history, which a new leader has to take account of. As already stressed, 'everything in Liverpool lies in history'. More than in most authorities the history of the last twenty years is for all the leading councillors a major factor in the present, starting with the advance of the Liberals through community politics 'which we invented here', going on to what is described as 'the Hatton regime'. Harry Rimmer as leader saw his role as restoring sound local government and putting finances on a firm basis. The early months symbolised for him what he achieved, although they were traumatic, involving compulsory redundancy and the award of the ONYX contract for refuse collection, against traditional Labour attitudes.

## Hung authorities

Hung authorities, or authorities in which no one group has a majority, illustrate the variety in local government. There have always been hung authorities, but in the past many were authorities where the party system was not fully developed and Independents held the balance. In the 1980s and 1990s, hung authorities, involving party balance, became more common. In 1995, 149 of the 395 English authorities were hung (Rallings and Thrasher, 1997).

### Adjusting to the experience

Hung authorities were for many councillors and officers a new and often disturbing experience, challenging past ways of working based on majority control. The period was treated in some authorities as one of abnormality, to be lived through until normality returned. Interviewing in a county that had been hung since 1981, just before the 1985 election, I was assured by officers and leading councillors that it would be only a few months before normality returned, yet the authority has been hung ever since.

Where 'hungness' is accepted, procedures may be adopted and conventions agreed, as in Cheshire (Wendt, 1983). These were used as a model in other authorities. Where it proved possible to agree conventions, authorities did not need them in practice, because relations were good, as indicated by the making of the agreement. The Liberal Democrat leader in Basingstoke and Deane said 'Although we agreed conventions, we put them away and have not needed to look at them.'

At first in many hung authorities, attitudes were determined by past experiences. Counties which became hung in 1981 and 1985 illustrate this point. In some where the Conservatives lost control, they assumed they would continue to hold the chairs, particularly where they were the biggest party. They had done so since the county began and felt it was their natural position. Labour often concurred, for they were the party of opposition and the national party discouraged alliances with other parties, although it later adopted a more flexible approach. In 1981 one Labour leader said 'It was the first time in thirty years the Labour Party nationally had shown any interest in us.' In Humberside, Labour, which had previously been in control, demanded a majority on committees which the other parties were never likely to concede. The Liberals often looked for a sharing of chairs, since a share of power was often their aim and they saw hung authorities as 'balanced'. Not all these attitudes were universal. Emily Blatch, the Conservative leader in Cambridgeshire, interpreted the results as a defeat, even though they were the largest party, and therefore did not seek the chairs when the authority first became hung, or as she called it 'unhinged'. In some authorities, Labour formed a minority administration with Liberal support, as in Cheshire, or supported a Liberal administration, as in Devon. Positions taken did not necessarily last for the life of the council. The Conservatives in Oxfordshire found that holding chairs was an embarrassment, since they were often defeated in committee. They did not find it comfortable to be chairs of committees whose decisions they disagreed with. The budget was often the breaking point, marking the end of previous arrangements. An administration that could not carry its budgets treated defeat as a vote of no confidence (Leach and Stewart, 1992).

Gradually, as hung authorities came to be a common part of experience, ways of working developed for the hung position. The abnormal came to be seen as normal. Labour generally came to recognise, as Councillor Wheeler the Labour leader in Hampshire said, that 'In a situation, where you have not got a majority, it is better to put 80 per cent of your policies through and have an influence on the other 20 per cent than to be in opposition' (Mac-Donald and Arnold-Foster, 1995, p. 20). Sometimes traumatic events had an impact. In Berkshire there was a twenty-five-hour budget meeting (with adjournments for group meetings) which forced reconsideration.

The history of hung authorities is marked by events that reson-ate afterwards. The exploitation by Labour in Avon of a tempor-ary majority on the council (because of a bye-election) to pass their budget was seen as an act of bad faith by the other parties. As a consequence Liberals and Conservatives moved closer together. Events in the election can have an impact . A Labour group that came near to gaining power in a county resented an unexpected gain by the Liberal Democrats which made them reluctant to negotiate for their support, leading to agreement between Con-servatives and Liberal Democrats. In a few authorities conflictual attitudes dominated. This is more likely where there are annual elections, so that the hung position could be treated as a tem-porary abnormality to be corrected at the next election, unless it re-emerged. In others where the party groups were strongly opposed to each other, either because of personality or ideology, conflict remained almost endemic. Leaders of former majority parties often did not find leadership in hung authorities accept-able and soon resigned.

*Forming an administration*

Different approaches to forming an administration developed in different authorities. Coalitions were relatively rare at first, although over time they have become more common, as hung positions have become accepted as normal and as the attitude of the Labour party nationally has become more pragmatic in the light of realities at local level. Coalitions usually involve the Lib-eral Democrats, normally with Conservatives in Labour-dominant authorities and with Labour in Conservative-dominant authorit-ies. It is the natural alliance of former oppositions in reaction to the defeat of the previous majority. In Berkshire, Labour and Lib-eral Democrats – and the Berkshire Group (of Independents) –

formed an alliance that involved informal electoral pacts in key wards. Lawrence Silverman, the Labour leader, pointed out that 'the very concept of coalition government...is something quite unknown at national level (except during the war). The strangeness of the idea means that we cannot actually use the word' (MacDonald and Arnold-Foster, 1995, p. 20). In Lincolnshire there was a 'partnership administration' between Labour and Liberal Democrats. In Wolverhampton, Conservatives and Liberal Democrats formally set up a single group in order to gain a majority on each committee under the proportionality rules, but continued to meet in separate groups. In Solihull, Conservatives and Ratepayers formed a single group for a time to create an administration, and ceased to oppose each other in local elections.

Some shared administrations fall short of being full coalitions. Shared chairs can be between two parties on an agreed basis, but allow for policy differences, as over nursery vouchers in Norfolk. In North Norfolk a formal agreement between Liberal Democrats and Labour was passed at the annual meeting of the council, setting out a 'working arrangement' in which each group was 'free to vote as it wishes', subject to provisos about keeping each other informed. Sometimes a shared administration arises without any prearranged agreement, depending how the votes fall, particularly where Liberal Democrats differentiate their votes, although the chairs may be refused by one or both the other parties in those circumstances. It can occur, as once in Shropshire, where chairs are decided by committees, by the accident of who is present. In Surrey the chairs were determined by secret ballot as a result of a previously unused and unnoticed standing order. It resulted in shared chairs, with Labour refusing to stand. There have been instances, where chairs were shared out among all parties according to their strengths. Chairs were shared in this way for one year in Solihull and for a period in Clwyd until the majority of the Labour group refused to co-operate.

The most common approach is a minority administration. Sometimes it will be conceded automatically, as in Cambridge, to the largest party. In Waltham Forest a protocol recognises the minority administration as having a special relationship with the officers. A minority administration can be brought about with the tacit or open support of another party, but often, as in Cheshire, with procedural changes to remove the status of the chair, as

Andrew Stunnell, the then Liberal leader claimed to have done, although the position of chair carries a weight with officers that cannot be removed by changes in procedure alone. Where either Labour or Conservatives form a minority administration, Liberal Democrats sometimes show their strength by transferring support in mid-term, often over budgetary issues. This pattern became less common, because disagreement lessened when authorities spent at the cap.

Where Liberal Democrats form the minority administration it can be challenged only by Labour and Conservative agreement, which is unlikely. If however the Liberal Democrats over-exploit the position, it can lead to at least tactical agreements between Labour and Conservative. In Gloucestershire, Labour and Conservatives agreed to vote down the Liberal administration in mid-term, on the basis that the Conservatives would hold the chairs for one year and Labour for the next. Alternatively a challenge to a Liberal Democrat administration may lead to 'no administration'. 'No administration' means there are no chairs in the traditional sense, but chairs for the meeting only. They can be chosen in different ways. In Oxfordshire it was on the basis of an agreed rota (although at one time the Conservatives refused, adopting an oppositional role). In Bedfordshire chairs were decided at each meeting. In Cambridgeshire senior county councillors, often former chairs of the council, took the role for the meeting only. In Leicestershire at one time the authority took counsel's opinion on whether meetings required a chair at all. The advice was that it was not necessary if the committee found a way of conducting its business.

This discussion of hung authorities shows their variety. Many factors are at work. The arithmetic of the hung authority is important. There are differences from the relative strengths of the parties and not just the three main parties. In Stroud the hung authority had five groups, with Independents and the largest Green party group on any council. Chairs were shared, with the key arena being a strategy group on which all parties except the Conservatives were represented, until the Greens left over an environmental issue. Decisions in a hung authority can turn on the vote of a single Independent. Some do not welcome this position. In one county it was regarded as fortunate that two Independents cancelled each other out.

Past history is important. Where there is normally a particular party in control, the former opposition parties will be drawn together. Past personal relationships are important, particularly between the leaders, making co-operation easy or difficult. One Labour leader, explaining why he had made no approaches to the then Alliance said 'I like the Tories, I respect the Tories. You know where you are with them.'

### Returning to majority control

Once an authority has been hung, the politics of the authority can be changed even when it returns to majority control. In one county, it was said that the opposition gained from the experience of sharing power: 'They know the right questions to ask', 'They know what information is available'. Working relations that have been established while hung can continue. In one authority that had been hung for nine years, Labour could have used the previous mayor's vote to take the mayoralty again and gain control. There was a reluctance 'to ride roughshod'. Regular leaders' and spokespersons' meetings can continue after the hung authority experience, depending upon the attitude of the majority party and the leadership style. One Labour leader felt the party was so effective in such meetings despite being in opposition that 'we put up motions to be defeated to hide the fact that we get our way on so much council business'. On the other hand, in another county a group of young Turks elected in 1989 wanted an assertive Conservative group and looked back on the hung position with distaste. In the return to majority control as in the hung authority, there is diversity of experience.

## Relations with the party

There is a separation between the party outside the council and the group on the council. Yet there is a connection between them. The group requires party support for elections. The party looks to the group to achieve party policy.

Party organisation takes different forms. Paralleling the council, there may be an organisation covering the area of the authority.

However, except where the authority's boundaries match those of the parliamentary constituency, the district or county party may not represent the main party unit and is merely a convenience for the local electoral process. It may claim – and, in the Labour Party, has claimed – a greater role, but nationally the Labour Party has sought to restrict the role of former 'city parties' to local government issues.

Different models of party–group relations can be found. There is a greater tendency in the Labour Party than in other parties for the local party to assert claims to determine policy. In a minority of authorities, the district party chooses the leadership positions, either jointly with the group or separately, their views being normally accepted by the group. While the Labour Party model standing orders allow for the expression of party views on the leadership, they do not allow the party to decide the leadership, and such practice is rare, although that practice may change with the introduction of new forms of political executive.

The manifesto can be a source of conflict. Not all parties issue manifestos and even where they do, they can be anodyne. On the other hand some manifestos are detailed. In the Labour Party, 'while it is the function of the local party to determine election policy, it is the definite responsibility of the Labour group to decide group strategy and action on the Council' (Game and Leach, 1995, p. 17). That can be a source of conflict and the group can be criticised for not implementing policies. Disagreement is not inevitable, and the manifesto may express clear agreement on policy between group and party. In some authorities, such as Sheffield, the council formally adopted the manifesto. That left open the issue of the extent to which the authority can implement the manifesto because of its financial or legal positions. One Treasurer said, 'This council has adopted two contradictory documents, the manifesto and the budget.'

At the ward or constituency level the relationship is important to the councillor, since problems in the relationship can lead to de-selection, which is probably as common in the Conservative Party as in the Labour Party. As Game and Leach point out, de-selection in both main parties is considerably more frequently personal than political (Game and Leach, 1993).

In the Labour Party the local district party can develop an assertive role, and party–group conflict can develop. It is not inevitable.

Some leaders, such as Graham Stringer in Manchester, based their challenge to the previous leadership on the local party and maintained its support, involving it in major policy decisions. In Walsall the local party backed the Tribune group on the council during their years of opposition to the leadership. The district party committed the group to decentralisation in its manifesto in both Walsall and Rochdale.

The Conservative Party is probably more accustomed to accept a leadership role. National habits have their influence locally, and leaders face less possibility of a challenge from the party organisation. One leader on being interviewed about the manifesto could not find his copy and had clearly forgotten its existence.

The Liberal Democrats are likely to lay less emphasis on party dominance or party discipline. In the same way that their councillors will emphasise their right to follow their own views, so the party will respect group views and their independence. Some manifestos have laid the basis for immediate action, such as the Liberal Democrats' manifesto in Kingston-on-Thames which expressed a commitment to decentralisation, as had the Liberal manifesto in Tower Hamlets.

Hall and Leach have characterised the different patterns:

(a) A significant overlap of membership between party group and active local party, but a strong sense of the distinctness of the two pieces of machinery.

(b) An acceptance that the local party should take the lead in manifesto preparation, but with input from committee chairs into relevant manifesto 'working groups' to ensure a sense of realism in manifesto proposals.

(c) A leader who takes the local party seriously, reports back regularly, and who tries to generate local party support for, or at least acceptance of, proposals from the group on the council – but who will ultimately resist pressures from the local party if it is out of line with a legitimate interpretation by the party group of its brief.

(d) Considerable use of informal channels between key actors in the local party and the party leadership, and a recognition that most problems can be resolved in this way rather than by the passing of formal resolutions.

(Hall and Leach, 1996, p. 17)

*National party organisation*

While party–group relations can be a source of variation at local level, there are also national influences. Both the Conservative and Labour Parties have local government officers with supporting staff. They are small in relation to the scale and diversity of local government. Many local government officers ascribe an unreal influence to such bodies: 'Millbank has insisted on it', or 'Conservative central office had a word with them'. The party headquarters issue guidance, but that does not mean it is necessarily followed. The Labour Party's guidance on group policy in hung authorities had to be modified because it was being ignored in practice. Conservative authorities varied greatly in the extent to which they pursued competitive tendering when urged to.

There can be specific interventions by national parties, possibly through their regional offices. The Labour Party intervened in disputes over decentralisation in Walsall and in group disputes in Tower Hamlets and Hackney, suspending councillors from the party or the group. The Liberal Democrat Party held an inquiry into the Tower Hamlets. Such interventions rarely resolve issues, since situations can only be fully understood within authorities rather than from outside.

The Liberal Democrats have not developed a local government section in the same way as other parties, because of the existence of the strong Association of Liberal Democrat Councillors, based in a disused nonconformist chapel in Hebden Bridge, close to the West Yorkshire town that provides the setting for *The Last of the Summer Wine* television programme. It marks out the independence and character of the Association, remote from the metropolis and committed to community politics. When I visited it, I recorded 'The big hall of the Birchfield Centre was full of feverish activities – piles of paper, posters over the wall, divided into areas for different activities or organisations.'

The Association gives guidance, not rules to be followed, but advice on strategy and tactics. Their paper on how to manage a balanced authority has been influential – and not merely on Liberals, as they found in one county: when the Liberals met representatives of the Labour group, shortly after it became hung, they found them sitting with copies of the publication in front of them. The Association employs staff who act as advisers. Their influence depends not on formal authority but on the quality of their advice.

It can be argued that the national parties are an influence for uniformity, but their influence is heavily mediated by local circumstance and by local actors.

## Varying cultures

The politics of a local authority are played out in a setting with its own political culture, itself a product of history and of local circumstance. As Hoggert has argued, 'Local political cultures specify the ground rules for the acceptability of local political action.' Yet as he also argued, 'operational styles are embedded in cultural traits but not in a fixed way' (Hoggert, 1991, p. 133). The styles are the immediate product of the political composition of the council, the membership of the groups, their relationship to the local parties, and the nature of the leadership. Personalities play their parts but in a particular setting which has its own influence on political style.

On my visits to authorities I encountered diversity as I went from one authority to another finding the particularity of political style. Westminster, Wandsworth and Bradford were well known as flagships for the Conservatives under Margaret Thatcher. Socialist republics were once spoken of in Islington or Sheffield, or in a different sense in Lambeth or Liverpool. Tower Hamlets became well known for the Liberals' policy of decentralisation. Variety has been seen in the description in this and the preceding chapter. Some pen-portraits provide further examples.

Kensington and Chelsea is divided sharply between an affluent area returning Conservatives and an area of deprivation returning Labour. There is an assured Conservative majority with seats rarely if ever changing hands. The majority do not feel challenged by Labour and are ready to involve the opposition on certain issues. Stability is dominant in the culture. The leader had been longer in local government than the chief executive. It is a traditional Conservative authority 'devoted to the interests of the residents' and conservation, responding to the active pressure of 120 residents' associations. It has out-sourced certain activities, not as a matter of general policy but for practical reasons.

In another London Borough the leader saw his role as to bring stability to the Labour group which was in an overwhelming majority on the council, but faced difficult financial conditions. The group had been able to cope with successive financial crises, but had almost come to regard crisis as the norm. 'Crisis brought its own excitement', and 'the adrenalin flowed'. A group accustomed to crisis found it difficult to face the possibility of longer-term thinking.

Durham County Council, grounded in mining traditions, has been Labour-controlled since 1926. It sees itself as belonging to the traditional Labour movement. It was conservative in administration, with heavy involvement of councillors, a concern for detail, appointments of chief officers based on six standard questions and relatively untouched by management fashion. It is changing, but in a way other authorities changed some time ago; it remains 'a canny authority going about things in a canny way'.

Rotherham brought together in 1974 an old steel town with many mining villages. The miners' lodge, the miners' welfare, the local party and the local council were linked with particular individuals playing a role in all settings. The mining background proved most powerful in the Labour group. Leading figures from the five former urban districts and rural districts share the comradeship of the NUM. Mining has left the area, but the leadership in this authority looked back and talked readily of mining. Inevitably there was continuity, with in 1991 leader and chairs having been in the same position since the 1970s. There is virtually no opposition, with some seats unopposed. In the former mining villages, if there is a contest, 'all you need to do is ring a bell and they come out'. Stability of control and of practice went hand in hand, yet new members of the group were restless and challenge was possible.

Rochdale seemed to be an authority preserved from old times. It had two wards held by the Liberals since Gladstone's day. It was hung until 1980, although it did not know the word, with chairs allocated without regard to party. Labour, on gaining control in 1980, changed that, committing themselves to either control or opposition. In 1982 Conservative and Liberals joined to form an administration. The Labour leader eventually retired in his seventies and was succeeded by a man in his twenties as a result of district party involvement. He was full-time leader, ever-seeking initiatives in a group that did not fully support him. However, with district party support he ensured a commitment to decentralisation.

An East Anglian authority controlled by the Conservative was a council of farmers. They were not given to much involvement in council business, but were prepared to make judgement on officers, and by implication their proposals, as they would make judgements in the market. Instinct made them suspicious of change. Passions could be aroused but only over issues like straw burning.

In Dwyfor, 78 per cent of the population spoke Welsh, and councillors who were largely elected as Independents felt deeply about the culture of the Welsh language. They saw themselves as protecting a way of life against an alien culture. Tourism in certain forms and second homes were seen as threats. Planning issues were crucial: 'The local councillor must represent the area; the others have to represent the authority.'

These pen-portraits, all drawn at a particular time, are merely examples. In every authority particular features can be found. In one Merseyside authority, council and committees can be noisy and angry, which could be as easily directed at officers as against other parties. 'You have to have a very thick skin to be an officer in Merseyside.' In a Welsh authority, Labour lost control and Plaid Cymru formed an administration in a hung authority. It was a period of uncertainty as 'political innocents were out-manoeuvred by experienced politicians', or so an officer saw it. South Lakeland when I first visited it was an authority of Independents in which the politics of geography centred on the dominance of Kendal as perceived by the councillors from Ulverston and far-flung rural areas. In Wychavon, 'tree preservation orders were charged with drama'. In Corby, following the rejection at the election of the previous Labour leadership who stood against official Labour candidates, a leader and deputy leader were elected who although on the council since 1979 had never held a chair of a committee. Thurrock saw itself as a safe Labour area in which new members had to work an apprenticeship which could last ten years. The loss of the parliamentary seat led the group to recognise the area was changing. In Barnet, while Margaret Thatcher was MP, her presence was felt. 'A well-known person connected with the borough' was a phrase often heard.

# 10 The Process of Management Change

## Dominant management ideas

Under the impact of the challenges set out in Chapter 8 the need for management change in local authorities has been widely recognised. In most of the authorities visited in the last five years, there has been a 'management change programme'.

These were influenced by emerging management ideas. Management gurus such as Tom Peters were brought over from America to address local government conferences. Management courses propagated the ideas and the Audit Commission was a powerful force in codifying the ideas.

Many of these management ideas were developed in the private sector and applied sometimes unchanged and uncritically in local authorities and sometimes sympathetically transformed. There was a widespread adoption of these ideas and legislation reinforced them. Certain local authorities become known for the extent and nature of their innovations. Many innovations take place in particular authorities, and then through local government's networks of communication and conferences become well-known. The Wrekin was marked by a focus on organisational culture. The then Chief Executive was known for sitting at the reception desk in the council offices for half an hour each week. It provided a symbol of cultural change, which became recognised in the world of local government. York introduced service contracts specifying the form and level of service and how redress could be obtained. It was followed by Islington and Lewisham, and influenced the government's approach to the Citizen's Charter and the response of other authorities. Southend and Wandsworth pioneered contracting out, as Solihull and Cambridgeshire pioneered financial devolution to schools: in different ways these ideas were then translated into national legislation.

As a result of all these influences certain themes became widely accepted:

- An emphasis on *organisational values*, as local authorities produced statements of the values they sought to promote within the organisational culture.
- A stress upon *closeness to the customer* as local authorities sought new relationships with the public.
- The development of *strategic management* as local authorities sought to clarify their direction in a changing environment.
- The devolution of management responsibility to *cost centres*.
- The use of *performance management* with managers of cost centres being held responsible for specified targets.
- The conduct of internal relationships between units on the basis of *service level agreements*.
- The development of *human resource management* through staff development and communication to reinforce organisational values.

It was almost as if there was a new management ideology, widely accepted throughout local government as the one right way to manage authorities. This set of ideas was found by research into what were seen as well-run authorities by their peers in local government. One authority described by Leach and his colleagues depicted what it called 'old think' and 'new think'.

| *Old think* | *New think* |
|---|---|
| • provider/producer driven | • consumer driven |
| • expanding and stable revenues | • declining revenues |
| • municipalism | • compulsory competitive tendering, buy-in and joint ventures |
| • establishments and vacancies | • cash limited budget |
| • slow rhythm of change | • fast rhythm of change |

Another made the following contrast:

| | |
|---|---|
| • traditional, static | • change-orientated |
| • insular | • open, communicating |

- centre-focused
- incremental short-term

- rule-driven
- passive employment policies
- no recognised corporate culture

- finance/treasury driven

- customer-focused
- business-orientated; planned
- flexible
- active employment policies

- corporated (*sic*) culture geared to management style and purpose
- more policy driven

(Leach *et al.*, 1993)

There were exceptions on my visits. It was said in one authority, where the language of the new dominant ideas was notably absent, 'You must realise that in the language of diffusion theory we are late adaptors.' In Gateshead it was asserted 'We are not interested in the current fads. They come and go.' The impression remains of widespread adoption of at least the new language of management, although there was diversity in the meaning given to that language in practice. Management change was not restricted to these ideas. Politics had its own impact, and particularly in Liberal Democrat authorities and some Labour authorities there was interest in decentralisation to areas.

Although certain ideas were dominant in most management change programmes, what happened in practice varied from authority to authority. The changes take place within authorities conditioned by past practices and local traditions and influenced by political attitudes.

There is also in any management change the likelihood of uneven development. Change may be more readily accepted in some parts of the organisation than in others. Change in structure is more readily achieved than change in culture. Change in management processes may not be matched by change in political processes. Indeed there can be false expectations of councillors. 'We do not need councillors who are managers but councillors who can question them', as one chief executive said. The Nolan Committee expressed concern – 'Proposed new methods of working will not make progress if they fly in the face of local experience' (Nolan, 1997a, p. 14) – pointing out that councillors commonly seek office to run things and to help their constituents; not to 'exercise strategic direction', 'hold officers to account' or 'any of the other fashionable statements of purpose' (ibid).

Nevertheless, despite the exceptions and the variations, the management changes have to be understood as a significant transition in many, if not in all, authorities.

## The process of transition

Periods of transition in the working of authorities are often marked or initiated by change of personnel. Change in personnel does not itself bring about change, but can initiate a process of transition. In appointing a chief officer or in selecting a new leader, a local authority may be looking for change. A chief executive may be appointed 'to bring about change' without the nature of the change being clarified, motivated by a feeling that old ways of working are no longer appropriate. This mood reflects the tension between the inheritance of history and present challenges. It is given expression in phrases such as 'getting away from bureaucracy', 'narrow departmentalism' or an aspiration to 'corporate working' or 'community leadership'.

A new party group coming to power may be committed to change. They may feel frustrated by the chief executive or chief officers, if they seem reluctant to change. Ironically it can be the effective dominant chief executive who is seen as the obstacle. It is not that such a chief executive does not accept the need for a political change of direction but that he represents a style of working alien to the new group. They look to his retirement and a new appointment for change in the way of working with which the chief executive was associated.

In one London borough, the need for change and even its possibility was realised by councillors only during the job interview. They had advertised for a chief executive based on the model of the one who was about to retire, who had seen his role as that of the traditional clerk. One candidate applied, setting out his views on management, stating that if appointed he would want to change the role and bring about management change in the authority. He said he should not be appointed if that was not what they wanted. The members were impressed and appointed him.

It is not always necessary for a change of person to occur. Some leaders and chief executives have recognised the need for change, and sometimes a continuing need. John Foster, the chief executive of Middlesbrough, held the position over twenty years, but had the capacity to remotivate himself and redirect himself for new challenges and new changes. A change can come suddenly and unexpectedly. At a management team in Brent the leader surprised the team by announcing that he wanted all services market tested, not previously the policy of the group. This initiative started a process of management changes, which developed their own form. Robin Wendt as chief executive of Cheshire felt after eight years that more was needed than for the authority to be 'a well-run hung authority', and proposed to the council a diagnostic consultancy, which identified a lack of strategic direction, to which the chief executive responded, proposing a new structure which gained political support. Brian Flood who was leader of North Tyneside for over ten years was committed to a continuous process of change as necessary to the creation of a learning organisation. Councillor Hall, the leader of Stevenage since reorganisation and before, supported changes in the 1990s to build community governance, involving area committees and new relationships with other organisations in the community. Councillor Dennis Heptonstall who had been Labour leader in East Staffordshire since reorganisation, developed, with the support of the long-serving chief executive, ward action service plans as a new means of community involvement.

Change is not easily brought about in large-scale organisations. One Northern city leader expressed his frustration at the difficulty of bringing about 'almost any change' in a large authority. Change is more easily achieved in a small authority when there is commitment by the chief executive and leader. It is no accident that many of the authorities most marked by the range and extent of change, as opposed to particular changes, are small authorities. In different ways and periods, Arun, Braintree, South Somerset and the Wrekin come to mind. The recently appointed chief executive of Craven produced an analysis of its strengths and weaknesses. Strengths included a small loyal staff deeply committed to the area and a knowledgeable group of councillors involved in many local organisations. Weaknesses included lack of communication across departments, over-long hierarchies and little focus on service users. She proposed a strategic review leading to a radical reorganisation.

In a number of instances the initiative for change was brought about through the stimulus of management consultants. They can be brought in by councillors frustrated by officers' reluctance to change. In some instances the consultants' report has led to the retirement of the chief executive, who did not feel able or willing to introduce the new structure. And sometimes it has led councillors to seek retirement. In one authority, while the councillors would not accept reorganisation proposals by the chief executive, they agreed to consultants being brought in, whose recommendation followed similar lines. Consultants have been an important influence on local authorities in the process of organisational change, as a source of innovation. They can be a force for uniformity in their general acceptance of dominant management ideas.

There is among councillors a tendency to see structural change as the key element in the transition, with the danger that it becomes an end in itself. It is a visible change with the clear attractions 'of unravelling old ties'. Structures have the apparent advantage that they can be described, discussed and implemented. Structures become symbols that communicate the idea of change, although the communication can mislead. Perhaps the greatest danger is that structural change and management change are equated, so that too little attention is paid to the need for change in processes, in culture and in communication.

In one metropolitan district a new chief executive, appointed with an expectation of change, concentrated on developing management processes and on cultural changes. He had deliberately avoided structural change as a distraction from the main process of change, and achieved much. In conversation with leading councillors, there was a sense that 'nothing had changed' because there had been no structural change.

## Examples of management change

A variety of examples can be given. In East Cambridgeshire, the chief executive had become the only chief officer. He had two assistant chief executives, who along with a corporate support manager formed a client core, surrounded by a group of providers, who can be the local authority itself, business management centres, voluntary bodies or private contractors. The relationships were governed by contracts, service-level agreements or statements of accountability.

In Mendip, it was said 'if you look about the council offices, it is impossible to tell without knowing it, who works for the authority and who for a contractor'. There were ten contracts covering staff, including finance, with the finance adviser from the private sector sitting in the management team.

In Fareham, a new chief executive introduced a new structure and processes, arguing that client–contractor splits were oversimplistic. The following roles were identified:

- a core role, concerned with the council's overall purpose, style and standards
- a programme role, developing strategies and programmes
- a purchaser role, turning programmes into detailed action plans
- a provider role, covering both service and support providers
- a support purchaser's role, helping users of support providers to obtain the services they require.

In Brent, business units had to meet defined outputs within the overall resources given. They operated within a corporate framework of rules on finance, personnel, property and IT, which are kept at a minimum. Thus the authority rejected the Audit Commission's emphasis on central purchasing, except when asked by business units. Their view was that purchases are best arranged locally by a business unit manager. Equally the units worked out their own accounting systems to suit their own needs. Each business unit had its own account and its own cheque book – a powerful symbol in convincing managers of the extent of the change. Central ledgers had been dismantled and central requirements for information reduced to the minimum required by external bodies and to ensure overall financial control. The business units were divided into contractor units, commissioning units and core units.

In Sunderland, a management model was introduced involving strategic planning with vision, aims, values and ten strategic objectives. It provided the framework for medium-term financial and services plans. A system of performance appraisal was introduced. There was a performance review process involving an in-depth examination of activities on a three-year rolling programme.

In North Tyneside, traditional departments were replaced by 15 (initially 16) new functions each of which carry full responsibility for service delivery in linked areas. Five (originally six) directors of equal status were appointed to carry through strategic issues without a chief executive, although a head of paid service had to be appointed. The directors are given lead responsibility for particular strategic issues, client groups and geographical areas; provide links with outside agencies and oversee a number of functions but with no individual budgetary responsibility (LGMB, 1997).

'There are still traces of civilisation in Dorset' said the chief executive, reflecting a 'Dorset way of doing things' in an authority seeing itself as set in the traditions of rural England. Change is pursued gently if persistently. Performance management has been introduced on a voluntary basis, extending through peer pressure. 'Simple SLAs procedure' avoids an excessive bureaucracy, with invoicing normally on an annual fee.

*The cracks are beginning to appear*

The changes have been introduced in organisations whose structures, processes and culture have been moulded by history. There can be tensions between this inheritance and these new approaches. The tensions are not merely because of inertia. There is an inherent tension between the new management approaches carried to extremes and the nature of local government.

Thus while a stress on the customer has been valuable in sensitising local authorities to the views of the users of the service, the word 'customer' cannot capture the multifarious activities of the local authority, involving rationing, arbitrating, balancing and regulating. In addition an emphasis on the public as customer can lead to a neglect of the public as citizen. And through the public as citizen, the local authority is constituted as a political institution.

The need to set objectives has a value in making explicit what may have remained implicit. For councillors, the difficult task is not to set objectives but to achieve the right balance – for example, between economic development and conservation or transport and the environment – and that task is often neglected in management approaches.

The development of service-level agreements between service departments as clients and central departments as providers has led to previously non-existent discussions over the nature of the service received, which have a clear value, but have also exposed the weakness of the client, who is often dependent on what the provider offers.

Roles can become complex. One chief executive was also the treasurer. When he asked for information from computer services, which had been constituted as a trading unit, he was asked whether he wanted it as chief executive formally in charge, or as treasurer with access to it. In both cases he was entitled to it, but if it was as a client he should be denied it. 'People had become very silly. Clients and contractors tended to act as they thought business acted. It got very fraught. We are now seeking more of a spirit of partnership based on recognition and mutual interest. It's taken a lot to get back to some sort of partnership after years of cut-throat stuff' (Rao and Young, 1995, p. 41).

The development of cost centres and the separation of client and contractor can create a series of separate units which focus on particular tasks, reducing the capacity of the authority for organisational learning and for responsiveness to community issues. In Lewisham, Barry Quirk, the chief executive, has argued, 'The task is now to move beyond devolving responsibility to front-line managers and empowering them to act. We need to realise the advantages of being one organisation.' He seeks to combine the benefits of 'a small team' as strategic managers '(economies of scope) with the benefits of a large organisation (economies of scale)' (Quirk, 1997, p. 9). In Brent, which developed a series of business units, the 'risk of fragmentation was recognised. Specific measures are needed to ensure there is one united single face, that we are not giving customers the run around from one service point to another and that the council remains overall more than the sum of its parts.'

Management change is likely to continue as weaknesses in new management approaches appear, and efforts are made to overcome them while realising their strengths.

**Response to change**

Patterns of uniformity and diversity can be explored by examining particular changes in response both to national legislation and government policy and to local political and other factors. In the remainder of this chapter discussion will focus on the following selected changes, which were important in the period covered by my visits:

- The impact of CCT
- Financial pressure and the budgetary process
- From co-ordination to policy direction
- The pattern of industrial relations
- Toward decentralisation
- Emerging issues

*The impact of CCT*

Uniformity of response should never be assumed, and the process of management change shows variety both in approach and in outcome. In different local authorities there have been different responses even to legislative requirements.

Christie distinguished two approaches to CCT. One was 'to accept the structures of CCT, try and survive for the foreseeable future and hope that in the long-term the legal environment will favour' in-house provision. The other was 'to accept that competition is a way of life for local government and that the emphasis must be on matching the capabilities of the organisation to the environment, building on its strengths and facing up to competition' (Christie, 1991). Walsh and Davis found four basic political attitudes:

- A hostility to the principles of direct labour and a desire to see work done by the private sector where possible.
- A neutral stance of opting for internal or external provision according to what was best value for money.
- An attitude of preferring the DSO to win but accepting the value of contractors when they could provide a better price.
- An approach of making every effort to help the DSO to win.

                                        (Walsh and Davis, 1993, p. 26)

These differing attitudes were found on my visits. In one Northern metropolitan authority, trade union values were seen as paramount. It was assumed without question that the authority would do everything possible to retain work in-house, except reduction in pay and conditions. No departure from national agreements was even contemplated. This authority was untouched by management change, holding as far as possible to traditional ways. This was the type of the authority identified by Geddes and Wahlberg, 'that tended to have a strong and effective direct labour sector, often supported not only by trade union involvement amongst the workforce but also by the presence of trade union members on the council' (Geddes and Wahlberg, 1996, p. 22). It was contrasted by them with authorities which were 'finance-driven' and ready to consider externalisation, and with authorities 'implementing government policies in a fairly straightforward way' (ibid, pp. 23–36).

In Sunderland, the policy of the Labour council was 'to maintain a viable in-house workforce which is capable of winning tenders and providing services to the required standard with a public service ethos'. In Berkshire, on the other hand, both the Conservative administration and the shared administration in the hung authority supported a widespread programme of externalisation. To the chief executive it was seen as a way of making a large county manageable. The Labour leader supported it as avoiding the constraints of CCT. One researcher has commented on Berkshire, 'It has externalised so much that you wonder just what the county is – the county is now being run by the private sector' (Painter and Goodwin, 1996).

The Conservative Leader of Wandsworth argued, 'operational inefficiency can be overcome by a combination of three key measures, specifying services carefully, vigorously pursuing competitive tendering and using surveys to ensure customers are getting what they want' (Lister, 1995, p. 10). On the other hand, Bromley, another Conservative authority, had a policy that 'Except where we have a statutory duty to do so, a performance centre will not be tested in open competition simply because it has distinguished its client and contractor functions and set up business systems.' From different attitudes different patterns of management emerge, not merely over CCT but in relation to market mechanisms generally.

*Financial pressure and the budgetary process*

Elcock and his colleagues identified that the main features of the traditional budgetary process were:

- A narrow range of focus for each department and committee, together with a narrow span of control for each chief officer and committee chairman.
- The preparation of Estimates in isolation from other Departments and committees.
- The 'Base' or 'committed' expenditure in the Budget will go largely unscrutinised and unchallenged . . .
- The absence of overall policies governing the preparation of the Budget.
- The absence of means to prioritise the bids made by committees for resources.
- The absence of attempts to assess the overall impact of committees' expenditure plans until late in the budgetary cycle.

(Elcock et al., 1989, pp. 69–70)

　　The traditional budgetary process normally consisted of preparation of estimates by departments which were then subject to appraisal. The process tended to be dominated by the treasurer and a few leading members who would sometimes conduct 'sweat-sessions' or 'Spanish inquisitions' (Greenwood *et al.*, 1977) to reduce budgetary demands to acceptable levels. The clerk, and later even the chief executive, might not be involved in the process. In one county the former treasurer was described as 'playing the work of resource allocation as a hidden mystery'. Variations had developed. Marshall described the predetermined rate procedure in which departments worked out their budgets within levels set for them (Marshall, 1960).

　　From the mid-1970s the assumption of growth changed to the reality of constraint and later of cutback. The management of constraint could for a time be moderated by increases in the rates or by 'creative accountancy' (Davies *et al.*, 1983). Creative accountancy solved immediate problems at the cost of a future which soon became the present. Eventually, all local authorities had to face the reality not merely of constraint, but of cutback.

The Conservative government developed a combination of controls that were impossible to avoid. The capping of local authority expenditure was achieved in a way that minimised political costs. By announcing the criteria in advance the government ensured that nearly all authorities capped themselves, rather than set budgets above the cap and have a cap imposed, with the uncertainties and costs involved. The Labour government has modified capping, but retained it as a reserve power and in 1999 did not specify criteria in advance or cap any authority.

Capping removed from practical consideration in most authorities the decision on the level of expenditure, and therefore, apart from the use of balances, the level of local taxation. In doing so it reduced political debate. One Conservative leader in a London borough, whose party lost control, said 'we could not campaign against the Labour Party by saying they would increase expenditure, since we were already spending at the cap'.

Local authorities will again face budgetary choice on the level of expenditure and the level of council tax if the government merely retains capping as a reserve power to be used only rarely and does not specify the criteria in advance. The budgetary choice involves the balance between the need for expenditure and the costs of taxation. Making that choice is difficult because the political costs are not clear, with no recent precedent as a guide in many authorities. There has been choice on the budgetary process but it has been choice on the allocation of expenditure or on *where* the cuts will be made; even where there has been actual growth, the general perception has been of cuts. 1999 has seen the tentative re-opening of budgetary choice.

Under constraint, the budgetary process spread over time as decisions became more difficult. 'It seems one has only got this year's budget out of the way before we are on the next year's', or 'You can only have a fortnight off between budgets.' There is now a greater tendency to undertake in-depth reviews as the search for savings has grown, and to identify priorities rather than impose an across-the-board cut. The budgetary issues are no longer the monopoly of the treasurer. Chief executives and sometimes the management team are involved. There have been authorities where the chief executive has sought to bring the budgetary process under his direct control, serviced by a budgetary office. More councillors tend to be involved in the process, at least in the majority party or more widely in hung authorities. The public are more often consulted, if only to ensure their understanding of the constraints under which authorities operate.

Although there are general tendencies brought about by the experience of constraint, there remains considerable variation. While there has been a tendency to ensure greater councillor involvement, there remain important differences in the extent of that involvement. The budgetary process can vary in the extent to which parameters are set at the outset of the process and whether there are different percentage reductions on different services. There is variation in the extent to which priorities are identified. In Sandwell in 1991, priorities were determined on the basis of questionnaires to all councillors (Collinge and Leach, 1997). Some authorities pursue zero-based budgeting, but the impracticality of scrutiny of every item is likely to lead to a rolling review. The presentation of information can vary, with Middlesbrough distinguishing mandatory from discretionary expenditure. Dudley, among other authorities, has resorted to the sophistication of decision conferencing, using computer modelling to assist budgetary choice. In the end, a budgetary choice has to be made, which is a matter of judgement. It can be an informed judgement and one widely shared, but that is not necessarily so. There is variation in judgement as well as in processes.

Financial constraint has been greatest on capital expenditure, leading to a search for other sources of funds. Authorities have differed in the emphasis given to the search and in their success in achieving it. Some authorities explore every source – European grants; lottery funds; single regeneration budget; disposal of property; private finance and other forms of partnerships – and have developed the skills and knowledge required. Others lack the skills and knowledge and have not sought to attain them.

*From co-ordination to policy direction*

Chapter 4 emphasised that there had been a continuing concern for co-ordination of an authority's activities. Co-ordination was seen as about bringing together separate parts for effective administration. There is now a growing emphasis on co-ordination for policy direction.

The Maud Committee stands at the point of transition. In its recommendations it emphasised the administrative efficiency that can come from co-ordination. But it also saw the need for management processes to set objectives for the authority. Its recommendations for a management board to be in effect a political executive was universally rejected but led to a majority of authorities creating policy committees, later to become policy and resources committees (Greenwood *et al.*, 1969).

In the national world of local government certain ideas and forms came to be widely adopted following the recommendations of the Bains Report:

- the policy and resources committee
- the chief executive as head of the paid service and the council's chief policy adviser
- the management team as the expression of corporate management
- the process of corporate planning setting out the policies of the authority.

The part played by the new roles, and the ways the processes developed, however, varied. In some authorities there was little change. The policy and resources committee was a finance committee writ large. The chief executive was the former clerk with a new title, but playing the same role. The management team was a collection of service heads maintaining their territory. Processes of corporate planning became a routinised listing of the authority's activities. New models were built on old ways of working.

Many of the attempts at corporate planning were based on assumptions about growth which were soon challenged by the experience of constraint and cutback. The forms of corporate planning adopted covered all the activities of the authority with the same emphasis and in the same detail. They did not discriminate between important and unimportant. They gave no guidance on how to deal with the changed financial position of the authorities.

In the 1980s and 1990s there came a new interest in policy planning processes as a means of ensuring co-ordination in policy direction. Strategic management was promoted by the Audit Commission, starting with their guidance to local authorities entitled 'The Competitive Council' (a strange title for local authorities

encouraged to enter into partnerships). Continued financial pressure led local authorities to recognise the danger of using short-
term measures. The need to consider long-term effects and to
identify priorities was recognised. Concern for the 'wicked issues'
became priorities as authorities identified community safety, the
environment and poverty as requiring a special focus.

Local authorities became concerned with the new fragmentation within, as departments devolved responsibilities to cost centres
or established trading units, either under the impact of compulsory competitive tendering or as part of the general development
of management in the authority.

Leach and his colleagues identify 'five different ways in which
fragmentation might become apparent':

- If the authority's learning capacity was inhibited or impeded
  (e.g. across the client/contractor split).
- If the authority found it impossible to carry out mandated
  functions effectively (e.g. if a service planning role became
  problematical because of the variety of service providers).
- If the authority's capacity to respond effectively to problems as
  experienced and presented by individuals and communities is
  frustrated.
- If the authority's capacity to secure necessary co-operation
  amongst external agencies in the pursuit of mandated functions is restricted.
- If the authority finds it impossible to (at least) influence outcomes in relation to its strategic agenda.

(Leach *et al.*, 1996)

Some authorities recognise the need for direction, if the authority
is not to become a series of separate units that conduct their relationship with each other through fixed contracts or service-level
agreements. The need for co-ordination between departments
has become the need to give direction to a fragmented structure.
It has not been universally recognised. Leach and his colleagues
identify some authorities as adopting 'a reinterpretative' response
to fragmentation, in the sense that they have seen that differentiation within the organisation requires integration, but they also
found authorities with an *ad hoc* response, authorities resisting

change and enthusiasts for market mechanisms who did not see the issues of fragmentation as relevant.

Recognition of the need for strategy means an authority reviewing its policies and organisation in relation to a changing environment, involving choices on the direction of the authority and its priorities. There is a general tendency, but also considerable variation: a distinction between strategic management, which involves that process of review and choice, and strategic planning, which is the most common approach to strategic management and involves procedures leading to a plan. In 1994, 74 per cent of all authorities had adopted a mission or core value statement and 59 per cent a corporate or strategic plan. Others were considering them. On the other hand, there remained 19 per cent of authorities which had not prepared the former and 24 per cent the latter and were not even considering it (Local Government Management Board, 1995). Some authorities have produced a mission statement or its equivalent but have not produced a strategic plan. It is easier to produce a mission statement than to translate it into practicalities.

Mission statements and strategic plans can be prepared by officers and ratified by councillors, sometimes without much discussion, for there is often little that can be said about the more anodyne of mission statements or of objectives in strategic plans. Who could disagree that the authority should aim at a healthy environment or that it should be caring? The process can, however, be driven politically, giving expressions to manifestos, and lead to significant variations between authorities.

Leach set out a list of most popular themes, showing such variations as: 'business-like; competitive; value for money; partnership; citizenship; community; customer-orientation; service quality; communication; consultation; equality; accessibility; valuation of staff; civic pride; caring' (Leach, 1996).

In Tower Hamlets, the chief executive said she had 'tried to avoid a grand mission statement, which is like apple pie and motherhood' but to have one with meaning for staff. It contains passages such as: 'we should remember what it feels like to be on the wrong end of public service ... we've all been on the blunt end of rudeness, stupidity and inability to communicate from the private sector. If it's difficult to deliver services well that people want and have choice over, the task is much harder in multi-service, complex public services.' 'We will aim to always surprise and please our users with responsive and caring services.'

In Somerset, core principles were set out:

- To disperse power
- To encourage active citizenship
- To put the environment at the centre of our thinking
- To ensure services of the highest quality
- To ensure staff are motivated
- To provide as far as possible equitable access
- To improve access to services by decentralisation.

The processes vary considerably, whether focusing on the environment and the community or on the organisation. There is a distinction between those authorities which see strategic management as a continuing process of organisational learning, guiding the authority in adjusting to the environment, and those who see it as the production of a vision for the community or the organisation.

Collinge and Leach argue,

A corporate strategy is a set of decisions about the overall direction of an organisation, decisions which integrate its various activities and plan the response to contextual changes in the medium or long term. To be worthy of its name a 'corporate strategy' must therefore be based on conscious or deliberate decisions rather than merely the de facto direction in which a council finds itself heading. Councils differ and may be classified according to their 'strategic' direction – the orientation of the corporate strategy which they are currently pursuing.

If we step back from the substantive strategies which are being pursued, then authorities may also be classified according to their 'strategic decisions at the corporate level'. (Collinge and Leach, 1995, p. 344)

In some authorities, strategic planning is selective, focusing on a limited range of issues seen to be of strategic importance. It is an expression of strategic choice. Sometimes that is avoided. In one Scottish region the councillors identified sixteen priority objectives until it was pointed out those objectives covered everything the council did, so that there was nothing that was not a priority.

In others, strategic planning is seen as covering the whole range of activities and plotting their future direction. It can be argued that such programmes are useful management tools from which service plans setting targets for service units can be derived. Yet it can be a means of avoiding strategic choice. If everything is strategic then nothing is strategic.

In Coventry, the annual policy review following a two-day Labour group identified key themes:

- Managing for customers – both the public and internal customers.
- Managing the shifts of power, brought about by legislation and by changes in society.
- Managing in a commercial environment – internally within the council and within the city.

Those themes represented a significant change of direction involving a strategic choice.

Effective strategic management will always involve choice. In one authority the Liberal Democrats took control at a by-election, two years before the next election. They had many priorities for change including open government, economic development, equal opportunities, decentralisation, public participation, and so on. If they had attempted to do them all, none would have been done effectively by the next election – the pressure on management would have been too great. I facilitated a seminar in which the councillors recognised this point and made a strategic choice on their two priorities to be emphasised above all others. That may or may not have been strategic planning but it certainly was strategic management involving strategic choice.

*The pattern of industrial relations*

The pattern of industrial relations has changed over time and can vary between authorities. Manual workers had a strong basis in local government in the public utilities. Other staff were organised in NALGO (National and Local Government Officers' Association) after the First World War, but it was for long dominated by senior staff with leading positions held by chief officers. The world of local government was not marked by militancy. The nature of

NALGO argued against it. For other staff the existence of fair wages clauses provided safeguards. Local government experienced, especially with the growth of Whitleyism after the Second World War, detailed national terms and conditions and elaborate procedures for resolving disputes.

Industrial relations from the 1970s onwards became more militant. Different factors were at work: the growth of shop-steward influence; the reaction of public service workers to incomes policy seen to bear most severely on the public sector; the transformation of NALGO through the loss of influence of senior staff; and the emergence of 'educated radicals' amongst staff in certain departments. Militancy reached its climax in the winter of discontent in 1978/9.

In the 1980s and 1990s the pattern of industrial relations became more complex. Changes in union structure have taken place, with the emergence of MPOU (Managerial and Professional Officers' Union) as in effect a senior staff union, and the merger of NUPE (National Union of Public Employees), NALGO and COHSE (Confederation of Health Service Employees) in Unison, combining manual and non-manual workers. At the same time there has been gradual movement to greater flexibility in pay and conditions, with growth in local bargaining and some authorities opting out of national pay and conditions.

The impact of financial constraint and later of compulsory competitive tendering led to different responses depending on the approach taken by the authority and the degree of militancy in the unions. In some authorities there was a marked change in the attitudes of Labour councillors who had normally been supportive of manual worker unions, although often suspicious of NALGO as an officers' union. Attitudes changed when they were often opposed by trade unions in decentralisation or reorganisation and in dealing with financial constraint. In one authority the unions had been given a veto on any proposals for new technology, with equipment standing unused in boxes. Eventually the veto was challenged, leading to change after a strike in what was a traditional Labour authority. Councillors resisted what they saw as unreasonable or unrealistic trade union demands.

In dealing with the perceived threat of compulsory competitive tendering, councillors and unions came closer together in some authorities and there are still in many authorities close links between the Labour Party and the unions. The way industrial relations are handled will vary considerably from authority to authority, as Fowler argues, pointing out that 'The degree of elected member involvement is particularly variable' (Fowler, 1995, p. 133). Yet while variation exists, not least in the extent of militancy, there remain important forces for uniformity.

> So far the evidence suggests that labour market fragmentation has *not* driven a process of localisation of bargaining arrangements. Although central government has in some measures promoted the break-up of national employment systems they have proved remarkably durable mechanisms for labour market regulation. This durability derives not only from the corporatist interests of the bargaining partners, but from the fact that reference to national terms and conditions continues to provide a useful and efficient framework for wage negotiation and the mutual recognition of grading systems. (Doogan, 1997, p. 8)

### Towards decentralisation

Interest in area decentralisation in England derived not from national legislation but from local authorities themselves. In Scotland each new authority was required to prepare schemes of decentralisation by a year after reorganisation, while in Wales ten councillors can opt for a decentralisation scheme within an area, subject to approval by the Secretary of State. These developments for Scotland and Wales are recent. Interest in area decentralisation in England developed within local authorities in the 1980s.

Decentralisation within areas was not new, at least on a service basis. Services adopted area structures as part of the process of administration, but the emphasis of those structures was on the internal organisation of the services rather than on relations with the public or on political control. There could be area sub-committees particularly in the counties but they focused on particular services. The Maud researchers found area children's committees in some but not all counties visited. In education there was provision in the counties for delegation to divisional executives (Cohen, 1952).

Experiments in area management have been tried before, where new areas were absorbed into local authorities. Manchester set up for ten years a Withington committee 'in 1904 based upon a distinction between central and local functions'. At the end of that period a special committee of the council reported against this form of devolution and it came to an end.

> The reasons for the failure were obvious. The Committee has its own officials; clerk, surveyor, medical officer of health. They were under the control of the Committee and not under the head officials of the Town Hall. The district therefore had not the advantages of the services of the leading Manchester officials, who were responsible to different committees. The system was, in short, about as bad and as unworkable a method as the wit of man could devise. (Simon, 1938, p. 219)

Such was the conclusion of a member of the council, reflecting assumptions and beliefs which supported centralisation of services.

Centralisation was the dominant tendency in the 1960s up to reorganisation, when divisional executives in education were abolished. The dominant modes of thinking favoured centralisation to gain the alleged benefits of size on which reorganisation was based. The Bains Report recorded that 'we have received no substantial body of evidence which supports the creation of area committees. A number of authorities have in fact abandoned this concept and we can see no advantage from the management or administration viewpoint' (Bains, 1972, p. 33). The Bains Committee considered area organisation at officer level but discussed the issue virtually entirely about county services, because of the delivery problems over a large area.

The new authorities were reluctant to establish an area organisation at member level, seeing it as a threat to the new authority. There were exceptions. Stockport had area committees with area co-ordinators as a sounding-board for local views and local issues (Hambleton, 1978). West Norfolk, whose chief executive had been on the Bains Group, went further; three area committees were set up, responsible for a range of services with an area organisation (Bolton, 1974). Later the Department of the Environment launched a series of area management trials designed to increase responsiveness (Harrop *et al.*, 1978).

It was not until the 1980s that interest in area decentralisation developed in a significant way. There was growing interest in decentralisation in particular services as management ideas moved away from centralisation. However, the new movement went wider. It was concerned not with one service, but a range of services, with relations with the public leading to neighbourhood offices and with a political focus through area committees. The developments were driven mainly by Liberal and left-wing Labour politicians, although not in anything like all authorities. The movement was grounded in local politics. The chief executive in Islington said to me, 'The councillors brought into the authority a set of ideas that challenged all my past assumptions.' He found it an exciting experience.

The developments in Tower Hamlets and Kingston-on-Thames were set out in the Liberal or Liberal Democrat manifestos. Although grounded in local politics a diffusion process was at work. Walsall's neighbourhood offices became important symbols for other authorities. Later, Islington and Tower Hamlets became well known as models to be followed or avoided.

Because moves to decentralisation were based on local politics, there have inevitably been wide variations in approach. Even in Scotland where schemes of decentralisation are required by legislation there is marked variation in the approach. In England only a minority of authorities have pursued decentralisation. Chandler and his colleagues found that 38 per cent had decentralised some service delivery to geographically-based area offices, with only 20 per cent having devolved decision-making in one or more services (Chandler *et al.*, 1995).

Where decentralisation has taken place there has been variation in purpose and variation in form. Within the Labour Party, Beuret and Stoker distinguished three purposes: improving the delivery of services; an element in the campaign to transform local government; transforming social relations and politics (Beuret and Stoker, 1986). The left-wing leadership of Walsall, both in its creation of neighbourhood offices and in its abortive attempt in 1995 to devolve major functions to over 50 elected neighbourhood forums, was driven by the belief that 'socialism is more likely to be achieved in this country through participative democracy' (Burns *et al.*, 1994, p. 18). In the Liberal Party and its successors, community politics has been a motivating force. In Eastleigh, the role of area organisation is 'to facilitate community leadership and community development'. In Tower Hamlets, Councillor

Flaunders argued that 'the important thing was to take power from the officers and give it back to the people, and in a representative democracy the only sensible way to do that is to give it to the councillors' (ibid, p. 203), but in neighbourhood committees where '*you* will know *who* made all the decisions' (ibid). Gaster detected a change of emphasis over time in general approaches to decentralisation, from improving direct service provision in the 1980s to local co-ordination and exercising influence on behalf of local people (Gaster, 1995).

With different purposes it is not surprising that even within the limited number of authorities pursuing decentralisation there is considerable variation in approach. The Liberal Democrats in Kingston-on-Thames introduced neighbourhood committees composed of councillors elected for the area, as in Tower Hamlets, but they did not decentralise such a wide range of services or create separate neighbourhood organisations, although there was a neighbourhood services manager who works with a neighbourhood team of officers. South Somerset have decentralised most services to area committees with an area office structure, but have placed a stress, lacking in Tower Hamlets, on the role of the central policy and resources committee in developing strategies. In Harlow, a Labour-controlled authority, there is an important difference from these models, in that all committees reflect the political balance on the councils, as opposed to Tower Hamlets, Kingston and South Somerset or Labour-controlled Fife, where the committees consisted only of the councillors for the area, which in some areas gave the majority to other parties. Some Labour authorities are reluctant to pursue area decentralisation. In one Labour authority it was said area committees would be settings that Liberal Democrats with their commitment to community politics would be best placed to exploit.

Some authorities which have created area committees of local councillors have seen them mainly as sounding-boards. Bradford has area panels of councillors for each constituency which receive the views of an area liaison group composed of local community groups and representatives of neighbourhood forums. They 'listen to public comments in their meetings and advise the Authority on the co-ordination of services for the area' (Chandler *et al.*, 1995). A similar role is played by the area committees in Birmingham who are also allocated funds for local decision.

In other areas, such as Cumbria and Middlesbrough, community councils were set up as sounding-boards or with limited decision-making powers, subject to ratification by the authority. Such community councils can be open to the public, and have representatives of local associations or specially elected representatives, with their composition varying from area to area. Southampton has developed a community action strategy based on about 13 community action forums, supported by six community action managers. 'They have been a focus for organising local communities, identifying local needs, communicating with the councils and getting things done' (LGIU, 1996, p. 9). Their constitutions vary. Most include individual residents within their membership but some operate on the basis of representatives of local organisations. Some allow councillors to attend small planning meetings, but others do not.

Walsall intend to go further. Power is being devolved to seven pilot neighbourhood committees. 'Each of the seven neighbourhoods has been divided, with the advice of local people, into smaller constituencies of around 100 households ... with an electorate of between 150 and 300, this will be coming close to a sustainable scale of local democracy' (Walsall, 1997).

Even where area organisations are based on councillors only, they involve the public. In Stevenage the meetings of the area committees are open to the public and are attended by an average of seventy people. The councillors have become a part of the meeting rather than a separate committee. They have ceased to sit facing the audience but have moved to the front row and have begun to move into the general audience. Where decisions have to be made, the chair gets the audience view and then quickly seeks approval of the councillors as the formal committee, which is virtually automatic. The committees have small budgetary allocations and take discussions 'more seriously than many normal council committees'.

Development can take place at officer level. Coventry has established area co-ordinators in six areas of deprivation. Area co-ordination is said to be 'becoming a successful way of working to ensure that services are developed and co-ordinated in a way that meets local needs'. They have no independent authority but are accountable to the chief executive, which gives them influence. The Labour group had opposed area committees as 'weakening the power of the group', which leaves the relationship with ward councillors on an informal basis.

The variety of practice reflects a development grounded in local politics and local experience.

*Emerging issues*

Inevitably there is considerable variation in the response to new issues and new approaches. While all local authorities in a research study had an equal opportunities policy, 'there are tremendous variations amongst the local authority institutions in adopting and implementing equal opportunity issues' (LGMB, and SOCPO, 1993). Variation can be found in the responses on corporate issues such as community safety (LGMB, 1996), the environment (Audit Commission, 1997b) or community health (Moran, 1996). Local authorities vary in the extent to which they are organised to respond to European policies and opportunities (John, 1996). Walker records the diversity of the public relations function, which comes in many shapes and sizes (Walker, 1997). It is likely that there will be variation in the response to best value as there was to CCT.

Over time, as concern for these issues becomes established across a wide range of authorities, pressures to uniformity may grow, as they may with the new statutory requirements on community safety.

**Variation in response**

This chapter has discussed certain general trends in response to the challenges set out in Chapter 7. They show the general impact of those challenges but variation in the responses. There has been a widely accepted management model embedded in change programmes, yet some authorities have resisted that model, while there are significant differences in practice even in authorities that have adopted it. Those differences are likely to grow as local authorities wrestle with some of the problems in the application of that model within local government. Differences within a general tendency have also been illustrated in discussing the response to CCT, the developments of budgeting under the impact of financial pressures, and the development of strategic management as the need for co-ordination assumes new forms. In industrial relations there are significant variations, but also important forces for uniformity. The approaches to area decentralisation illustrate the variety of locally generated developments outside the dominant model, although in a minority of authorities. While emerging issues and approaches are often widely recognised, responses vary.

# 11 Changes in Officer Structures

The last chapter considered changes in the ways of working. This chapter examines the impact of those changes on the officer structure. The changes have taken place within the inherited assumptions, beliefs and conditions, which retain their powerful influence. The present organisation of local authorities reflects both change and continuity, and the emphasis can vary from authority to authority.

## The departmental base

The challenges of legislation and of management ideas have led to changes in the role and nature of departments. The model of the department as a professional bureaucratic organisation for the delivery of services has been challenged, although the extent and nature of change vary from authority to authority.

### The impact of contracting

The introduction of compulsory competitive tendering (CCT) meant that the role of client was separated from contractor or, put another way, of purchaser from provider and this can continue under best value. Where work is contracted-out separation is clear. Where the work is carried out inside the organisation, there can still be separation, although the extent varies. The provision of a service can be separated from the client department in a direct services organisation which often develops a culture of commercial success: 'Contractor units are real tigers' was said in one authority. In some authorities there is a further separation, with a technical clients unit dealing with contract management. In other authorities separation is within departments. In some authorities both approaches were used depending on the service. In Bolton it was laid down: 'The closer the activity subject to competition is to the strategic management of the service and to policy formation and understanding of customer need, the greater the case for a soft split and retention of defined activities within service departments', and 'The more stable and routine is the service being delivered the greater the scope for harder splits and integration with freestanding DSOs.'

When CCT first developed, there was an emphasis on separation, not merely in making the contract but in running and monitoring it. Relations were governed by the strict words of the contract. It could be more important to enforce the terms of the contract than to provide a service. In one authority visited, the direct services organisation regarded itself as independent, refusing to take part in corporate working. Within the workings of local authorities, relations between central departments and service departments became governed by service-level agreements, specifying services to be provided and payments to be made. Central departments in some authorities are divided into quasi-trading units. These changes 'mean that the centre needs to:

- draw a line between the provision of central services and the provision of corporate strategy and co-ordination
- shift the emphasis of central control away from routine intervention and towards more discriminating strategic guidance.'
(Campbell, 1991, p. 13)

It may make more important the strategic role at the centre and of policy units within it. 'The fundamental raison d'être of a policy unit is to provide a central point which links the corporate policy drive of elected representatives to the resource allocation processes and implementation practices of the bureaucratic structure' (quotation in Campbell, 1991, p. 26).

There have been widespread changes in the roles of the centre. Some authorities have created departments bringing together all central services. In two authorities (Kent and Hertsmere) the treasurer was freed from all departmental responsibility, acting as the council's independent financial adviser.

All these developments modify the traditional model of both service and central departments. Control by contract or quasi-contract replaces control by hierarchy. There is, however, considerable variation in practice. Carried too far, a bureaucracy of contracts replaces a bureaucracy of hierarchy. 'Paper multiplies and internal invoices flow. Management by contract involves a move from hierarchical authority to control at arm's length, with either internal or external providers actually providing the service. Paradoxically though, much of the development of contract management especially for complex services involves the re-creation of management systems that are essentially hierarchical in character' (Walsh, 1995, p. 136). 'Trust is not easily developed and there is evidence that relationships at the beginning of contracts are often poor, when the parties to the contract know less of each other' (ibid, p. 131). What has been seen in local authorities has been distrust embedded in separation reinforced by a paper bureaucracy. There has been a reaction in some authorities against the consequences of separation. It is being recognised that client and contractor have to work together. Trust has begun to be recognised as important. Relations are being re-established and separation modified. 'The arm's-length nature of the relationship tends to be modified by the development of trust-based mechanisms' (ibid, p. 136). The best-value regime may encourage this trend.

*Other changes*

Another modification of the traditional departmental model has been the development in a small number of authorities of area or neighbourhood structures which bring together departments at local level, possibly although not always responsible to an area committee of councillors. There has been considerable variation in the extent to which these developments have modified traditional structures. In some authorities officers at local level remain within their departments, although being encouraged to work together. In a few cases, those operating at area level are responsible to an area organisation with its own chief officer. Organisation by area has then replaced organisation by service, although within the area there will be organisation by service.

Nor is that all. In some authorities services have been separated off into arm's-length bodies. Partnerships have been formed with other organisations. Many such developments have been encouraged by government policies. In Chapter 10 it was shown that management change programmes had led to the development of cost centres, each with their own targets.

The combination of all these developments in various forms in different authorities means that the traditional model of departments based on hierarchy and with relations defined by bureaucratic professionalism cannot be assumed to be the only model. A combination of separation between client and contractor, whether within the department or outside it, of cost-centre management, of area management and the creation of hands-off organisations has modified the departmental model in many if not in all cases. One chief executive is recorded as saying 'the days of departments are numbered' (Walsh and Davies, 1993, p. 9). Rather, the forms are changing. The departmental inheritance is still powerful.

What is seen is a combination of the traditional model of the department and new ways of working. The extent to which past practices are maintained and new ways of working are adopted varies from authority to authority.

*The roles of chief officers*

The changes have made the roles of chief officers more complex since they face different relationships, hierarchical and contractual, and encompass decentralisation to areas or cost centres while still having overall responsibility. They are no longer in charge in the traditional way and have to find a new role. The appointment may be made on management grounds as much as on professional grounds, and at least in some cases not from the dominant profession. The chief officer will be expected to play a corporate as well as a departmental role. These changes have brought changes in role and in style.

The chief officer may also be challenged by the position of the chair, who may now have an office in the department – relatively unknown 20 years ago. Some councillors, both of the left and of the right, have been more ready to challenge chief officers. The politicisation of authorities was for some chief officers a traumatic experience. 'They no longer give us the respect to which we are due.' Some chief officers felt their status threatened by chairs who played an active role in the department. That status can still remain, inherited from the past and secure in its departmental base, as long as the chief officer maintains an alliance with the committee chair. That is hard to achieve where an officer has difficulty adjusting to the new political reality, and that political reality may change again with the introduction of political executives, whose members may well play an even more active role in departments.

Over and above the strengthening of political control there is greater informality in the relationships between councillors and officers. Contact has become more frequent and less time-tabled by appointment. Councillors have sought contact with officers at different levels of the organisation, and some officers are active in political parties outside the council, giving them easy access to councillors. Some chief officers felt threatened by these developments, while others accept and encourage contact, provided they are kept informed. A chief officer would, however, resent an officer who exploited his position in the political party to push for policies opposed to those of the chief officer.

The 'great chief officer' was long-serving. Time spans have changed. Contracts can mean that many chief officers serve only a short period, sometimes for only five years, due just as often to the chief officer not renewing the contract as to the council not renewing it. Early retirement with pensionable added years has almost become an expectation for many chief officers. It has become an exception to serve to 65 (Audit Commission, 1997a).

There have been changes in style. The days of the 'great chief officer' may be over if by that one means the long-serving chief officer set at the top of the hierarchy – a remote and authoritarian figure, whose word was paramount and whose signature appeared on every letter. Such an approach was perhaps not as universally adopted as believed. But it was a belief that influenced.

Now other styles are favoured. The model chief officer of today manages differently. There is an emphasis on leadership by motivation. Hierarchy has not been abandoned but modified. Management by walking about has taken the chief officer from the office to walk the corridors or visit staff outside. Management teams of senior staff have become important in the working of the departments and an emphasis is placed on communicating upward and downward.

These changes are general trends that modify traditional patterns. The extent to which those trends are followed varies. The new style influences behaviour, even where not fully adopted. Not all chief officers welcome such ways of working. There is nothing less effective than adopting a management style with which one feels uncomfortable. Management by walking about succeeds only if it is enjoyed.

*Strategic directors*

In a number of authorities, existing departments have been broken into service units, focusing on particular tasks, and service units are then grouped into directorates. Service units may be based upon professions, but directorates cross professions. The relationship of the director to the service unit varies, but the assumption is that the service unit will be responsible for operational management. The relationship between director and service unit is one of modified hierarchy.

In Kirklees, 70 per cent of the time of the executive directors is intended to be spent on the strategic role and 30 per cent on operational issues. As an expression of this definition of the role, the chief executive and the executive directors have a suite of offices which are deliberately separated from the offices of the service units which are grouped under them. In North Tyneside, where executive directors were established along with heads of functions, originally heads were linked to two executive directors in order to escape assumptions based on former hierarchies. Directors would focus on strategic issues, leaving heads of function focusing on operational issues, subject to appraisal by the directors.

This approach has been adopted in a number, although not the majority, of the new unitary authorities. In Milton Keynes, strategic directors were appointed for environment, resources, neighbourhood services and learning and development, with the children's functions of social services located within the learning and development directorate and other social services in neighbourhood services.

The Barnsley programme area directors are accountable to members not for the delivery of services (which is the responsibility of the service heads) but for council policy and for the performance of service heads under performance management arrangements. The joint review of social services in Barnsley stressed there was a need to clarify the responsibilities of the programme area director and the director of social services, finding a degree of uncertainty not merely in those responsibilities but in the role of the programme area committee and of the social services commit-tee (Audit Commission and Social Services Inspectorate, 1997).

The problem is to separate the role of strategic director and head of service. It is not always clear what is strategic and what is operational. In one authority it was said, 'What is strategic in prac-tice is what the councillors are interested in.' In another authority it was suggested that an issue was probably operational rather than strategic if the answer was Yes to a series of questions. They included, Is it short-term? Does it fall within existing policies? Has it been dealt with before? Has it limited or no impact on the envir-onment? There is a danger that the strategic director becomes too distant from operations so that strategy proves ineffective in practice. There is the opposite danger that the strategic director becomes so involved in operational matters that strategy remains undeveloped. The problem is to get the balance right.

In some authorities, it was envisaged that strategic directors would change their responsibilities. This change has rarely hap-pened because strategic directors tend to remain attached to their service responsibilities. Change is most likely to happen where the strategic director is not drawn from any of the services for which he or she is responsible.

## A changing professionalism

Professionalism remains important in local government yet there have been significant changes. Professionalism is starting to change itself through continuous professional development. Nearly all professionals now recognise that the assumption that basic train-ing can sustain a professional throughout a career is inadequate. Policies for continuous professional development ensure that knowledge is updated and new skills learnt, securing a systematic approach to what the good professional would do anyway. Con-tinuous professional development is, as yet, generally voluntary and is limited in its requirements. Nevertheless it represents a significant step.

It is no longer accepted that professional ability is the sole or primary requirement for senior staff. 'The managerial critique of professionalism has, to a considerable degree registered a success to the extent that former exponents of professional autonomy have accepted the need for the external review of professional performance by managerial criteria. Professionalism and managerialism now operate in a sometimes uneasy co-existence within local government' (Gyford, 1993, p. 18). The chief officer's role and that of the senior staff are no longer seen just in professional terms but also partly or wholly in management terms. Management development is seen as an important part of officers' experience and there has been a major growth in management courses. A Local Government Management Board working party identified skills required for future chief officers and senior management, including:

- Political skills
- Strategic management skills
- Decision-making skills
- Negotiation skills
- Intellect
- Personal Integrity and Flexibility
- People management/relationship skills
- Communication skill
- Influencing skills
- Results orientated/drive for achievement
- Operational management skills
- Change management skills
- Analysis and problem-solving skills
- Business and commercial skills
- Leadership skills
- Public service orientation.

(LGMB, 1993)

The list goes well beyond traditional professional skills.

On my visits there were striking contrasts between those who say 'I am a manager first and foremost. I use my professional knowledge, but I am not doing a professional job any more' and those who would still say 'I am the council's professional adviser and that is my main task.' There are examples of both, although there are growing numbers of the former. Some chief officers are appointed from outside the dominant profession or even from outside any of the professions represented in the department, although not where high-status professions are involved. An accountant and a social worker have been appointed as librarians in two counties. In directorate systems which group services together, the director may come from any of the previously dominant professions or less often from none. Career patterns are changing, so the whole career might not be spent in departments based on the profession, but with some time being spent in, for example, a policy unit attached to the chief executive. Yet for all these changes the professional chief officer with a career based on the profession remains the most widely accepted model.

The political challenge has had its impact on professions. Young has contrasted a new style of professional chief officer with the traditional model. He sees the new style as 'chief officers who less often have claims of specialised and unchallengeable knowledge, who accept the political priorities of their councillors and take those policy dispositions as the framework within which they work to secure the success of politically determined council policy. Far from being detached they typically see themselves as working alongside the members' (Young, 1988, p. 64). Not all take that position. Some resent councillors challenging their 'professional judgement'. In many authorities the professional view is still accorded respect. The political challenge varies in intensity and direction.

There is no simple model. Stoker identified five categories:

1. The De-skilled Professional: these professionals have been reduced to a subservient position in their employing organisations.
2. The Constrained Professional: these professionals have been obliged to accept some sharing of their autonomy within their home authorities.
3. The Contracting Professional: these professionals have moved to something resembling a model of private practice providing their services to the local authority or other public service on a contract basis.
4. The Technocratic Professional: these professionals are the advisers to the lay non-elected *elite* that are assuming a large role in the new governance.
5. The Managerial Professional: these professionals have taken senior positions within local authorities and define their role as manager.

(Stoker, 1993, pp. 6–7)

## The management team

The management team is composed of all or some of the chief officers or all the directors in local authorities. In most authorities before the reorganisations of 1974 and 1975 there were chief officer meetings, although some are of recent origin. In Cheshire, regular meetings of chief officers were established in 1959 by Alistair Hetherington, the newly appointed clerk, although occasional meetings had been held before, particularly for civil defence during the war (Lee, 1963). Past chief officer meetings often focused on household matters. Some were described as mainly concerned with car allowances. The Bains Report said, 'In some authorities they appeared to be convened mainly for the purpose of a collective consideration of the agenda for the next meeting of the council; in others Chief Officers only meet together to discuss the occasional problems that affect them all' (Bains, 1972, p. 48) – or back to car allowances again.

The Bains Report argued for a different type of meeting:

> We believe that the officers' management team should have a corporate identity and positive role to play in the corporate management of the authority. It is the counterpart, at officer level, of the policy and resources committee. Its members do not attend primarily as representatives of particular departments, though on occasion it will be necessary for them to speak in that capacity; they are there as members of a body created to aid the management of the authority as a whole. (Bains, 1972, pp. 48–9)

The Bains Report led to the general establishment of management teams, but their nature varied greatly, as they still do. They vary in size and composition. In one small district the team consists of the chief executive and two assistant chief executives. There are teams of sixteen or more which have their own problems. With small management teams there are dangers when significant officers are excluded. In two authorities visited, one county and one district, the treasurer had been excluded, almost inevitably leading to conflict between him and the team. In other instances, central officers dominated, causing resentment amongst service chief officers. Management teams vary in the relationships between their members. Some teams work well together, but some are marked more by conflict than by co-operation.

I have visited authorities where the management team was in disarray, aware that they were not dealing with major issues. The blame was put on the chief executive, but that meant chief officers were evading their own responsibilities. In one county, the dominant members of the management team were described by others as 'very skilled in killing ideas'. In another county, the chief officers' weekly meeting was seen as burdensome. It was attended by eighteen, many of whom 'had been there too long', and it was felt nothing new ever came out of the meeting. In another, old conflicts remained unresolved, and everybody's position was well known. 'It is only the old game and there are only the old moves to be made.' In one London borough, there was a tacit agreement to keep divisive issues off the agenda, so important issues remained undiscussed. In another, a chief executive was seen as gaining his way through 'intellectual bullying' and over-weighting the meetings with members of his staff. In a Northern city, the chief executive had abandoned his early belief that the management team could be made effective, relying instead on the leader's meetings as the only means of challenging 'baronialism'.

Especially in the early days, management teams were in danger of over-burdening themselves with detail. The chief executive sought to secure that any important issue facing a department was considered by the corporate team. In effect, they sought to do departmental management corporately. Meetings were held weekly and became like a council committee struggling through its agenda. The consequence was they never got round to identifying and dealing with corporate issues.

Management teams that work well together devote time and effort to the working of the team. Away-days are used to establish team-working, often with an outside facilitator. Attention has been given to the role of the team and its ways of working. In one authority the need for three types of meeting had been identified, each with its own requirements for timing, frequency and form: information exchange; current business; strategy. In another authority a protocol or rules of the game had been agreed between members of the management team. Chief officers in the team can be given a specific corporate responsibilities. In one authority, three service chief officers were each given responsibility for a geographical area. Two others were given specific roles for promoting the city and for learning from the public. They were supposed to devote 10 per cent of their time to these responsibilities. In this way corporate roles provided a counter-balance, admittedly limited to service roles.

Some newly appointed chief executives, facing hostility from their management team, sought and succeeded in bringing about changes by retirements. Others have widened teams to bring in supporters. In one shire district a chief executive added the personnel officer, the assistant chief executive and the executive manager, with roles associated with his own.

There are dilemmas in the working of the management team. One issue is whether its members' main role is in corporate management or in management of the services for which they are responsible. In the management team the key role may appear to be in corporate management, but individuals cannot deny their service role even there, and in most cases the majority of their time will be spent on their service role.

One way of resolving the dilemmas has been the development of strategic directors. The management team then consists of these directors, but that is not without its problems. In one county where the directors' board was seen as effective by its members, it was felt by some service heads that it had two dangers because of that effectiveness. It was centralising, drawing issues up to itself. It was also too ready to institute changes, without regard for the operational consequences. But that was perhaps the 'conservative' speaking.

Dilemmas are inevitable in the working of a management team. How they are resolved, if at all, varies from authority to authority. In part that depends on the role played by the chief executive, who can be leader, chair or colleague, or all three.

## The chief executive

*From clerk to chief executive*

The Maud Committee recommended the recognition of the clerk 'as head of the authority's paid service ... to have authority over the other chief officers so far as this is necessary for the efficient management and execution of the authority's functions' (Maud, 1967, para. 179).

The post of chief executive became generally established after the 1974 and 1975 reorganisation, although some authorities such as Coventry had already adopted the title as a symbol of change from the previous role of the clerk. The Bains Report recommended the appointment of a chief executive as the authority's 'chief policy adviser'. Chief executives were to be given authority over chief officers, except in professional matters, and lead the chief officers' management team. The post was to be open to all professions. They were to be freed from departmental responsibilities.

While the main recommendations of the Bains Report were adopted in most authorities, change was less than anticipated, at least at first. Most of the posts in the new authorities were given to former clerks, some of whom saw little need to change. There were authorities such as Manchester, West Glamorgan and Hull where the title of clerk and responsibility for the clerk's department were retained.

Certain names stand out as establishing the role of chief executive, although some had begun to do so before reorganisation. Sir John Boynton, the chief executive of Cheshire, believed that 'The chief executive must assume a responsibility for the whole of the affairs and activities of the authority. His corporate role must spring from a conviction that the authority is – or can be – something more than the sum of its different parts' (Boynton, 1986, p. 2). Those who sought to establish the role of chief executive stressed corporate management. Derrik Hender, as chief executive of Coventry, built corporate management through the development of management systems (Greenwood and Stewart, 1974) and provided strong leadership to the management team in the West Midlands County. John Barrett, as chief executive of Cambridgeshire, built the corporate role through gradual change over a ten-year period.

There were impressive chief executives with an individual style. Kenneth Abell, the chief executive of Dorset, was a dominant figure, reflecting in the role the power that a county clerk could obtain. He invited me to visit Dorset, 'while civilisation still existed'. 'Whilst I believe it is not now typical of local government, I find I can adequately do my job if I have a word with the chairman of the county council by phone once a week, the chairman of the policy and resources committee once a month and the chairman of the majority group as seldom as possible.' Gordon Moore, the chief executive of Bradford, provided dynamic leadership, but as an individual rather than through the management team. He came to feel that nothing could be achieved through the team, believing in 'management by by-passing'. It was his claim too that five votes of no confidence had been moved against him in the council, although none had ever been passed. He had a capacity for surprises – 'Bradford is a city of surprises' – and a bias for action. He was seen as getting his way, so normally he did.

*Variation in roles and ways of workings*

Over time the role developed. The background of chief executives has widened, first with a growing number of treasurers being appointed, but then more widely. Norton found in 1990 that only 46.5 per cent of chief executives had a legal background and 19.7 per cent had a financial background. An increasing emphasis was laid upon the corporate role and on building the links between the officer structure and the political structure. Many chief executives provided leadership in management change programmes. Increasingly chief executives have developed their role in community governance.

The Audit Commission defined the chief executive's key tasks as:

1. Managing internal relationships.
2. Converting policy into strategy and strategy into action.
3. Developing processes, people and management skills to ensure that the authority is and will continue to be capable of delivering its strategy.
4. Reviewing performance against stated objectives.
5. Thinking and planning ahead.

(Audit Commission, 1989)

The reality is, however, that there is and can be no standard model (Clarke and Stewart, 1998). Conditions vary from authority to authority, not least in the political process, an aspect neglected by the Audit Commission. Studies of the chief executives have found considerable variations in the way the role is played.

Gyford and his colleagues found that 'the self-perceived and actual role of the chief executive still varies considerably from the familiar primus inter pares (and sometimes hardly even that) to the 'policy maker and director' (Gyford *et al.*, 1989, p. 118). That variation is confirmed by the researches of Norton (1991), Morphet (1993) and Travers and his colleagues (1997).

One reason for the variation lies paradoxically in the shared characteristics of the role, which means that how it is performed depends on the relationships established, to a greater extent than any other officer's role. The chief executive is the head of the paid service. As such, the chief executive has responsibility for the staff and formal authority over them. It is, however, an uncertain authority in practice, since to be exercised effectively it requires members' support. The role differs from other chief officers' in lacking defined routines or tasks. One treasurer appointed to the role of chief executive said he spent the first six months looking for the role and all he found were crises. The role has to be made and re-made in the relationships which determine its potential.

Key relationships are with the leader and leadership of the council, yet chief executives cannot ignore their relationships with the opposition; to do so builds suspicion for the future – should change in control occur. The chief executive may build wider relationships with councillors generally. The chief executive has important relations with the management team and the chief officers, and may seek wider contact with staff. The role is set at the point of interaction between the political and officer structures. The success in managing both sets of relationships determines scope for action and shapes the nature of the role. Increasingly, as emphasis is placed on community governance, external relationships grow in importance. The role of the chief executive can be seen as determined by these three sets of relationships and the interrelationship between them.

Within the pattern of relationships, different roles and ways of working will develop, which depend on the personality of the chief executive, the personalities of other key actors, the conditions of the authority, the political process and the attitude of other organisations. There is a contrast between a chief executive who sees herself as a change agent, probably serving for only a limited period, and one whose emphasis is on organisational continuity. A chief executive can place an emphasis on contact with staff, experiencing their work and holding meetings at all levels. Other chief executives work through chief officers rather than having direct contact with staff generally. Some chief executives see building the management team, and working with it, as the most important part of the role. For others the management team plays a more limited role with emphasis on one-to-one relationships with chief officers rather than with the corporate group.

*Differences in style*

A chief executive's relationship to the political process may be focused on the leader. Contact can be close – almost daily – or more limited. Some chief executives welcome an informal relationship, whilst others see that as dangerous. Chief executives vary in the emphasis they give to the role of the authority in the community. One survey found time spent on this varied from 1 per cent to 88 per cent with an average of 11 per cent (Travers *et al.*, 1997). A chief executive may face critical change when an authority used to majority control becomes hung. The chief executive can play 'the honest broker role'. Others will not find the role easy or may not be trusted sufficiently.

A chief executive's role is governed by local conditions. That makes it difficult to determine what makes an effective chief executive; it may be easier to identify what makes an ineffective chief executive. Certainly, a chief executive who cannot read the nature of the organisation and its environment is unlikely to be effective. I have been impressed by the way certain chief executives who have moved from one authority to another have changed their approaches. In part that is the learning that comes from experience. In part, it is a recognition that there is no one way in which the role should be carried out. It must be grounded in local conditions, even when the aim is to change them.

A chief executive who does not believe in local government and in the local political process is unlikely to be effective. Some chief executives denounce councillors as lacking ability, and regard the political process as an obstacle to be overcome. These chief executives undermine the conditions on which effective local government depends.

Some chief executives barely develop the corporate role. Stories are told about them, often perhaps unfairly, once they have retired or in some cases been retired. One newly appointed chief officer asked to see the chief executive, who saw his main role as maintaining protocol in a major city. The chief executive said he could not see why the chief officer wanted to see him; he should get on with his job. Another chief executive did not see his job as concerned with the impact of CCT. 'I hope it is happening' was all he had to say. A housing director asked to see a chief executive about ideas for developing the service. The chief executive said, 'I have no issues about housing on my agenda.'

Other chief executives are seen as more concerned with bureaucratic detail than effective organisation. In one county, the previous chief executive was seen by councillors as 'walking in treacle – nothing ever happened; it was always too difficult'. In a shire district based on a major town, the same phrase was used: 'overwhelming treacle'. In one London borough the new chief executive found his first task was to sign swimming passes for children. His response was 'I do not care if the chief executive has always signed them – you must find another way.' That response was its own message. In another London borough, a chief executive found he had the support of only half a personal assistant when first appointed. He was not surprised that his predecessor retired through ill-health. In a shire district, the newly appointed chief executive asked his secretary how many meetings were in the diary, and was told there were none. His predecessor was presumably either an isolated figure or one who had freed the authority from meeting-itis!

An appointment of a chief executive can often reverse tendencies in the previous chief executive or the authority. One chief executive in a Northern city said of his predecessor 'He was more intelligent than myself – he was full of ideas. My contribution is to put ideas into action.' One county which had had a traumatic and divisive period of management change under the previous chief executive, appointed a chief executive who saw the need to quieten things down – almost to a point 'where nothing happened'. The next chief executive sought to learn from both experiences, opening up issues, but cautiously.

Chief executives vary in style because of local circumstance but also because of personality. One chief executive was described as 'relaxed and not committed to any position, letting discussion guide him. He surprised his colleagues with new ideas but will let them fade away if not taken up.' Another was described as relying on influence and discussion – 'almost management by hinting, but the hints are accepted'. Some chief executives emphasise the need to change culture. One stressed personal communications, lunching regularly with different groups of staff. Another chief executive saw the task that absorbed most time as sorting out conflicts between chief officers. A chief executive was described as 'adding a buzz' to the organisation, but he could be seen as 'over-enthusiastic'. Another metropolitan district chief executive 'prefers to make changes in bite-size bits'. He resists elaborate systems, preferring guidelines within which departments work.

Relations with councillors can also reflect personal style. One chief executive spent much time wandering the corridors talking to councillors, believing informal contacts gave him political feel. Another chief executive sought a 'proper' distance between chief officers and councillors, banning the use of first names, although I found some underground users of such names. In one Independent-dominant authority there was such confidence in the chief executive that he was expected to allocate committee places. Some chief executives lack political sensitivity. Over lunch with councillors, the chief executive continuously referred back to a previous authority as an argument for the ideas he was advocating. For the councillors it was clear they had heard it often before – so often that for them it had become an argument against.

One county chief executive devoted considerable time and effort to developing contact with the chairman of the county council, the leading political figure. The chief executive found himself dealing with what he considered were issues of minor importance, but which were necessary for building confidence. In one Independent-dominant authority in East Anglia the chief executive said he had to be 'the political conscience', reminding them of a world outside. A metropolitan chief executive stressed a 'no-surprises approach' with councillors. That approach had built confidence about the management changes he was introducing, so they told me 'we like what he's trying to do, but we don't really know what it is'.

One chief executive spent time outside the council offices; he would talk to members of the public, spend a day sitting in classes in schools or out with the refuse collectors. A London borough chief executive saw the important task as working with other organisations. She had inherited an isolated authority. A county chief executive learns about the strength and weaknesses in the impact of the authority by patterns drawn from letters, complaints from councillors and MPs and key informants both inside and outside the organisation.

Some chief executives emphasised the development of management systems. In one authority the chief executive had been the previous treasurer and the chief executive had not supported his ideas. He described it as his 'years of exile'. In a short period of time he created a comprehensive system of interlocking elements involving a strategic management process, a corporate business process and a system of accountable management. In Bexley the chief executive established a comprehensive system of management targets and monitoring processes.

Some have devoted major efforts to developing the skills and knowledge of seeking external sources of funds, giving it considerable personal attention. One chief executive saw as his major personal achievement, building up the capacity of the authority to access new resources in an authority where such opportunities had been neglected. He found excitement and personal satisfaction in the search for resources.

## The diversity of role

The diversity of role and how it is played can be illustrated by a series of examples showing both the impact of personality and of circumstances and the interplay between them. There is a broad distinction between those chief executives who see their role as change agents, and those who focus on the continuing work of the organisation, although the difference may be blurred in practice. Paul Sabin, the chief executive of Kent, was appointed to bring about change and argued that the role of chief executive was

> all about managing change. This requires leadership on the officer side in partnership with the political leadership. It involves spelling out the vision, setting the style, changing the culture and establishing the key management principles. The chief executive must also take responsibility for strategic management, ensuring the political and managerial expectations are matched by the organisation's capacity to deliver. The chief

executive also has a key role to play in developing external relationships, particularly in respect of strategic concerns. Ultimately, however, the chief executive's role is to provide the interface between the political and executive arm of the County Council. (Sabin, 1989, p. 122)

There are different approaches to the role of change agent, reflecting personality as well as local conditions. One chief executive in a metropolitan borough has made an impact through style. When staff bring him problems he is ready to acknowledge that he does not know the solution, asking who can help. He surprised councillors by asking them to arrange a visit for him to their wards as part of a learning process. When the leader was treating an officer-member working party as a sub-committee, he startled the leader by saying at the start of the meeting 'Is it your turn or my turn to chair the meeting?'

A London borough chief executive was excited by ideas, but frustrated by problems of implementation. 'He wants to build the new Jerusalem tomorrow', and that does not fit easily into committee cycles and departmental procedures. He responded by 'writing with a heavy hand' to shake the organisation out of its torpor. Team building did not come easily to him. He wanted action.

A metropolitan district chief executive believed 'the chief executive is boss', and in new appointments is re-writing terms of reference to make that clear. When first appointed, he gave a talk, later written up, about the sort of organisation he wanted to build, that was effective in implementation stressing performance management. He saw the councillor's role as to make policy, advised by officers, and then for it to be carried out by them, even if silly, 'since councillors have to learn from their mistakes'. He believed councillor frustration was high because of failures in implementation.

There is a difference in style, too, amongst those chief executives who focus on the continuities, not ruling out change, but not seeing it as the dominant concern. One such chief executive described himself as a 'one-off sort of person'. He believed in immediate responses and his conversation jumped from topic to topic or as people wandered in and out of his room. His office reflected his interests, with books piled in corners – some to do with work and others not. He was closely in touch with individual chief officers but not in any systematic way.

One chief executive had been treasurer in the county borough before being appointed chief executive in the newly formed authority. He was a dominant figure whose knowledge went back many years. He relied on his many contacts to enable him to anticipate problems and curb developments to which he was opposed. Councillors respected him and yet saw him as the problem.

In an Independent-dominant authority which opposed any councillor playing a lead role, the chief executive had come to play that role, attending all committees. With only 160 staff 'the authority was his department'. He was a public person in the town, recognised by many. Political impermanence had made his continuing presence important.

Another chief executive was described as 'a cold fish' by some, but others saw him as a 'a breath of fresh air'. He was a puritan for 'proper procedure', insisting on the right of an officer to give advice publicly and openly even before a critical by-election. With clear logical thinking he would normally set out a solution to any problems raised, but could have difficulty seeing other choices to the one his logic prescribed.

*The life-cycle*

There is a life-cycle for chief executives. When they are first appointed, they may be newcomers. That provides opportunities: 'In the first six months the chief executive has a unique opportunity to introduce change. Indeed he will be expected to do so.' It also provides problems, if those changes are opposed by experienced chief officers backed by their chairs. In one authority the chief executive believed she had political support for change, but when her proposals were developed they were defeated in the group, leaving her in a difficult position, which was resolved when she was appointed to another authority. Another chief executive, looking back, reflected, 'I shudder at how naive I was.'

The chief executive may not be a newcomer, which can be an advantage but also a disadvantage, particularly if he had worked his way up from a junior position. 'I always felt they still regarded me as the junior solicitor', said one chief executive after he had moved to a new authority where he felt more sure of his position. One county chief executive had at first felt constrained because he had been appointed over the heads of chief officers, when he himself was only a deputy chief officer. A treasurer found his first year as chief executive frustrating, trapped by what he felt was an unsatisfactory role based on that of the previous clerk. It was only when he recognised the need to change the role that he found a management style that suited him, but it was different from his role as treasurer. Words like 'motivating', 'experiments', 'innovation' describe that style.

The role changes over time. Some chief executives serve for a long period. The time can come when the chief executive will have been involved in the appointment of all or most of the chief officers. Jeffrey Greenwell had been chief executive of Northamptonshire since the 1974 reorganisation when he retired in 1996, and was clearly the most experienced senior officer to whom others turned for advice. Brian Hill in the last period of his 'quinquennium' relied on the deputy clerk to run the department and concentrated on issues that interested him: 'It gives me the opportunity to go mad.' Chief executives can maintain their motivation over a long period provided they can set new goals for themselves.

While some chief executives have sustained their motivation over long periods, others become stale, and recognise it. One district chief executive felt after ten years he had exhausted his capacity for innovation. Chief executives have felt threatened by the 'continual machinations' of councillor and officers. 'I was almost destroyed as a person' was said to me by one chief executive after he had decided not to renew his contract. This pressure may be one factor in the tendency to serve for shorter periods of time and retire earlier. It is rare to find the chief executive serving for twenty years, as with some clerks before reorganisation. Even then there were problems, but they were sometimes hidden. Tales are told of a county clerk with a severe drink problem that often left him ineffective, but about which neither officers nor councillors were willing to take action.

In the past, it was rare for a clerk to move from one authority to another, although the clerk of Cornwall became clerk of Kent and, as Rodney Brooke has pointed out, ran both counties for a time from his flat in London until forced to choose. 'Mr Platt was properly resentful at the imputation that he could not do both simultaneously!' (Brooke, 1998, p. 14). It has become more common to move at least once, particularly as movement between types of authority has become more common. Michael Lyons had moved from Wolverhampton to Nottinghamshire before becoming chief executive of Birmingham. One chief executive moved from Southwark to Sefton and then to West Glamorgan.

Chief executives who move between authorities do not necessarily adopt the same approach. They themselves will have learnt, and circumstances vary. John Harwood on moving from Lewisham to Oxfordshire found that councillors did not seek the same heavy involvement typical of a London borough. When Roger Paine became chief executive of Cardiff, staff expected him to sit at the reception desk, as he had done at the Wrekin. He saw his priority as learning about the organisation, visiting all departments and meeting all staff. He had moved from an organisation that understood and supported his approach to one in which he had to build anew. Heather Rabbatts faced a different position in Lambeth from that in Merton, where she found a smoothly running organisation and her emphasis was on meeting the need for a corporate capacity rather than wholesale organisational change. In Lambeth she found an organisation that had almost broken down.

*An uncertain position*

A number of authorities have abolished the position of chief executive, because they were critical of the role played by the chief executive. Often they associated the post with that role rather than recognising, as was sometimes the case, that the chief executive was not necessarily playing the role.

One approach has been to rename the post. Taunton Deane appointed a general manager in place of a chief executive, Wolverhampton a principal officer and policy co-ordinator, while East Sussex appointed the county personnel officer as head of the paid service. In all these cases the newly appointed officer played the role of chief executive. In Cleveland where the treasurer had been appointed as co-ordinating officer for two years, there was a reluctance amongst councillors to accept a role beyond co-ordination, but crises meant that a wider role as chief executive came to be accepted.

Other authorities have sought to replace the chief executive with a collective leadership: the management team with a particular chief officer designated as chair – as happened in Humberside – or even a rotating chair. In Newark and Sherwood, the chief executive was replaced by a management team of four, but the need for a chief executive came to be recognised. In Northumberland an inner triad of officers replaced the chief executive, consisting of the director of finance, the county secretary and the director of property. In the end the arrangement was abandoned and the director of finance was appointed as managing director, a title chosen to distinguish it from the previous position of chief executive. Rarely do such arrangements last, although North Tyneside could be seen to be an exception, where a group of newly appointed strategic directors replaced the chief executive. Even there, legislation required the appointment of one of them as head of the paid service.

*Support for the role*

A chief executive must be satisfied she has the resources to do the job required. Heather Rabbatts in taking up her appointment in Lambeth laid down conditions about the process of staff appointments and about staff she wished to bring with her. She faced a crisis that required exceptional measures: 'It was an authority that had almost ceased to work... the levers no longer connected with action. It was held together with sticking plaster' and with the commitment of some staff who carried on regardless of the chaos around them. She required staff in which she had confidence and new directors with a proven record to achieve organisational renewal.

There has been a change from the model of a chief executive without a department. In part, this trend is because of financial pressures leading to a reduction in the number of chief officers. A chief executive may protect his position by retaining or assuming departmental responsibilities. One treasurer in a London borough appointed as chief executive insisted on combining the posts. 'Nobody but a fool would have taken the post without a department.' Another chief executive felt the position under threat and brought the secretary's department under his control.

In some authorities there has been a proliferation of special units, covering issues such as anti-poverty, disabilities and community safety. In one authority there were twenty-six special units in the chief executive's department, which an assistant chief executive sought to co-ordinate. In many there will be a policy unit directly under the chief executive. Such policy units can be resented. One large one was seen as 'twenty bright members of staff with nothing to do but ask questions'. It was said that staff 'spend so much time justifying what they are doing that they never have time to do anything'. Needless to say, that was not the view of the policy unit.

In one London borough the chief executive found he did not have a department with a budget of his own, so he had 'very limited flexibility to promote new initiatives'. He felt the chief executive 'needs to be able from time to time to call upon a large pool of experienced and competent staff whose undivided efforts will be devoted to addressing urgent issues having corporate implications'. He proposed a new department headed by himself as chief executive and director of finance responsible for central services, finance and IT, policy and partnerships and quality and communication.

## Conclusion

Changes have taken place which have affected the role of professionalism and the nature of departments. Management teams have become generally established and the role of chief executive has replaced that of clerk. Yet the inheritance remains powerful. The professional base remains important in its influence on the nature of departments. Management teams cannot ignore the roles of chief officers. Where strategic directors have been introduced there is often uncertainty of role. The development of the chief executive's role has to be worked out against this background. There is both change and continuity.

The working out of the changes varies from authority to authority. Superficially certain features appear widely shared – chief executives; departments; chief officers; management teams – but under the shared titles there is wide variation. This is illustrated by the role of chief executive. Local circumstances and personality mean that how that role is carried out varies from authority to authority and over time. There is diversity within the general uniformity implied by the widely shared role.

The creation of new political structures proposed by the Labour Government is likely to affect the role of chief executive and chief officers, giving to mayors or cabinets a more direct involvement in the management of authorities. A new structure based on a council manager, would on the other hand build up the role of the chief executive. These propositions represent the formal position. What will happen in practice will depend on how the relationships between councillors and officers develop and that will reflect the dynamics described in the next chapter. Diversity will remain, even within what will be apparently similar structures.

# 12 The Dynamic of Councillor–Officer Relations

## The tensions in the relationships

In the interactions between councillors and officers two worlds meet. Councillors and officers are cast for different roles and are drawn from different backgrounds.

| Councillor | Officer |
|---|---|
| Political | Non-political |
| Lay | Professional |
| Often part-time | Full-time |
| Recruited outside the organisation | Recruited by the organisation |
| Elected | Appointed |
| Representative | Non-representative |
| Allowances | Salaried |

Councillors and officers have different agendas and different codes of behaviour. The councillor is the outsider drawn from beyond the organisation, yet formally within. The officer is the insider and a part of the organisation, appointed to it and carrying out its business. Councillors can become insiders, almost a part of the organisation – although then they may begin to lose their distinctive contribution. Against this background, conflict or tension is often found. Councillors and officers can have difficulty understanding each other; finding a common language; appreciating each other's points of view.

Chapter 4 described a model of councillor–officer relations as part of the inheritance. The model never described reality in all its variety, but it had a major influence on the workings of authorities. In part it was sustained by separation. Thus in one authority it was said to Leach, 'In the early days (over twenty years ago) members confined themselves to attendance at committees. They saw that as their main job. I don't think I ever saw a member here unless there was a committee in progress. Nowadays it's unusual not to find a member wandering round the place, even though we have substantially reduced the number of committee meetings that we have' (Leach *et al.*, 1997). Sir Robert Wall recorded that 'a former leader of Somerset County Council who was also Chairman of the planning committee forbade members of the planning committee to go into the planning department. It was well into the 60s before members of Somerset County Council dared to tread in the planning department and then very gently' (Wall, 1993, p. 40). Such separation was probably more common in the counties than in the county boroughs, where committees met more frequently. Gyford and his colleagues, however, found one metropolitan district where until recently 'members were not encouraged to come into the town hall, except for formal meetings or by appointment' (Gyford *et al.*, 1989, p. 125). The model had its impact, founded on at least a formal mutual respect. Hasluck, no respecter of councillors, records in the 1930s:

> The tradition in Local Government Service is for officers to treat Councillors with equal respectfulness however inept and stupid they may be and irrespective of their activity or somnolence. The Councillor is always Sir to the officer, even though the former may be an ignorant local shopkeeper and the latter a brilliant expert in his profession. Courtesy costs nothing, and no profession is more respectful towards its employers than the Local Government Service. This does not imply obsequiousness; there is simply a traditional attitude of grave and respectful attention to the words of wisdom which are presumed to fall from the elected representatives of the democracy. (Hasluck, 1936, pp. 90–1)

The conditions on which the model rested have been transformed by challenges and change. In a period of management change, problems can grow if the changes appear to threaten the roles of the councillor. The intensification of politics has disturbed protected worlds for certain chief officers. 'They are morons', said one director of education, who found his committee 'challenged my professional judgement where heretofore there had been respect'. Another director of education resigned his position because of the development of 'corporate management', but he may have mistaken corporate management for the assertion of political priorities. Such disturbance was not inevitable. Brian Hill, the chief executive of Lancashire, saw his key task as 'maintaining the culture of courtesy and respect between councillors and officers' as well as 'between officers'. There are still authorities relatively unaffected by politicisation. One chief executive who had moved from a highly political county was surprised to find in his new county a different approach. Two incidents reflected the change. When he returned from holiday he found no messages from councillors. Councillors did not contact the chief executive unless asked to. When a major paper was presented on economic development he had to insist on a chair's briefing. The chair did not understand what was happening; it had never happened before.

Laffin and Young record change:

> The basically collaborative and harmonious relationship between officers and members which obtained under conditions of growth was based on what we term the *principle of mutuality*. Essentially this relationship was one of partnership, reflecting a broad consensus between the members and officers as to goals and as to the basically collaborative nature of their relationship. Increasingly, political partisanship, financial constraint and member assertiveness have disrupted this principle. Even leaving aside increased pressures from central government and community groups, the conditions of mutuality in this relationship are clearly disappearing fast not only in the larger urban authorities but elsewhere as well. (Laffin and Young, 1985, p. 42)

They also recognised that there are wide differences between authorities. In some, 'officers and members are working well together, albeit with understandings that would have shocked a town clerk of thirty years ago. In others, relationships have almost broken down into extreme resistance and defensiveness on the part of the officers and an aggressive determination to put the officers in their place on the part of the members' (ibid, p. 43).

As the researchers for Widdicombe said:

> Responses to the different aspects of politicisation and their effects varied. We found that many members clearly welcomed the enhanced role which, in most cases, the process implied for councillors. Some, however, looked back nostalgically to the bi-partisan politics, inter-party courtesies and unproblematic chairman/chief officer partnerships of the past. Some officers found the changes challenging and invigorating; other resented the passing of the comparative order and security of the local government world they had known as a recently as five or ten years ago. (Widdicombe, 1986b, p. 198)

The model generally no longer encompasses the reality of changing politics. David Blunkett, while leader of Sheffield recorded his views on a new balance to be achieved, challenging the view that the councillors are concerned with policy and officers with implementation. 'Both officers and members know that is not true: that officers are inherently involved in the formulation of policy ... and that members are involved in carrying these politicies out. And they have got to be because changing policies is about knowing whether they are working and being able to monitor and evaluate the success of what's taking place' (Baddeley, 1989, p. 49).

Frustration will grow if political change is not accepted. One officer said to me, 'You mustn't get worried about councillors contacting your staff rather than yourself. If you worry that's the end.' Where there is frustration, it is expressed in the conversations of local government. Officers will speak of the low calibre of councillors, and be reinforced in that view by their colleagues in other authorities. They will say, as if it is a proven fact, that there are only five or six able councillors on their councils. Others are spoken of in patronising, and far from complimentary, terms. Yet it will normally be found that the five or six able councillors are the leading councillors whom the officers meet frequently. It could be that that is more the explanation than the mysterious quality called 'calibre'.

Councillors do not impugn the intelligence of their officers – if that is what is meant by calibre. If frustrated in the relationship, they will question the politics of the officers. 'He's really a Tory', 'She's one of them' are commonly heard phrases to explain perceived failures to take on board the priorities of the council. Such sentiments surface most strongly among councillors when control changes. Councillors are often surprised that officers serve the new administration as they did the previous ones. But suspicion will re-surface at moments of frustration. If a party's priority does not appear to have been responded to, the reason may be that it has not been understood because what the party is seeking is outside the experience of the officers. Yet the explanation that often comes readily to councillors is political bias.

Relationships can vary. In some authorities there is an emphasis on formality. In others, value is seen in informal relations. In one district, councillors and officers met for a drink after council meetings as a long-accepted practice. The members' dining room in one county was important in the working of the authority since it was used by chief officers. In some authorities councillors will openly attack officers in committee and council in circumstances in which the officers cannot readily reply. This was a feature of some traditional Labour areas where the senior officers were seen as well-paid, secure in employment and living in fine houses well away from the authority, as opposed to councillors and constituents. In a Welsh authority, councillors said 'When we want advice from officers, we will tell you. We do not want to be polluted by officer advice.' Suspicion of officers was a feature of some Conservative authorities where councillors saw the officers as bureaucrats to be attacked. In some authorities such behaviour would be stamped on by the leader. 'Attack me but not the officers. I am responsible for what happens here.'

In one northern authority, councillors saw officers as hostile to their aims. Some of the directors are regarded as 'independent pashas within the Ottoman Empire'. Officers regarded councillors as ignoring facts because they did not accept an officer analysis of indices to identify areas of deprivation. They spoke of councillors as of low calibre, unable to appreciate policy issues but only specific cases. In another northern authority it was said to me, 'you have to sack someone to make a impact'. Councillors'

suspicion of officers can lead to a reluctance to delegate responsibilities, often producing a structure of numerous committees and
sub-committees with over-burdened agendas adding to frustration
as councillors feel they are controlled by the agenda rather than
controlling it.

In some authorities councillors felt frustrated, and officers were
distressed at what had become for them an alien world. Newman
has described the vicious circle of a blame culture. 'Members don't
trust officers to deliver their political agenda→Members tend
to be critical of officers, don't give political support→Officers
put energy into avoiding being blamed→response to change is
shallow (focus is on compliance rather than delivery)→mixed
messages to staff→change is not delivered→members don't
trust . . . and there are other vicious circles produced as officers
pass blame down the organisation or to each other' (Newman,
1996, p. 94).

Change in councillor–officer relations can come suddenly with
changing politics. In some of the radical-left councils elected in
London in 1981 with ambitious programmes, impossible burdens
were placed on what were often weak structures and processes
inherited with little change from small metropolitan boroughs.
Faced with frustration councillors blamed the bureaucracy and
took matters into their own hands, rather than building effective
structures and processes. In one authority it was described as 'like
a medieval court, with councillors like princes being sought for
decisions'. In one radical-right authority in London it was said
by officers, 'You have to argue back and shout back – otherwise
you are not respected and are swept aside.'

These problems express the potential for frustration but there
are more examples of good relations particularly between chairs
and chief officers. Sometimes those relations are seen as too good
by fellow-councillors. 'He is in the pocket of the officers' is a
common complaint against a chair, if he or she and the chief
officer have established good working relations.

The relationship between councillors and officers is at times
difficult because of different priorities and ways of working.
However, within that general statement there can be a variety of
relationships which can take different forms, determined by both
the traditions of the authority and the personalities involved. 'It
is clear that there exist enormous variations in local government

in the way the relationship works, both broadly and in detail'
(Nolan, 1997a, p. 38). What is remarkable is that so often the
relationships work well.

## Relationships distinguished

*Leader and chief executive*

The relationship between the leader and chief executive was
described in one authority as 'the pivot on which the authority
turns'. Leach and Collinge argued that 'there is an implicit
bargain or series of bargains – which underpin the relationship.
The first is *informational*; both chief executive and leader can, in
normal circumstances, provide an exclusive and privileged source
of information for the other. The second implicit element of the
bargain is *joint (though not necessarily equal) participation in strategic
direction* in both proactive and reactive senses' (Leach and Collinge,
1998, p. 57).

At a seminar held for political leaders and chief executives,
leaders came to

> a clear view about the need for a good and strong working
> relationship; respect and compatability; and the mutual under-
> standing of each other's problems. They also saw the relation-
> ship as providing a 'window' on the organisation, and expected
> it to provide a balance in terms of ideas and thoughts... Most
> difficult, however, was the situation where it was becoming
> clear that some of the basic conditions for a successful relation-
> ship were showing signs of weakening.
>
> For *chief executives* the highest expectations were attached to
> consistency, mutual support, open communication and the set-
> ting of high standards of behaviour and approach... There was
> a clear desire for a leader (and a political group) which brought
> a strategic approach and had clear objectives. (Clarke and
> Hunt, 1997, p. 4)

It is common for leader and chief executive to talk together at
least every week, if not more often. This will normally be a scheduled but informal meeting, although where the leader works and

the authority is rural and dispersed, phone calls will be a substitute, if not always a satisfactory one.

The scheduled meeting will not be the only times leader and chief executive meet. They are likely to attend many of the same occasions in the authority and the same events in the community and may travel in the same car together. The leader may 'drop in' to see the chief executive. In one small district, his ability to do just that was for the leader a token of the success of the chief executive in contrast with the formal style of predecessors. In one county the leader and chief executive saw each other several times a day, and often ended the day with an informal discussion. On the other hand, one leader in a Welsh Labour county felt the need for only a weekly half-hour meeting with the chief executive, assuming that the authority would run smoothly without his detailed involvement.

Leaders and chief executives differ in their styles so there can be no set pattern of relationships. Chief executives, if they are to be successful, have to adjust to the style of the leader, and the leader has to accept the style of the chief executive. A change of leader either within the party or because of a change in party control means the building of a new relationship with all the difficulties involved. One chief executive said, 'I decided to retire when the leadership changed for the seventh time.' A new chief executive is likely to have been the leader's choice, unlike a new leader, over whom the chief executive has no choice. But even with a chosen chief executive a relationship has still to be built. One new but strong chief executive had to learn to work with an equally strong leader by 'not claiming credit'. A chief executive faced with a change of control from Labour to Conservative knew the leader sought a new direction for the council, but lacked a clear steer. The chief executive worked with the management team on a management change programme, expressing their view 'of what a Conservative authority ought to be doing'.

One chief executive who served for twenty years had three leaders. The first saw his role as maintaining group stability and gave general support to the chief executive in developing management in the authority. The second opposed management change, slowing down management developments. The third was as committed as the chief executive to developing management and they worked together in partnership.

The relationship can be affected by length of service. A leader and chief executive who have long served together are likely to have built up an understanding. A long-standing chief executive may be seen by a new leader as an obstacle to be overcome, being set in his or her ways and dominant in the authority. There is a difficulty if a chief executive is close to the leader – when the leader changes there will be a natural suspicion. There is a greater danger if the leader is not close enough. In one authority the chief executive was close to the leader. Power changed in the group and a new leader was elected. The chief executive felt he was distrusted as too associated with the previous leader. He determined not to get so close to future leaders, but then became too distant.

Incidents or even phrases can breed suspicion. In one county the chief executive had difficulty establishing close relations with the Alliance administration in the hung authority. He was not asked to attend the informal meeting of chairs as he had with the previous Conservative administration. He blamed himself. Words he had used jokingly about the hung authority giving officers power had been seen as significant.

There needs to be a balance in the relationship between formality and informality. 'I always wanted a business relationship in a sense. I would never refer to our chief executive in a meeting by first name ... It does not have a good effect when members of the public are sitting there and the chair of committee is asking "Geoffrey" if he minds saying this and Geoffrey is the Treasurer' (David Church, former leader of Walsall: see Nolan, 1997b, p. 277).

Relations can break down. In a district council, relations had broken down so much that leader and chief executive never met except at committees. It could not last, and the chief executive retired. A leader may face differing attitudes amongst her councillors. In one authority attitudes differed sharply. 'Councillor X believes that all staff are wasteful bureaucrats. I see them as doing difficult jobs well.'

Leaders and chief executives constitute a varying and variable relationship, which deeply affects the workings of the authority.

### Chief officer and chair

The relationship between chair and chief officer mirrors that between leader and chief executive in all its variety and variation.

There is however a critical difference. The chief officer's role is defined by the services for which he or she is responsible. The role differs from that of the chief executive, whose role is defined by relationships rather than by services. The chief officer can see the primary role as running the service, and professionalism as marking out the contribution to that task. Professionalism can be a barrier in the relationship between chair and chief officer. The phrase 'my professional judgement' can be seen as meaning 'councillor keep out', and professional judgement can be subtly and perhaps unconsciously extended in range and depth. Professionalism can be a support where the chief officer sees the role as professional adviser, giving views but not pronouncing certainties on matters of judgement.

The chair's role can vary considerably because it is in no way defined beyond chairing the meeting of the committee. The chair has no formal authority, but gains the authority from his or her political position, the traditions of the authority, including the attitudes of the officers, and his or her own personality, ability and skills. A chair cannot make formal decisions. Decisions can be delegated to officers. Yet as the County Treasurer of Hampshire said, 'It would be a brave chief officer who did not take soundings on some of the delegated decisions that he was taking' (Nolan, 1997b, p. 246). In practice, different models of the chair's role can be found:

- *The ministerial model*, based on the belief that a chair should be like the minister in charge of the department.
- *The minimal model*, who sees the role as mainly chairing the meeting and 'I'm there if the chief officer wants to consult me.'

Within and between these models are many different approaches:

- *Anti-bureaucratic*, who can come from the left or from the right – 'I'm there to bring the officers into line'.
- *The policy enthusiast*, who has certain clear policy aims that occupy most of the chair's interest, energy and time.
- *The caretaker*, whose main concern is to see nothing goes wrong, or rather that nothing that goes wrong gets into the hands of the press.

- *The would-be professional,* who builds up a real expertise in the services for which he or she is responsible.
- *The manager,* who sees the role as running an effective organisation.
- *The public person,* who is mainly interested in public appearances.
- *The advocate,* who sees the role as securing political support (and financial support) for the services with which the committee is concerned.
- *The strategist,* who is concerned to set broad directions but is not interested in detail.
- *The case-worker,* who is mainly interested in particular cases.

How the chair plays the role will necessarily influence relations with a chief officer.

In one Welsh county the Independent chair refused to meet the director of social services, because it would bias his approach at committees. On the other hand a chief officer can resent what is seen as overmuch intervention by the chair in the running of the service. Where a chair has an office in the department, he or she can come to see themselves as head of the department. Equally a chair may feel barred by a chief officer who guards his or her departmental empire. Councillors in reaction may develop contacts at different levels of the department through party activities or in the normal working of the authority.

In one authority a director was under attack from the chair as previous directors and deputies had been. The chief executive raised the issue with the leader who backed the chair, his wife. In this instance the group felt the leader had gone too far and voted him out. Some chairs and chief officers make good relations difficult, but normally understanding is built over time by frequent contact.

In some authorities there are strategic committees and service committees, all with their own chairs. There can be uncertainty as to whether the main relationship of the chair is with the strategic director or service head. It is easy to say the relationship is with the strategic director on strategic matters, yet issues do not always fit easily into such boxes.

The introduction of contracts under CCT changed the relationship between chairs of service committees and those providing the service. Where the service is provided externally there will be no direct relationship. The chair's main relationship will be with the client chief officer, and some chairs have had difficulty adjusting to the hands-off relationship. A related issue arises when a contract is made with a direct services organisation outside the department for which the chair's committee is responsible. In that case the DSO is likely to be subject to its own committee. The relationship between the chair of that committee and the head of the DSO differs from the relationship between other chairs and chief officers. It is illustrated by committees being called DSO boards, implying a different way of operating. The work of the DSO is governed by the contract. The chair of the board cannot be concerned with the policy being followed. The board and its chair focus more on its operations as a business. It is a changed role which not all councillors easily accept, although some welcome it.

*The opposition*

The opposition in a local authority is a part of the authority and therefore of the process of governing. The councillors in the opposition have 'a right to know'. They are members of committees and are therefore part of the decision-making process. Officers are servants of the whole council and have a formal duty to keep all councillors informed.

Opposition councillors, as members of committees and of the council, have contact with officers. They consider they have a legitimate complaint if denied information. Officers recognise they have responsibilities to the council, including the opposition, although they have to balance it with recognition of the 'administration'. The wise chief executive or chief officer will give information to the opposition when requested, but will not give them access to the advice given to the majority group or to working papers prepared for it. It is not always as simple as that. When that group has rejected the chief officer's advice, she can still be asked 'What is your advice on this issue?' in committee, which differs from the question 'What was your advice to the chair?' A difficult and delicate path has to be found through the political minefield. Councillor Gorrie, the leader of the Liberal Democrats in Edinburgh, said in his evidence to the Nolan Committee, 'some of our officials try and draw a distinction between information and advice, but I think they should give advice, though they need not tell me what advice they gave to the Labour group' (Nolan, 1997b, p. 88).

The wise chief executive and chief officers maintain contact with opposition leaders and spokespersons. With the tacit approval of the majority group, many have regular meetings, although not so frequently as with the leadership of the council. Failure to do so builds suspicion amongst the opposition, which may be dangerous if control changes. One chief executive in a large city had little contact with the opposition. The only committee he attended was a one-party committee containing the leadership of the majority group. When control changed he found his post was abolished. Both chief executives and chief officers have to guard their backs.

Local authorities differ in the likelihood of the opposition coming to power, which can affect attitudes. Where such a possibility appears remote it can mean the opposition is disregarded, although that can be dangerous. In the early 1990s many 'safe' Conservative authorities saw Liberal Democrats or Labour in power.

*In the hung authority*

In the hung authority there is no majority group and many of the patterns of behaviour appropriate to the majority system do not apply. Effective working may require the chief executive to act as broker, even to the point of suggesting an alliance when the parties are not able to do so. In Wiltshire in 1985 the chief executive identified that the only practical outcome was an Alliance administration supported by Labour, and he encouraged that outcome. In one district council in 1996 the Liberal Democrats had allied with Conservatives and Independents in a loose administration, but were unable to achieve their policy aims. The chief executive brokered a shared administration between Labour and the Liberal Democrats on the basis of their similar manifestos. In Lancashire the chief executive brought the leaders of the parties together after a traumatic first meeting of the council at which Labour refused the chairs it had been agreed they would take as the largest party, because the other parties combined to elect the Conservative leader as chair of the council.

Different forms of administration are found in hung authorities. Where a coalition is formed, the relation between officers and councillors is closest to majority control although officers have to be sensitive to both or all parties involved and to possible differences between them. With a minority administration, shared chairs or no administration relationships are different from the majority situation. The chair cannot have the authority of an assured majority, although because of past habits, the position of the chair will still have special weight with officers.

A chief officer supported by three spokespersons can be in a powerful position, where there is a readiness to work together. Spokespersons' or leaders' meetings have their own dynamics. In some instances, one group may adopt an oppositional stance, coming to such meetings but being reluctant to reach agreement. There can be differences in their readiness to reach agreement at these meetings, some leaders or spokespersons reserving their positions until their groups have been consulted. Chief officers may find themselves managing such meetings and the relationships involved in all their variety.

The almost hung authority can present special problems. At a meeting of one county council the Alliance and Labour found themselves able to defeat the Conservatives because of the absence of a Conservative member. They carried a series of resolutions. They asked the chief executive for an assurance he would implement the motions. According to an Alliance councillor, he declined to give that assurance. They therefore added to each resolution a rider, calling for immediate action. This incident followed a previous occasion when the chief executive did not implement a decision to restore school cleaners to previous terms and conditions. He argued that further decisions were required and he could not implement it on the basis of the county council resolution alone. It was a difficult and delicate set of circumstances.

*Backbenchers*

The relationship between backbenchers and officers is often limited. The main relationship lies in the committee or sub-committee. These settings are often not for discussion but for 'getting through the business'. The councillor will also deal with officers in casework, and constituency issues often focus on complaints or particular cases. Neither contact provides a good basis for building a relationship.

Some chief executives cultivate a wider relationship, drawing on the knowledge of the local councillor. One chief executive periodically offers the councillors in each ward a visit for which he invites them to draw up their own programme. It builds his understanding of the area, using the often under-used insights of local councillors.

## The settings

While the relations between leader and chief executive or chief officer and chair will often take place in informal settings, there are a number of regular settings for contact. Some are part of the regular cycles in the work of the council and mark its particular rhythm. Each setting shapes a different pattern of behaviour.

### The committee

The committee is constituted as a formal setting for authoritative decision-making – conditioning the councillor–officer relationship. The nature of the committee room with its long table suggests formality. The committee meeting is governed by its agenda – normally largely prepared by the officers. The chair controls the meeting, but with the chief officer by his side, often supported by an array of officers from the relevant department and from central departments. Staff from the committee section guide on the formalities and take the minutes.

Officers' roles are defined by traditions. They are there to advise the committee, rather than to take part in discussion, although the line between the two is not always clear, and officers and committees interpret it differently. Officers present reports and answer questions, but the committee belongs to the members. Officers' behaviour is therefore controlled behaviour. They will laugh politely at a member's joke, but it would be out of place to laugh at serious points. Chief officers vary in their approaches. Some present all the reports which stand in their own name, emphasising the hierarchy of the department. Others call upon officers in their department to present them, spreading responsibility and credit or the lack of it. The committee meeting is usually a formal game, governed by committee procedures and the formalities of party behaviour. It remains an important element from the inheritance.

There has been a general tendency to reduce the number of committees and to increase delegation to officers. The number of committees has fallen over the last thirty years from 10.4 at the time of the research for the Maud Committee (Maud, 1967) to 5.6 in 1994 (LGMB, 1995).

In a few authorities there have been moves away from the undifferentiated cycle of meetings. In Clwyd, each meeting was treated as a stage in the management process, with separate meetings for strategy, budgeting and review as the main business, with operational issues decided by sub-committees. In Avon, implementation sub-committees enabled the committee to focus on policy and review. In Stroud, as a hung authority, agendas were planned over a twelve-month period by officers working with spokespersons.

There is one example of an authority breaking out of the mind-set imposed by the inheritance. In Clackmannanshire, there were only twelve councillors. Yet, like other district councils, it operated through a committee system, which meant committees of, say, eight councillors were meeting and then reporting to the other four councillors at the council meeting – a time-consuming procedure. The solution adopted is so obvious that one is surprised that any other approach was ever used. Clackmannanshire decided to abolish all committees and instead the council meets more frequently, with councillors as spokespersons for particular services. The new unitary authority has maintained this approach, even though the range of services is wider. Clackmannanshire's approach was not followed by the other authorities of similar size. To them, abandoning the committee system was almost unthinkable. Clackmannanshire was the exception which proved the rule or rather challenged the assumptions still dominant in most authorities.

*Emerging settings*

Until recently, apart from the council meeting, the committee was in many authorities the only official setting for councillors. Increasingly, new settings have been developed. Working groups and panels have been set up in which the emphasis is less on the formalities of decision-making and more on discussion of issues,

although with a variety of forms and purposes. They can be constituted as joint officer–member groups and can even be chaired by
an officer. They can be member groups with officers in attendance,
but less constrained by the formalities of decision-making. They
are likely to involve backbenchers and be less affected by party
conflict. Officers may be drawn from different levels of the organisation, widening councillor–officer contact. Working parties
explore a policy issue or review performance. Quality panels
assess the quality of service and scrutiny panels monitor the work
of appointed boards in their area.

In some authorities, working parties are virtually unknown.
In others, the authority appears threatened with take-over by a
proliferation of such bodies, ever talking, but never reporting.
In others, clear procedures are laid down. Cambridgeshire had a
self-imposed limit on the number of such bodies at any one time.
In such authorities, the remit, reporting procedures and time targets are specified.

East Cambridgeshire moved towards a 'Council without Committees'. The emphasis is on members' advisory panels advising
the full council (chairman's advisory group, recreation and tourism, monitoring resources advisory, strategic development, and
value-for-money panels) along with time-limited working parties.
Committees with executive powers were retained for appeals and
complaints, grants, licensing, personnel and planning. In Cumbria, select committees have been set up in which a group of
members – mainly backbenchers – take oral evidence as well as
receiving written evidence. Their reports are considered at full
meetings of the council and have covered devolution in the
county and the youth services.

Kirklees has developed scrutiny commissions and quality
reviews. 'Kirklees believes that the Council is Local Government –
not just a service-providing agency. As such it has a remit and
responsibility to investigate any issue which has an impact on the
public of Kirklees and to lead public debate. As a consequence of
this, the Council has established a system of Scrutiny Commissions
to examine major issues. Their investigations cover issues for which
other organisations are primarily responsible and major issues
within the Council, but not within the remit of any one Service
Committee.' Quality reviews have been set up to review the experience of services; a number of 'service sampling' activities have been

established. Sometimes this involves a visit by a group of elected members to a particular facility and in other cases might involve a structured meeting with a group of service users. The key question here for members is "How does it feel for our customers?"'

In Haringey, public scrutiny has been developed. Services are identified as subjects for scrutiny, and submissions are invited from the public and from interested bodies. Hearings for the public are held by panels of councillors along with officers' views.

In different ways, authorities are breaking out of the limitations imposed by the inherited committee system, while generally maintaining that system. The pattern of behaviour in such settings is very different from in committee, although where such groups are held in committee-rooms ingrained habits die hard, and some councillors, long-used to committee working, find it difficult to adjust to a different style. The informalities should, and often do, enable discussion to flow easily between officers and councillors.

*Area committees*

Some authorities have introduced area committees of councillors as part of a process of decentralisation. They can be mainly sounding-boards, at which local issues can be raised and reports asked for, as in Birmingham. They can, however, as in Kingston-on-Thames or in South Somerset, exercise substantial powers.

The area committee, whether a sounding-board or a decision-making body, is likely to differ in its way of working from other committees. There is a greater balance of expertise between councillors and officers. All the local councillors have understanding of the area and the councillors' understanding may be greater and certainly wider than that of the officers. The chair has less of a special position, because he or she has less access to special knowledge. If the meeting is held in the area, as is normal, the public are present in greater numbers and contribute to the discussion. Party divisions can be overwhelmed by the pressures and problems of locality and are resented by the public. Area committees permit greater contact between councillors and officers in a setting that may be relatively informal. The formal meeting can more easily merge into the informal, and the public, who resent over-formality, provide a constant pressure for informality.

*Agenda meetings*

While the emphasis has been placed on informal contacts between chairs and chief officers, two other settings involve chairs and chief officers. The pre-agenda meeting considers what is to be on the agenda and the nature of the reports. The agenda meeting is a briefing meeting, after the agenda and reports have gone out, to enable the chair to prepare for the meeting. These meetings vary in their nature and in some authorities the chair may be content to clear the agenda on the phone.

The pre-agenda meeting can be a fairly routine occasion, going through the business. It can however be a point where the tension arises between the chief officer's formal responsibilities to the council and responsibility to the majority group. The chair may object to an item on the agenda or the nature of a report. The chief officer is likely accept the chair's view if no issue of principle arises. Yet in the final resort the chief officer may have to assert her duty to the council.

*An informal political executive*

The legislation which eliminated one-party committees did not eliminate meetings of the party leadership with officers, but made them unofficial, although almost inevitable in a majority-controlled authority. Leaders' meetings, chairs' meetings or their equivalent are common and recognised as such. Edward Lister, the Conservative leader, has said that in Wandsworth there had been a cabinet style for about 15 years (Lister, 1995). In some instances the majority group executive or the group officers will play this role attended by the chief executive and chief officers. In one Northern city the leader initiated a weekly meeting of group officers, chief executive, central chief officers and four trade union officers. In Bolton there was a weekly meeting of the leader and chairs with chief officers known as the liaison group. In Leeds the meeting of the leader, chairs of strategy committees and equivalent officers was known as the 'cabinet'. Such meetings are not formal decision-making meetings, but can be the most influential meetings in the authority. Held in private they enable in-depth discussion, both of long-term policy and of immediate issues.

There can be suspicion of such meetings amongst other councillors. In Independent-dominant authorities there are particular fears
of elitism. In East Cambridgeshire there were regular meeting between the chairman and vice-chairman of the council and the management team. To lessen suspicion it was agreed that any councillor
could attend the meeting. None had, but it overcame resistance.

Attendance at and frequency of meetings vary. Their style can
vary from a formality that resembles a committee to the informality of a discussion group. It can be 'blunt and outspoken'. Ideas
can be tested and crises dealt with. The leader can dominate the
meeting or facilitate the discussion. In these meetings all the variety of local government can be found.

There can be a merging of the political leadership and the chief
officers in the management team. In Newport, the management
team consisted of the leader, leading chairs, the chief executive
and the four directors. In Cumbria a management board, composed of four leading Conservative councillors and three chief
officers, replaced the management team in the 1970s.

In some authorities, general contact between leading councillors and chief officers has been rare or almost unknown. When I
visited North Tyneside, I was told my meeting with chief officers
and leading councillors was the first time they had met together
for discussion. It was itself a stimulus to the changes that followed.

The Labour Government's programme described in Chapter 7
proposes legislation enabling local authorities to create political
executives including cabinets, which could be composed of
members of the majority party. A number of authorities have
introduced transitional arrangements, giving a role to informal
political executives taking over functions of service committees.
Until legislation is enacted these 'cabinets', as they are called,
must remain outside the official structure and their decisions
have to be ratified by a committee whose membership represents
the political balance on the Council. These transitional arrangements show a diversity of practice.

*Meetings of the group*

Meetings of the political group can be attended by officers, normally on a particular issue. Thus when the budget is being considered, explanation of the background by the treasurer and the

chief executive aids an informed discussion. Granted that in majority-controlled authorities effective, although not formal, decisions are taken by the group, direct access to officer advice seems common-sense. Even a well-briefed chair may find questions or issues raised on which he or she does not have the immediate answer. One chief executive said 'I'd much rather be in there, influencing things, rather than have them come along later and tell me they'd made some really stupid decisions' (Gyford *et al.*, 1989, p. 132). Yet the Widdicombe research showed that in 259 of the 390 authorities replying, the chief executive never attended the party group, and the figures for other chief officers were higher. There were significant differences between types of authority. In Scotland and in metropolitan districts, chief executives occasionally or frequently attended groups in a majority of authorities.

Where officers attend political groups there are usually safeguards for their position to ensure the preservation of their political neutrality. Officers normally leave the meeting before discussion begins, after their presentation and questions. Indeed in East Staffordshire a procedure has been introduced where the first half of the meeting is constituted on a regular basis for this purpose as the leaders' advisory group. In Tamworth, 'there is a system whereby reports of a major strategic, policy or budget significance are presented by officers to an informal meeting of members of the majority group. The officers answer questions and then withdraw before there is any discussion. This process is carried out openly and in full knowledge of the opposition' (Nolan, 1997b, p. 436). Or as Lord Tope, the leader of Sutton, said, 'we have an agreement with the parties on our council that officers may attend a party group meeting to inform and advise on a matter before the council. Their role at that group meeting is exactly that – to explain, advise and answer questions. They leave the meeting before there is discussion, let alone decision' (Nolan, 1997b, p. 273). Demands usually come from the majority group, but officers will normally insist on their right to accept invitations from the opposition groups.

### The tactics of the game

There are inevitably conflicts between the worlds of the officers and of the councillors. Those conflicts are resolved in different ways on different occasions. Councillors have formal authority, but it is not always easily exercised. Councillors are dependent on officers for advice and information and for implementation. Councillors will not readily go against 'the best professional advice', unless they are sure of their ground. On most occasions councillors do not openly ignore officer advice, and it would not be acceptable for officers to refuse to implement the council's decisions. Yet there are many stages to be played in the game of councillor–officer relations.

A series of myths have importance in the game. They are myths in the sense that they depend for their influence not upon their truth, but upon their repetition in common discourse. They will normally have some basis in reality, but their use may extend in the tactics of the game beyond that reality.

> The myth of statutory constraint is a powerful influence in many local authorities. The belief is widely held that the local authority's existing activities are largely required by statute and that the local authority has no discretion in carrying out those activities. The myth has a basis in reality. The local authority is a law-bound organisation. It normally carries out activities only when specifically authorised by statute. Many of its activities are mandatory. That is the basis of the myth. It does not follow, however, from the fact that many of the activities of the local authority are mandatory, that the local authority has no or very little choice over those activities. Although the local authority has mandatory duties as well as discretionary powers, statutory duties are not drawn as tightly as is widely believed and in the final resort 'A local authority is responsible for its interpretation of the law and therefore its level of expenditure.' (Stewart, 1981, pp. 146–7)

The myth of statutory constraint can be used to protect expenditure on existing activities. Yet when it is said that expenditure is required by statute, it is not necessarily the case that either the existing level of expenditure or the present form of activity are required by statute.

Responsibility to the whole council can be prayed in aid by an officer is faced by demands by a chair for the alteration of a report. Yet in a sense it is only half the story, and on other occasions the officer will accept the views of the administration. The inherited model of councillor–officer relations was its own myth. It had and can still have influence even when recognised as not fully grounded in reality.

Warnings about surcharge have had an impact (Nolan, 1997a, p. 54). Surcharge gained greater prominence in the confrontations between a group of Labour-controlled authorities and central government in the early 1980s. Surcharge was actually imposed on Lambeth and Liverpool councillors with the penalty of disqualification. In this period a Northern Labour leader, who had been subject to a minor surcharge of £50 for reasons long-forgotten, used to say to his left-wingers seeking to defy the government by setting an illegal budget, 'You only talk, I am the one who has been surcharged.'

'The auditor will never stand for it' can be a weapon in the treasurer's armoury if councillors are proposing to run down balances. 'Ultra vires' can drift across the conversation. The statutory positions of the chief executive, the monitoring officer and the chief finance officer are in practice, used more in the game than in the application – used more often as a threat than they are applied in practice. The Nolan Committee said that 'like the threat of surcharge, officers told us privately, the statutory powers kept councillors on line' (Nolan, 1997a, p. 40). Few statutory officers have used or would use the ultimate weapon of a report to the council identifying mispractice. Treasurers and monitoring officers have to live with the consequences. For most officers the statutory roles and the duties that go with them are a resource referred to occasionally rather than used. 'If the council so decided, I am afraid I would have to prepare a report on it.' The monitoring officer in an authority visited by Nolan had only once had to prepare a report, but 'found that the possibility of writing a report worked wonders very frequently' (Nolan, 1997a, p. 30).

The neutrality of the officers is a powerful myth. The neutral officer will serve with the same devotion whatever the administration, yet the reality can be different. Councils may appoint officers sympathetic to their policies, and officers can have strong views on policy. Yet the myth survives and perhaps must survive in authorities where control changes.

There are other tactics. One county chief executive had persuaded his Conservative administration of the value of devolved management to cost centres on the grounds of efficiency and value for money. Control changed and the arguments for the proposal changed for the Alliance administration, to closeness to the community.

Councillors have their own tactics and create their own myths. 'We expect our manifesto to be implemented', or 'The group has decided brooks no argument' can create dilemmas when confronting the myth of statutory constraint or the reality of financial limitation. 'I've received a lot of complaints about this', or 'People are up in arms about it' expresses the role of the elected representative. 'I am accountable to my electorate' asserts that role. 'Who runs the authority?' can challenge the officers. Russell Goodway's (leader of Cardiff County Council) statement to the Nolan Committee illustrates the power of the manifesto as a myth:

> At the same time, they [officers] have to understand they operate within a political system and that the people who have been elected have been elected on the basis of a manifesto that they inherited to translate into a policy direction for the authority over the lifetime of that administration. It is their duty to work to that administration and help us translate that series of manifesto commitments into policies that we can take through the council and implement within the community that we serve. (Nolan, 1997b, p. 36)

However, as Gyford and his colleagues have shown, 'Manifestoism ... is still confined to a limited number of highly politicised authorities' (Gyford *et al.*, 1989, p. 132).

Some tactics can be over-used. Councillors will challenge arguments used too often. 'The crumbling of the roads' is no longer believed in one authority. The county surveyor had used the argument too often to protect his highways maintenance budget.

Other phrases have significance in the workings of authorities. 'The councillors will never stand for it' is a phrase commonly used by officers to oppose proposals even if the councillors had never heard of it. A newly appointed chief executive seeking a radical reorganisation met that response from his management team and yet his proposals were accepted by the council. Staff in a department may have proposals rejected by a chief officer on the same grounds. Yet unless the councillors hear the proposal there is no certainty they will reject it.

*Developing new relationships*

Despite frustration or tension in the relationship, it is possible to find ways through it. The first requirement is wider discussion between officers and councillors. Away-days or weekend seminars can have a role in creating settings at which issues can be discussed in depth. They can focus on policy so that across the boundary that divides the councillor from the officer world, understanding can develop of what is sought and what can be achieved. On such occasions the apparent certainties of the manifesto can be used to open up possibilities. Financial barriers may not be impenetrable if there is a readiness to explore. At one away-day, the chief officer for planning and transportation took the manifesto commitment for mixed housing development and gave it a series of different meanings. The issue was exposed not in opposition but in clarification, and once exposed could be discussed.

In the Central Region of Scotland, member–officer groups introduced a new style of working:

Openness of debate between members and officers was of critical importance to the quality of recommendations produced, and trust developed that would not normally have happened. As a result of the freer flows of information and of the exposure of differing points of view, the groups not only developed recommendations close to the manifesto commitments of the Labour Group, but also had the technical and professional input to make them viable. In the past, manifesto commitments often bore little relation to the policy developed by officers for the Council. However, logic suggests that a policy has more prospect of being delivered if both officers and members have ownership of that policy. (Central Regional Council, 1995)

Discussions can focus on ways of working. In one authority, chairs and chief officers took part in a weekend seminar with outside facilitators. The first task was for groups of councillors and groups of officers to identify the agenda for the weekend. To their surprise they identified the same issues – a first step in understanding. Understanding is critical to handling tensions, although there will be occasions when they are unmanageable. Many a structural reorganisation has been undertaken to remove chief officers seen as obstacles by councillors. Officers, to be effective, require political awareness and political sensitivity. These attributes are not the same as political commitment. Indeed to councillors suspicious of officers when control changes lack of awareness and sensitivity may give the impression of political commitment. The politically unaware may not appreciate the extent to which their own assumptions express political values. Words can fuel suspicion. Failure to see the importance of an issue to the new majority can cause resentment. The officers with political sensitivity and political awareness appreciate these issues. Those without it create problems for themselves.

There is a continuing need for political sensitivity. Although the model of good practice made policy implementation the responsibility of the officer, it is often in implementation that political issues arise. The letting of a council hall may seem a clear-cut issue for implementation, but in one city it raised such political feelings that the council itself voted on the matter. The issue was, of course, the letting of the hall to an extremist organisation. The politically sensitive officer will see the political in the apparently routine. Training has a role in building political sensitivity. Equally, councillors may need training in 'making the organisation work for you', which is unlikely to be achieved by aggressiveness that can come from frustration.

Too often attempts have been made to clarify relationships by a reassertion of old models in new guises, asserting the role of councillors in policy and the review of performance, and deploring their involvement in particular cases. What has to be appreciated is that policy may lie in the particular. At a meeting of the leader's panel in one county, most discussion took place not upon the strategy paper, but on an issue about grass-cutting of verges in one district. The county carried out one safety cut each year. Other district councils carried out additional amenity cuts. This district council did not, in part because of disputes over agency arrangements which up to now had been refused, but were now being conceded. The issues raised were:

- whether because of local feeling an area panel (which allocated county resources) should be given an extra £17,000 for grass-cutting to aid the agency agreement
- whether, if that was done, equivalent sums should be given to other panels – otherwise it would be seen as unfair
- whether the resources should come from the environment committee budget or from the county's special reserve.

Discussion aroused great interest – about 15 of the 20 there took part. It would be easy to regard this example as councillors getting absorbed in particular cases, but the discussion raised important points:

- county–district relations and the appropriate role of each;
- responsiveness to local needs and distributive equity;
- the discretion available to area panels;
- the principles of budgetary control;
- the role of the council's contingency reserve;
- whether verges should be cut at all.

In a particular case principles can be explored and can test policy. The way forward is to work with the grain rather than against.

## Conclusion

The settings in which councillor–officer relations are played out express the uniformities of local government, although their variety is growing with a movement away from reliance on the committee setting. Within those settings the relationship can take many different forms.

Councillor–officer relations are the force which drives the diversity of local government. It is possible to categorise councillor–officer relations in a variety of ways. Some authorities are described as officer-led, while in others councillors are described as dominant. One chief executive moving from an authority in the former category to an authority in the latter found his role had changed completely from, in his words, 'chief executive to chief administrative officer'.

Yet such a categorisation captures only one aspect of the relations. The emphasis given to different settings; the relative formality of relations; the patterns of accepted behaviour; the spread or concentration of relationships, are all variables. And while past experience is an influence, the pattern of the relationship cannot be regarded as fixed. Rather, it is a dynamic whose impact varies depending on the mix of history, experience, politics and personality that drives it.

# 13 The Local Authority: Toward Community Leadership

## The impact of locality

Localities vary and in their variation have an impact upon local authorities. That impact is a dominant impression of my visits. Consider the differences between areas:

- The great industrial city confronting issues of unemployment which fall most heavily upon ethnic minorities, but still retaining affluent communities within its area.
- The London borough in an area of deprivation, with high unemployment, again focused on ethnic minorities, but with areas of gentrification.
- The suburban London borough set in commuter land, but with large-scale former GLC estates.
- The cathedral city proving attractive to industries based on new technology.
- The former mining area where few or no pits remain, but where the values of mining communities still dominate.
- Market towns and villages where the role of agriculture is declining in importance and an increasing number of houses are owned by commuters or used as second homes.
- Welsh hill country, in which a large proportion of the population are Welsh-speaking.
- The seaside town where holiday visitors have declined, but which has become a residential centre for older people.

Each area has its impact. How is that impact achieved? The answer lies through the publics of the locality. The public have an impact on the local authority through the electoral process but also through pressure and protest, demand and complaint, suggestion and aspiration expressed directly to officers and councillors or through the media.

The impact of the public on the authority is a force for both uniformity and for diversity. The public in different authorities share needs and aspirations. They are subject to similar influences from the media and experience a common society and economy. It is easy to see society as homogenous and therefore to expect that local authorities face similar publics, with similar demands and aspirations. The reality is that the publics seek both uniformity and difference, although individuals do not see it in those terms. They are concerned with the particularity of their demands and aspirations. Only when those demands and aspirations are assessed collectively do uniformity and difference become visible.

Although there exists a shared society and economy, a differentiated society and economy also exists. Society is differentiated by age, by education, by gender, by ethnic background, by health, by culture, and by experiences, in ways that interact with each other. The economy is differentiated by occupation, by scale, by industry, by success or failure, by technology and by employment conditions. Society and economy contain forces for uniformity and forces for differentiation.

The forces for differentiation generate pressures and aspirations and the balance between them varies from place to place. In some authorities there are no or few farmers, while in others they will be a major force. The pattern of occupations varies as does the extent of employment and unemployment. Class structures vary from area to area. Ethnic minorities are concentrated in particular areas. Thus the pattern of pressures, demands and aspirations differs from area to area, requiring, in as far as those pressures are recognised by the authority, different responses.

The task of the local authority is to reconcile, to balance and to judge the different demands placed upon it. The outcome will vary from place to place because the pattern of pressures will vary as will the political composition of the council. This role of balancing, reconciling and judging arises at local and individual levels, as well as at the authority level. In any area, individuals and communities interact, creating potential both for co-operation and for conflict: in a decision on a planning application at one level or on the budget at another. The local authority is at the meeting point of differing demands. Differences in the balance of demands between areas create pressures for diversity in local government, within the boundaries set by national pressures and the still powerful professional norms.

There is an economic environment with an impact both on the communities and on the authority.

> Important aspects of the strategic and discursive selectivity of the local economy include: its regional location, its proximity to large areas of populations, its communication linkages; its population density; the degree of financial infrastructural and political support from the centre; its eligibility for European and national funds; the political philosophy of the local authority and local business leaders; its networked linkages with Whitehall; the local lobbying power that can be mustered; the availability of land with 'development potential'; the quality of the housing stock and the local 'aesthetics of place'; the skill profile of the local labour market; the degree of local economic diversity; its physical, infrastructural and discursive proximity to mainland Europe; and the political make-up of neighbouring local authorities. (Hay and Jessop, 1995, p. 25)

Hill country, former mining areas, declining mill towns, inner-city areas, university towns, new towns, have their own character. Climate, physical geography, are determinants. Outdoor cafe life does not flourish in cold climates. The inherited physical structures have their impact, seen in the contrast between a new town and an old industrial town. Over and above the physical and economic environment there is a social environment.

In 'understanding the local political scene, the fact that local social structures are not the same as their national equivalents must be grasped, since this establishes a framework within which variability is more easily provoked' (Hoggert, 1991, p. 159). Different patterns of industrial and commercial development have their own impact, not merely in the present but from the past. Each area has its own history which influences the present, creating problems and opportunities. There is a culture felt to a greater or lesser extent by those who live in the area. The communities or publics who constitute the area are influenced by and influence the environment.

As Gyford has pointed out, locality studies have attempted to capture the complex interactions between locality and civil society. Thus Baggulay and his colleagues have argued: 'The character of any particular place depends upon its location in a number of spatial divisions of labour and on the particular way in which these are combined together, in a kind of "geographical" structure with economic, cultural and political components' (in Cooke, 1989, quoted in Gyford, 1991, p. 12). They showed the relevance of this concept for local government.

> How far, and in what ways, local government should become involved in the resourcing or enabling of sometimes competing local interests in civil society is likely to prove a contentious matter. Nonetheless, locality now looms large, both as the context and the substantive focus of much activity in civil society. For that reason local government now stands potentially at the frontiers of civil society and the state, and perhaps therefore on the threshold of a new conception of its role. (in Baggulay *et al.*, 1990, quoted in Gyford, 1991, p. 27)

On this basis, Gyford argues:

> Many observers of local government have commented on its great diversity, of procedures and of politics, occasionally in terms of some bewilderment. We can now see that such diversity is not necessarily a random phenomenon or the outcome of the arbitrary whims of forceful council leaders or chief executives. It can also reflect the accumulated impact of the particular changes in economic fortune and in social relations which individual localities have experienced over years and decades.
> If such diversity is then rooted in actual, lived social experience, rather than merely a random departure from some supposed national norm, then it may be argued that it has a valid claim for political representation. Traditionally local government as a political institution has been justified in terms of its contribution to the wider system of government, through dispersing power or avoiding central overload for example. Perhaps we may now argue that there is also a case for localities to be governmentally represented by virtue of their nature as what Rose (1988) describes as 'geographically variable trends,

of social life' which shape political expression in locally unique
ways. (Gyford, 1991, pp. 23–4)

The local authority exercises its responsibilities in a defined
locality and the nature of local government has to be understood
through its relationship with the locality and its social, economic
and physical conditions. That relationship is built up through the
multiplicity of the relationships between the authority and the
publics and organisations that constitute the process of community governance.

## The local authority and its public

The nature of relationships with the public and the relative
emphasis given to them reflect the perceived role of the authority.
If that role is seen as mainly a provider of services, then an
emphasis will be placed on the public as service recipients, sometimes misleadingly called 'customers'. If the role is seen as mainly
a political institution for local government, then an emphasis will
be placed on the public as citizens.

In the classical writings on local government the publics in their
complexity are almost absent, because the perspective was sim-
plified. The municipal corporation defined the local authority
or corporation as including the burgesses. As Redlich argued,
'the town council – that is to say the lawful representatives of a
municipality – is the sole organ through which the burgesses
express their collective will' (Redlich, 1903, vol. I, pp. 302–3).
The 'burgesses and their representatives alone form an integral
part of the municipal constitution' (ibid, p. 334).

The emphasis was placed on the public as burgesses, constitut-
ing by election the council as their representatives. The literature
of the nineteenth century and even later focused on the role of the
public as elector. What is surprising to modern readers is that so
little was written about relationships with individual members of
the public. The life of present-day councillors with their advice
bureaux, their surgeries, the letters and other contacts, belongs to
a different world. In part this difference was due to smaller elect-
orates. Councillors belonged to a particular social group, often
closely in contact. Many of the functions of the local authorities

did not involve individual members of the public and were more concerned with the infrastructure of the locality. The public were the collective public. Doctrines of municipal enterprise were built on the welfare of the city rather than of the individual.

Even in the literature of the first half of the century there is little reference to the public, beyond the role of the elector and of rate-payer, and these roles were linked. Discussion of the relationship with the recipients of services is conspicuous by its absence. In *A Century of Municipal Progress*, a series of essays in praise of local government (Laski *et al.*, 1935), there is no discussion of the service-user, or as modern works would say, of the 'customer', amongst the chapter headings. Professionalism was seen as a precious asset. The professional–client relationship was seen as unprob-lematic, needing no comment. The professional understands the client's needs and will provide the service required. If there were problems in the development of professionalism, it lay not in the expertise and knowledge, but in the absence of what were then characterised as administrative skills, but now described as management competences.

The 1980s saw a new focus on the relationship with the public, arising in part because of the growing challenge to the dominance of the professional. The immediate post-war years were probably the heyday of professionalism in local government. There was a confidence in the capacity of the professional to deliver, and the emphasis was on the growth of services guided by professional expertise. The achievements of that period came under increas-ing challenge for not delivering on their promise.

The disillusion caused loss of confidence in the professional. It could no longer be assumed that the professional definition of ser-vice was necessarily right. Partly for this reason and partly because of cultural changes the public themselves became more question-ing and less ready to accept that authority knew best. The ideo-logy that underlay the welfare state came under challenge from the Conservative government committed to rolling back the state and emphasising individual choice. This challenge led to ques-tioning both the role of the professional and the growth in local government expenditure, which were seen as linked in provider-dominance. While there was early resistance particularly by Labour-controlled local authorities to many of the measures of the Conservative government it became clear that the slogan of

'Defend Jobs and Services and Defend Local Democracy' did not receive a widespread public response. It led to a reconsideration by those authorities of the relationship to the public.

There was a new emphasis on the public as customer and then on the public as citizen. The emphasis on the public as customer drew in part upon management thinking represented by such works as *In Search of Excellence* (Peters and Waterman, 1980). Clarke and Stewart wrote about the need for a public service orientation, arguing that local authorities had provided service *to* people rather than *for* them (Clarke and Stewart, 1990). Authorities had looked inward to the organisation rather than outward to the public served. York and other authorities introduced service contracts setting out the standards of service aimed at and the means of redress. Training in customer care developed. Quality of service was pursued and an increasing number of authorities introduced quality assurance programmes. These movements both pre-dated and influenced, and then were stimulated by, the government's Citizen's Charter. Authorities introduced their own charters following the models of the service contracts but now as part of the charter movement.

The emphasis on the customer had strengths, but also weaknesses. It hid the variety of relationships with the public. Some services are available on demand; others are rationed. Some services are provided free of charge; others are charged for, possibly subject to a means test. Some services have individual customers, but in others it is hard to identify an individual user. Some services are compulsory, while in others the public is free to decide whether to use the service. Local authorities arbitrate between different members of the public. They control and even prosecute individual members of the public. It requires not one word but many words to capture the variety of relationships. The public can be client or customer, but also claimant, applicant, user, regulatee, defendant and even prisoner. They can be pupils, passengers, drivers, pedestrians, carers, and many more. The movement of language from client to customer marks the movement from a dominant professional perspective, to an emerging management perspective but a more complex language is required.

An emphasis on the public as customer reflects the dominance of the view of local authorities as a provider of services. If the local authority is seen as a political institution constituted for local government, then the emphasis will be on the public as citizen. But the public as citizen can be interpreted in different ways, depending on how the political institution is conceived. The local authority as a political institution is constituted through representative democracy. Representation can be reduced to the process of the election. That is a passive conception of representation and in that passive model the citizen is the elector and only an elector.

There can be a different conception in which representation is an active and continuing process. In that model representative democracy is sustained by participatory democracy. Too often representative democracy is seen as opposed to participatory democracy, reflecting only a passive concept of representation. If, rather than being a representative, the councillor re-presents the views of citizens, that demands an active process in which the councillor is informed by participatory democracy. Participatory democracy, far from weakening representative democracy, can strengthen it. The development of participatory democracy does not mean that the representative becomes a delegate. Indeed, if anything, it makes the role of representative more important and more difficult. People speak with many voices, expressing differing values and interests. The task of the elected representative is to seek to reconcile, to balance and in the end to judge.

The citizen can be a participant in the process of local government. For a citizen as participant the local election is important, but it is not the limit of citizenship but rather its starting point. It is possible to go further. The emphasis of citizen as elector and even citizen as participant can be on the individual citizen, but the role of local government in community governance suggests the role of citizen as a member of communities. To recognise the citizen as a member of many communities is to build understanding of the individual in relationship to others.

There is growing interest in these wider aspects of citizenship. Harlow prepared a citizen's charter based on five rights:

- to be heard and listened to
- access to the authority and those who speak on behalf of the authority
- to information
- to be met with fairness, equity and justice

- to be actively involved in the governing of the local community.

Such a charter is not a charter for customers but for citizens. Norwich set up a democracy team to look at ways in which 'the involvement of Norwich citizen in the democratic systems of the city could be improved'. It has organised a citizens' jury, question-time road-shows, quango watch and a sixth form management game. Fife set up a citizenship commission whose remit includes: 'The promotion and development of representative and participatory democracy in Fife' and 'The review of progress on the Council's aims and programmes for consultation, communication, community and consumer participation, decentralisation and democratic participation.'

It is increasingly recognised that there is as much need for innovation in democratic practice as in management practice. Citizens' juries provide one example of such innovation. After pilots sponsored by the LGMB in six local authorities, others have followed (Hall and Stewart, 1997). But that is only one example. A repertoire of approaches is developing, including public dispute resolution, new forms of public meetings, visioning conferences, environmental appraisal, public scrutiny and referendums (Stewart, 1995, 1996, 1997).

## The many publics and the many relationships

The local authority is distinguished from many organisations by the number of publics it faces and hence by the multiplicity of its relationships and the variety of forms that they can take, even with an individual member of the public. That member of the public can be an elector, who may or may not exercise the right to vote. She may write to her councillor about an issue, sign a petition or go to a public meeting expressing citizenship in action. She may receive many services but be denied others, have a planning application accepted or rejected, use a library but be fined for non-return of books, be required to have trees cut back and drive a car on the roads. She is a local taxpayer, working for a firm which has its own relationship with the local authority and is a member of a residents' association pressing for better street cleansing. She glances at the local authority newspaper but reads the evening paper to which she has written about environmental issues.

The local authority has relationships with all living in the locality and with those who work there and many who visit it. The variety and intensity of the relationships with a defined locality distinguish the local authority from most other organisations, whether public or private, and means that a local authority shapes and is shaped by its public and through the public by the locality. Each relationship has its own conditions and involves particular staff. The organisational problem which few, if any, authorities have solved is both to recognise the particularity of each relationship and to realise the potential of interrelationships. Even staff dealing with clearly related issues have difficulty co-ordinating their activities, as case studies of families calling on social services have shown. The danger is that mechanisms of co-ordination are created, building up bureaucratic controls and a series of meetings that, far from realising the potential of the multi-contact authority, become barriers to effective action. Part of the organisational dilemma which lies at the heart of local government as a multi-purpose, multi-activity organisation is how to realise the potential of the many relationships in their interactions, while achieving the effectiveness of action in particular relationships.

To discuss the relationships of the local authorities only by services provided by the authority is misleading. The local authority has relationships with citizens who place demands and pressures on it and who, as electors, can change the composition of its governing body. The relationships of the authority with the citizens who make up the communities within it are not entirely within the control of the local authority. The local authority cannot define its market and hence the relationships it sustains as can a private firm. It faces many publics who have legitimate rights to its attention. Pressure, protest, demand, suggestion and complaint can come from many quarters, and in advancing their claims or ideas the public are not only customers and clients but citizens, electors and taxpayers.

A local authority is subject to a variety of pressures from the community. The pressures are not on the whole the pressures of organised groups, if by that one means groups constituted on a continuing basis for pressure on the council or other public bodies at local level. There are such groups, which may be local branches of national bodies. There are important interest groups such as chambers of commerce and trade unions who will place demands upon authorities. But the set of relationship is in many ways more diffuse, although Stoker has shown the role of interest groups has widened and strengthened (Stoker, 1991).

Many of the pressures will be temporary, focusing on specific issues. Campaigns will form and disperse as the issue is resolved or as it becomes clear it cannot be resolved. The nature of those pressures will vary from authority to authority. When I visited Barnet under Conservative control it was pointed out that the authority had an articulate public containing an above-average number of solicitors. There was an ever-present threat of judicial review and of reference to the ombudsman. In Hertfordshire, stress was laid on the strength and experience of groups campaigning on education issues. The authority were 'amateurs dealing with professionals'.

In campaigning there is a new and informed group of the public as a consequence of the responsibilities given to school governors for the management of schools and above all for their finances, creating an informed public of 300,000 governors who are a powerful pressure on local authorities and on central government for resources for schools. The protests generated, particularly in the counties over the school budget cuts in 1995/6, led to the Conservative government seeking to protect education budgets. The hands of the chairs of education in local authorities and of the secretary of state in the cabinet were strengthened by the pressures of governors.

The local authority cannot deny the legitimacy of these claims, but equally it cannot necessarily meet them all. The resources are not available and the claims made are often in conflict. The public of the authority are not a single public, but many publics, marked by bonds of co-operation, but also by lines of conflict.

There has been a change in the appreciation of the public by local authorities, whether expressed as concern for customers or for citizens. These changes challenge the limited consideration given to the relationship with the public because of the dominance of a professional model and of a representative model both of which in their own way assumed that the authority 'knew' what was needed. Those models are still powerful. How effective the challenge will be remains uncertain. All that can be said is that relations with the public are on the agenda of concern. An emphasis on relations with the public in all its forms can lead to diversity, reflecting the diversity of publics and of localities.

## The environment of organisations

Local authorities are set in an environment of organisations – both public and private. They can be recipients of services, but they can also be providers of services both to and with the local authority and to the many publics of the locality.

*Public agencies*

Chapter 5 described the framework of community governance, involving many agencies and organisations. Many of the services of a local authority are closely related to services provided by these bodies. The work of social services and of other departments is related to the health services. The work of local authorities in economic development is related to the work of training and enterprise councils and of the new regional development agencies. The institutional framework can, whether by conscious design or by accident, enable co-operation or hinder it:

> Where organisational divides are necessary, structures can still be designed to encourage or to discourage co-operation. Due to a failure in organisational understanding, the structural division between health and social services was reinforced by organisational design. Divisions were built into structures by:
>
> - the difference in governance between the elected local authority and the appointed health authority;
> - the difference between the finance of health authorities totally dependent on grants and of local authorities with their own taxation powers;
> - the difference between the capital finance of health authorities through grants and of local authorities through loans;
> - differences in the management structures with no equivalent in health authorities, when first created, to the chief executive in local authorities;

- differences in the hierarchical relationship between health authorities and central government and the relative autonomy of local authorities.

The result has been different organisational patterns of working, different organisational assumptions and even different organisational languages, which reinforced rather than lessened the structural divide. That divide was further reinforced by the decision to place all doctors with health authorities and all social workers with local authorities, so that professional boundaries reinforced organisational boundaries. A profession has a capacity to communicate across organisational boundaries, but that capacity was not used to aid inter-authority co-operation. (Ranson and Stewart, 1994, pp. 141–2)

There is an interaction between the role conception of local authorities and the relationship with other public agencies. If the role is seen as mainly the provision of services, then the interrelationship will be focused on service provision. If, however, the local authority sees its role in community governance as concerned with the overall economic, social and environmental well-being of its area, then inevitably it will be concerned to a lesser or greater degree with all aspects of the bodies discussed.

### The three-tier system

County–district relations have their own particular character in the environment of governments, as have their relations with parish councils. Each tier has its own basis in local elections. Each tier has its own concern for and relationship with locality, and yet the meaning given to locality will be different, as the boundaries and areas are different, creating different balances of interest and concern.

County–district relations have not been easy. The former county boroughs resented their loss of powers to the county. Other districts often resented the perceived self-importance and even arrogance of the county, reflected in what was felt by the districts as a patronising attitude towards the district, as in 'There are one or two able people in the districts'. The county has often seen districts as a lower tier, with limited functions, while parish and town councils have felt ignored by both county and district.

The process of local government reorganisation gave expression to past resentment and created new hostilities. County and district saw it as in their interest to denounce the effectiveness of the other tier. Both cultivated parish and town councils, and were often met by the response that 'if they had really been interested in the parishes they could have shown that long ago'. Counties defending the existing system expressed a commitment to improved working. Five counties found partners in the districts with which they explored new ways of working. A number of counties and districts have built on that experience. Somerset has developed a different approach in each district. In Mendip it is built on town forums, whereas in South Somerset it is built on the area committees. An LGMB study concluded that 'most of the case study authorities felt that blueprints of prescriptive initiatives written for a whole county area would not work. They suggest that if the diversity of local government is valued, it is difficult to introduce changes across a county area' (LGMB, 1996, p. 7).

Both counties and districts have developed new relationships with parish councils. Partly because of reorganisation but also because of a growing concern to get closer to local communities there is a new interest in parish and town councils as the elected representatives of the community. Counties and districts can co-operate in such developments. In Bedfordshire, agreement was reached between the county council, two district councils and the Association of Town and Parish Councils on the principles of three-tier working, starting from 'the preparation of community needs statements which will require officers from all three tiers to work together'.

Developments in new relationships with the parish and town councils have to recognise differences in attitude and approach. A town council with a population of 10,000 will aspire to an extended role which a small parish council would not feel it had the resources to assume. Counties and districts have recognised these differences. Broadlands offered parish councils a role both in setting and in monitoring contracts. Hertfordshire offered parish councils the help of volunteer officers to act as parish friends. It was up to the parish councils how they responded.

## *Joint boards and joint committees*

Joint boards and joint committees have always been a feature of local government. Joint boards have a separate existence as a corporate body, constituted by legislation, to discharge local government functions over areas covering more than one authority. Joint committees can have similar responsibilities but are normally constituted by agreement between authorities. Joint boards and joint committees became more important following the abolition of the Greater London Council and the metropolitan counties. Flynn and Leach concluded from the experience of joint action:

(i)   joint action has never been popular among local authorities and has been difficult to achieve even with considerable pressure from the centre

(ii)  the proliferation of joint action has been widely viewed as being in conflict with the principles of local democracy

(iii) joints boards have tended to operate as 'independent' authorities over which their constituent bodies have had little or no control

(iv)  whilst joint committees have been cumbrous in their working, subject to numerous delays, and have found it difficult to reach agreement

(v)   joint arrangements have not been taken seriously by one of the commissions of inquiry into the structure of local government over the past twenty-five years.

(Flynn and Leach, 1984, p. 43)

Travers and his colleagues who studied joint working among local authorities in metropolitan areas, concluded, 'Joint boards are criticised for their potential to become isolated and unaccountable. Joint committees, although more directly controlled by their constituent authorities, have tended to be controlled by district or borough leaders' (Travers *et al.*, 1995, p. 31).

Leach and his colleagues concluded that in the typical post-abolition metropolitan district 'There would be no specific piece of machinery for briefing/post-abolition/mandating/reporting back or joint activities' (Leach *et al.*, 1991, p. 165); or as a director or administration said, 'There's next to nothing in the way of questions or discussions on joint board and joint committee matters at our council or committee meetings. Basically the members involved do their own thing' (ibid, p. 166). The only exception was over precepts or levies which may be discussed with the leaders of the local authorities concerned.

The role of the councillor on such bodies is part of a wider problem of the ambiguities surrounding local authority representatives on outside bodies. Representatives on outside organisations tend to see that role as separate from their role on the council. Their commitment can be more to the organisation on which they serve than to the authority that appointed them and to which they have been elected. It is the commitment that a committee member shows to its services carried one stage further. What binds together the members of the organisation are the interests of its services. It is easy to forget the local authority in the agendas of the organisation. In a few authorities, representatives or 'outside bodies' are briefed and report back. That is not common and generally authorities forget their representatives once appointed.

There is confusion over the role of elected members (and sometimes officers) on external bodies.

> In one authority that claimed to have extensive links with local voluntary and semi-private organisations we received three conflicting views on the representative role. One member claimed that his role was simply to defend the interests of the council (and especially those that fitted with his party's vision) and to ensure that the organisations he was on supported the council's activities. A second member (who was the council's representative on a local voluntary organisation) stated that she 'never really made any conscious connection between my role as a councillor and my role on the management committee – the two are entirely separate responsibilities'. An officer from the same authority, however, stated that 'now we have service level agreements with many organisations – contracts – members are in a much better position to unite the organisational strategies of the council and the voluntary bodies they are appointed to, rather than having to concentrate on how the money is spent.' With such diverse expectations and understandings of the representative role of members of external

bodies it is no wonder that this authority was unable to achieve a coherent set of policies towards them. (Leach *et al*., 1996, p. 26)

## *The private and voluntary sectors*

Historically, local authorities were close to the private sector. In the nineteenth century most factories and commercial undertakings were owned by families who lived locally and often played a significant role on the local council. Their names, such as the Pilkingtons in St Helens, appear in the roll of mayors, as their portraits adorn the corridors of town halls. The focus of the nineteenth-century urban authority on the physical infrastructure was close to the interests of industry and commerce.

As the twentieth century evolved, increasingly businesses became subject to a more distant ownership. Local families sold their shares and moved away. Factories and departmental stores became subject to national or even international ownership. The reality was that a managerial elite had replaced an ownership elite and it had no time or taste for council business, as Clements has shown in Bristol (Clements, 1969). The politics of local government changed, too, and with it the personalities on the council. Labour gained strength and the dominance of a commercial elite in the locality was no longer possible, even where that elite was still present. The relationship between local authorities and the private sector and, to an extent, voluntary bodies on which the local elite had also played a role – at least on the 'acceptable' ones – moved from personal relationships to official relationships which may take many forms.

The private and the voluntary sectors are recipients of services. In as far as they own property they will be users of property-related services but beyond that they benefit from a wide range of services. This relationship used to be more visible when local authorities were involved with public utilities – gas, electricity and water – and the relationship was that of industry and commerce as customer and the local authority as provider. The private sector and increasingly the voluntary sector are suppliers of goods and services. Local authorities have always had contractual relations but they have extended as local authorities have contracted out more services. Partnerships with both the private and voluntary sectors have developed and are likely to grow under the private finance initiative.

Local authorities taxed local industry and commerce through the non-domestic rate. In 1990 with the introduction of the poll tax, the non-domestic rate ceased to be a local tax and became a national tax, redistributed to local authorities according not to their rateable value but according to population. The lack of a business vote then became the basis for complaints of 'no taxation without representation', a complaint which ignored the reality that individual businessmen already had a vote as ordinary electors. A statutory obligation was laid upon local authorities to consult business on the budgetary decisions. The statutory consultation remains, although much of its meaning has disappeared with the local tax and hence the commitment to it, both of local authorities and of industry and commerce. The limited proposals of the Labour government for a local supplement to the non-domestic rate may not be sufficient to revive interest.

Local authorities have a wide-ranging concern for economic development, which involves them in a variety of approaches to attract inward investment or to support local initiative. The authority can assist with property, provide information or, in certain circumstances, give grants. The private and the voluntary sectors can be partners with the local authority. Indeed such partnerships are increasingly required of local authorities. Bids to Europe, to the lottery funds, or for the single regeneration budget – all require or encourage partnerships.

Local authorities may encourage the voluntary sector through grants, although contracts are replacing some grants. The voluntary body that operates under contract is in danger of losing its distinctiveness. It can become just another contractor changing the role and nature of the voluntary body. Some local authorities recognise the danger. 'Those local authorities that were most effective in their relationship with voluntary organisations were proactive in working to allow the local voluntary sector to reach its full potential to help the local community' (Bemrose and MacKeith, 1996, p. 11).

*The media*

The media play a special role in the environment of organisations. A local authority can in part see the public through the media. Many public relations officers interpret their roles as involving relationships with the media and little else. Through the media, authorities reach out to the public, and through the media they may hear voices of the public or what may appear to be the voices of the public, but may be the voices of the articulate and the letter-writer.

The local media can take a wide range of forms involving weekly, daily and evening papers and the burgeoning array of the free press. There has been a rapid growth in local radio stations and regional television has an important role. Each local authority faces its own media which vary from locality to locality, both in attitude and in intensity or density of attention paid to the authority and its activities. A large city may have its own daily paper, an evening paper, a Sunday paper, free papers, two or three local radio stations and regional television based in the city. Contrast that with a rural authority in which the main press interest is from a weekly paper. A London borough may have a local weekly paper, but for the *Evening Standard*, it will be but one London borough amongst many. On the other hand, it is more likely to receive the attention of the national media when some problem hits the headlines.

Differences in the media between authorities are an important source of diversity. Where in a large city the media are greatest in density and national interest is higher, the impact on politics and on the work of the authority is likely to be greatest, not necessarily in determining policies, but in presentation.

## New relationships in community governance

If the role of local authorities is seen as an agency of the delivery of services, the relationship with the public and with organisations is defined by the services provided. This limited concept led to the relationship between health and local authorities being defined by social services, neglecting wider concerns. The relationship with the private and voluntary sectors would, within this concept, be that of recipient of services or the provider of services, although the recipient of the service need not be the willing recipient when inspectors regulate their activities. If however a local authority is seen as a political institution constituted for local government, then the concerns of the local authority extend beyond the services provided. It will see the public not just as customers but as citizens. It will have a wider concern with other organisations and agencies. Its involvement with health authorities will be more wide-ranging. Its interest in economic welfare will make it aware of the needs of industry and commerce. The emphasis placed on economic development in a number of authorities in the early 1980s can be seen as a response by the local authority as local government.

The challenges set out in Chapter 7 have led many authorities to emphasise the role of local authorities as political institutions providing leadership in community governance. This involves:

- *a concern for the area* and the communities within, extending beyond the services provided to encompass the overall social and economic well-being of those communities and the environmental condition of the area, as required by the duty which the Labour-Government proposes to place on local authorities;
- *a readiness to work in many different ways*, providing services both directly and indirectly, working with and through other organisations, regulating, influencing and networking as well as enabling self-help and mutual aid;
- *the realisation of community resources* to the full in meeting the challenges faced;
- *closeness to citizens and their communities*, listening and learning, informing and responding, reconciling and balancing so that the authority in choice and voice reflects their concerns.

Three examples from authorities illustrate the emerging role. (1) Arun's ultimate goal is:

the Council managing on behalf of the community and making arrangements to see that services are delivered as required.

The challenge for local government is in maintaining and developing power for the people through the local democratic process.

Whilst most effort will be applied to identifying local needs and responding to local choice/local voice the council will not lose sight of its prime objective – the provision (both directly and indirectly) of public goods and services.

The vision is about a new local authority that promises community leadership and acts as the community's advocate and indeed is the champion for the community, campaigning when appropriate.

(2) In Cambridgeshire, an all-party members steering group proposed:

a direction that builds upon our past, but looks to the future. It is based on three key conclusions:

- Service provision is a fundamental role for the Council, but we must continually strive to improve its effectiveness and efficiency.
- The Council has a much wider role to perform, in governing Cambridgeshire and exercising community leadership on behalf of its citizens.
- The diversity and pluralism of the public sector means that we must learn to thrive and succeed in partnership and co-operation with external organisations.
- To sustain and enhance the quality of life for all the people of Cambridgeshire through democratic and accountable community leadership, the provision of services and the exercise of influence.

(3) A consultative document signed by all three leaders in Kent argued that 'A key role for KCC is to ensure that, in the more fragmented world of public services, high-quality, cost-effective and accessible services are provided for the people for Kent. This could be achieved by KCC direct action, through effective partnerships with others or by influencing other organisations', and 'working with others, KCC is well placed to promote and support informed, involved and active people and communities, and to reassert the role and value of local democratic government'.

Local authorities vary in the way the role in community governance is approached and the emphasis given within it. While there is a growing recognition of the need for the local authority to play a role in community governance, it is by no means accepted by all local authorities. Nor would all authorities who are playing that role necessarily accept that language. Yet much is happening that represents an assertion of the role of local authorities in community governance, and therefore re-defines their relationship to the locality. That role will be enhanced by the Labour government's policy on community leadership. A broad distinction can be made between those authorities which see that role as mainly involving the macro-level or authority-wide level, and those which see it as mainly involving the micro-level or the communities within. To an extent this distinction is between those authorities which emphasise the relationship with the network of organisations and those which emphasise relationships with the many publics of the authority.

*The macro-level*

*(a) Community leadership*  The first task is to enable a shared understanding among the relevant organisations about the locality and the communities within it. It is normal for the local authority to take the initiative in developing that understanding but not imposing it, for unless the understanding is shared it will not be effective in influencing the actions of other organisations and individuals. A shared understanding may aspire to a vision of what the area of the authority and its communities might be. But visions can beguile and mislead in a changed and changing world. An over-defined vision is unlikely to be achieved. Those who aim at a certain future may forget the need for learning, not merely now when the vision is formed, but over time as circumstances change.

It is wiser to set directions than to set a vision as an end-state. Directions should be set as directions towards rather than directions to. It is often easier to state the problems to be overcome than the exact way they can be overcome. Indeed, the starting point may be an appreciation of the problems faced by the communities within the locality so that different bodies and in particular public bodies can take account of those problems in their action.

The City Council in Bradford took the lead in setting up the Bradford Congress which:

- brought together key organisations in the economic and social life of the area – the chamber of commerce, the training and enterprise council, the health authority, the council of voluntary

organisations, the trades council, the churches, and institutions of higher and further education;
• undertook and encouraged others to undertake an analysis of the condition of the area, building on statistical work but using the insights and understanding of the publics about the key issues facing the area and reached a shared understanding on the issues to be faced, leading to an agreed statement.

Building understanding is the first stage, but community leadership is necessary to agree on actions. In Bradford the congress is moving forward from analysis of the issues to how they can be resolved, leading on to agreeing action to be taken by the different organisations. 'Often one partner takes the lead, with the support of others.' Other approaches are being developed to bring together different organisations in analysing issues within the locality and planning action. City Pride was an initiative by the Conservative government for Birmingham, Manchester and London that was designed for that purpose. Some approaches focus on the economy. The Leeds Initiative chaired by the council leader brings together leading industrialists, figures from commerce and the regional offices of central government. These developments are paralleled in other authorities.

The government sees community planning as the means by which community leadership is expressed. As described in Chapter 7, it proposes to require local authorities to develop processes for community planning, involving building both a shared understanding of local needs and agreement on action, with local people agencies and organisations (DETR, 1998b). The implications of this requirement will be discussed in the concluding chapter.

*(b) Community partnership*     Whereas community leadership involves local authorities in relationships with all or most of the main organisations in a locality, community partnerships involve relationships with a particular organisation or organisations. Community partnerships bring together different organisations – both public and private – to achieve plans, programmes or initiatives. The reasons for such partnerships can be a shared interest, as with the concerns of both health authorities and local authorities in community care. Partnerships do not require however that the interests are the same. What matters is that the partners join

together for action, even though their reasons for doing so are different. A local authority may form a partnership with a firm to undertake a development in which its main, although not necessarily the only, motivation of the firm is the opportunity for profit.

Partnerships take different forms. The local authority can join with another body to create a new organisation. The local authority can commission another body to take action on its behalf. Joint planning or programming procedures can be built. The form of community partnership varies with the action required and the organisations concerned. With some organisations, and particularly other public-sector organisations, the local authority may go beyond partnership on projects to partnerships to build joint working over a wide range of activities, as a health authority and a local authority might, not merely in community care, but in building the health of the community.

Lowenburg describes different examples of partnering for service delivery:

- Bexley Community Leisure Ltd as a not-for-profit trust registered under the Industrial and Provident Society Acts.
- Hounslow Community Initiatives Ltd to run leisure services activities as a not-for-profit charitable trust registered under the Companies Act.
- Greenwich Leisure Services as a not-for-profit workers' co-operative.
- Thamesdown leases out indoor sports and recreation facilities to two community associations operating as a charitable trust.
- Somerset has an agreement with a commercial company covering all aspects of highways work.
- Lewisham has an arrangement with Serviceteam covering all services previously undertaken by the DSO, run by a subsidiary to whose board the council appoints a non-executive director.

(Lowenburg, 1997)

The Labour Government's proposals 'to strengthen councils' powers to enter partnerships' (DETR, 1998b) is likely to increase the range and the variety of forms of community partnerships.

*(c) Community monitoring*    Local authorities have developed a role in monitoring other governmental agencies involving some of the following:

- The preparation of registers, setting out the public's rights in relation to appointed boards and their role and membership.
- Scrutiny panels to examine issues faced by such bodies. In South Lanarkshire scrutiny commissions 'will consider evidence from representatives of the Council, external organisations and the community about a matter of broad concern in the area and will produce a set of recommendations to influence the actions of the council and other agencies'.
- Accountability forums in Bromley where these bodies can explain their plans and be questioned about them.
- Drawing up a code of good practice on public accountability by the West Midlands metropolitan districts which other agencies were invited to adopt.

There is a possible tension between the monitoring and the partnership roles, although it need not be the case. The monitoring role can be welcomed by appointed boards concerned about their public accountability. Much depends on how monitoring is conducted. If in a hostile vein, it will lead to conflict and refusal to co-operate. A local authority carries more conviction in this role if it shows concern about its own accountability. The scrutiny panels in Kirklees are applied with rigour to community issues which involve the local authority as much as appointed bodies.

## The micro level

*(a) Community responsiveness*    Within the locality there are communities of place centring on neighbourhoods, villages or small towns. North Kesteven aims at 'one hundred flourishing communities'. Local authorities have given recognition to such communities by:

- area committees of councillors, meeting in the area and providing opportunities for public participation;
- neighbourhood forums, open to the public, often with representatives of community groups or elected neighbourhood representatives;
- building on the representative role of parish and town councils.

They enable the concerns of local communities to be recognised and responded to within the workings of the local authority.

In Bedfordshire, a pilot project was started in Dunstable based on the town council and extended to other areas. The aim was to test county council policy at the local level. Emphasis was placed on local service provision, where the local town councillors put their views to the officers concerned (e.g. on library hours), agreed initiatives (e.g. on hypothermia), and monitored local service provision (e.g. rota visits to residential homes).

The local authority recognises communities of place more readily than other communities, for a local authority gains its identity from locality and councillors are elected for place. However, as well as communities of place, there are communities of interest, communities of concern, communities of age and communities of background. Within any community of place there can be minority interests that may be neglected or even raise hostility. Many local authorities have created a variety of such forums to represent different communities: for the elderly, for environmental concern, for youth, for ethnic groups or for transport interests, etc. Such forums can and should take many different forms as different groups have different needs and different ways of working.

*(b) Community Empowering*   The local authority can empower directly by devolving certain of its powers to the communities within. Local authorities have:

- given effective decision-making powers to neighbourhood forums, as in Islington, even though formally the decisions have to be ratified by the local authority;
- built tenant management of estates or transferred estates to tenant co-operatives;
- developed user control of leisure facilities or community centres.

The local authority in Tendring developed a policy of passing facilities over to users by specially created trusts. Westcliff theatre was leased to a theatre trust with a limited subsidy. Bowling greens were leased free of charge to bowling clubs. Two new sports pavilions were made the responsibility of the hockey and cricket teams. Six posts were created to help organisations: e.g. sports and ground maintenance officer; a building advisory officer.

The extent to which decisions are devolved and power given varies from case to case. A local authority has to be clear on any limits it has set, otherwise a sense of frustration will build, as previously unappreciated barriers are met by those believing themselves empowered. Devolution of power within a policy framework can still be liberating for those so empowered, since what may seem a detail at the level of the authority can be of critical importance to those affected. Yet it will not be liberating if that framework is not appreciated, until confronted in frustration.

*A variety of approaches*

In the search for a role in community governance the route cannot be predetermined. Each authority has to find its own route in response to its own publics. Stevenage developed partnership and scrutiny approaches at the macro and micro levels. The Stevenage Partnership brings together different organisations, each represented by the 'highest officer' responsible for its activities in Stevenage. It includes representatives of the county and district, the health authority, the police, the chamber of commerce, the council for voluntary services, the further education colleges and the association of secondary heads. It has undertaken projects, each led by one of the partners: the needs of young people; local income; poverty and debt; and community safety. Against this background of good working relationships a monitoring committee has been established 'to make non-elected bodies providing services in Stevenage more accountable to local people, at the same time developing partnerships with them to ensure quality services that meet the needs of Stevenage people'. Stevenage has also created six local committees jointly with the county council which can be attended by other agencies.

The complex interaction between different publics and organisations in the light of local conditions influences the approach, or indeed the extent to which a role in community governance is pursued. As community planning develops it is likely to involve many different publics and organisations at both the macro and micro level. One of the key issues to be faced is the relationship between developments at these levels.


## Conclusion

Development of the role of local authorities in community governance is likely to deepen the relationship between local authorities and the locality. The diversity of localities will be given greater emphasis in the diversity of local authorities, as relationships develop both between an authority and its publics and with the environment of organisations. The interactions between authority and locality are already strong, as a few pen portraits will illustrate.

In East Staffordshire it was said to me in the 1980s that the council 'would never oppose a brewery firm', for the heart though not the whole of the authority is Burton-on-Trent. Redditch was described to me as a 'new town with the tradition of a small industrial town', marked by the continuity of councillors, with the leader having served on the council more than thirty years and the former Conservative leader having served longer. North Warwickshire is an authority whose geography means that it can appear to lack identity. It covers the area in between such powerful neighbours as Birmingham and Coventry. Inevitably the authority is united in defence of its territory.

Bury was described to me in the 1980s as 'right-wing, Anglican, innately Conservative as a garrison town with strong Church of England institutions'. Towns change, and authorities change. Portsmouth is a proud city, once devoted to the clear task of being 'the principal service base for the world-wide role of Britain and the empire'. It was concentrated on that task with a singleness of purpose appropriate to its island area. The council expressed the search for a new role, when it was realised that the army barracks would never be occupied and much of the defences was now an ancient monument.

In the London Borough of Richmond there was such a conservationist culture that the decorations in historic York House, the municipal offices, could be the subject of public controversy. 'We have hidden the new technology away, lest they object.' In parts of Nottinghamshire the miners' strike brought divisions into the council between striking and working miners. In Tunbridge Wells there was tension between advocates of conservation and advocates of the new Croydon. Sleepy Tunbridge Wells and the cautious style of the authority suited each other, but change in the area was matched by change in the authority. Trafford was an authority without an identity that came from a core centre. The new chief executive's slogan was 'First in sport, now first in local government'.

In Colwyn, most councillors came from the seaside area. While only a minority of councillors came from the rural area the values of rural Wales were seen by councillors generally as important to the authority. In South Wales, a Plaid Cymru councillor said 'In the valley councils . . . there is clearly a heavy Labour vote and it seems likely that the general civic society does not accept the way that the Labour Party as a British party thinks. They are rather inward-looking areas where communities are very close and people are interrelated' (Nolan, 1997b, p. 3).

The interactions between an authority and its area are many and complex. These examples show how important they are in understanding local government. Those who know the great cities, such as Birmingham, Leeds, Liverpool, Manchester, Newcastle and Sheffield, will know the differences in both authority and area. History and present pressures mark out the differences which both justify and explain local government. The development of the local authorities' role in community governance will reflect those differences.

# 14  Present and Future

## Present uniformity and present diversity

The chapters of this book have illustrated the diversity to be found in the workings of local authorities but also the uniformities, as well as continuity and change.

The forces for uniformity are easier to identify and to describe because they are necessarily shared. They underlie many of the texts describing local government. Broadly these forces are the impact of a shared society and economy, of legislation and the policies of central government, of national organisations of which the most important are political parties and professions, of the impact of the media both national and specialised and of the national world of local government, including its shared history.

The forces for diversity are more difficult to identify and to describe because they are necessarily diverse. Broadly they can be divided into the impact of locality, of the organisational context and of the personalities involved. It is the forces for diversity that require elaboration, because they are so often neglected.

The nature of locality can be seen as in part the local expression of the national society and economy that has been described as a force for uniformity, but it is also a source of diversity. Finer wrote sixty years ago that 'In a population of 40 million, scattered over an area diversified geologically, topographically, economically, and in relation to manners, customs, dialect and local tradition, there are bound to be differences in purpose, character, and behaviour. It follows that several thousand local representative bodies have points of view different from each other, as well as different from each other' (Finer, 1933, p. 7).

While there have been powerful national forces towards uniformity that have operated since Finer wrote, there have equally been forces for differentiation in society and economy. Differences are no longer largely explained by class alone. Society is differentiated in many ways – in the importance of ethnic minorities, in patterns of employment, in attitudes to new cultural patterns and in social norms.

The organisational context reflects the established way of working, itself a product of history and of the experiences of officers and councillors. Part of that history and experience comes from the shared world of local government. Through professions, conferences, journals and under the impact of legislation and government policy, beliefs about the workings of local authorities become part of the experiences of councillors and officers and a force for uniformity. But experience is also grounded in the authority and there are and have been distinctive practices and distinctive cultures which have been illustrated in this book.

There are links between the organisational context and locality, as illustrated in Chapter 13. Political processes and pressures are important elements in those links, for although generally the national parties dominate local politics, differences in style and beliefs are related to locality.

Thus the area which has been dependent on traditional industries, such as mining and ship-building, will be an area where the experience of much of the population and of the councillors has been formed by trade union experience. The council will have a culture which reflects established procedures both within the dominant Labour group and within the council. Some counties or districts grounded in rural areas will have a traditional conservatism, seeing a value in local authority services but concerned for economy. Both these types of area are changing. Mining and the dominance of farming lie in the past, and with those changes the councils are changing.

Whereas some authorities appear to fall into such simple typologies, the nature of locality and its interaction with the council are more complex with countervailing forces at work. A suburban authority will have councillors whose driving force is the preservation of amenities, while others will be driven by managerial values. Public pressures will be many and various. A major city will have councillors drawn from different backgrounds, as is appropriate given the range of communities and interests. The diversity within as well as between localities is reflected within councils.

The diversity of locality is however not the only source of organisational diversity. Locality is not perfectly reflected in or by the authority. There are time-lags, with past values no longer dominant in the local economy still being powerful on the council. Certain interests and attitudes will be better represented than others. Pressures vary in strength. Personalities have a role to play, not least in changing the workings of authorities.

As well as uniformity and diversity there are forces for continuity and for change. Some are themselves forces for uniformity. Legislation as a force for uniformity is in past legislation a force for continuity, and in new legislation a force for change. Locality as a force for diversity is a force for continuity but also for change as it changes.

Yet national pressure and the nature of locality are inadequate in explaining continuity and change. A series of questions can be posed:

- Why was management change in Kent carried further than in adjoining counties?
- Why did North Tyneside carry out a major organisational change?
- Why did South Somerset develop area committees to an extent paralleled by few other districts?
- Why did Kirklees introduce its major organisational change?
- Why did the culture of Westminster differ so strongly from that of Kensington and Chelsea?
- Why was the Wrekin marked by major cultural change?

Similar questions could be asked of all the authorities where there has been significant management or organisational change. There is the challenge of national legislation, but that does not explain the differences. There can be factors in the locality. Here one must have regard to the personalities involved and their politics and experience. Often the emphasis will be on the leader working with a chief executive, supporting and giving expression to their views. The combination of Councillor Hart and Paul Sabin in Kent or of Councillor Harmon and Robert Hughes in Kirklees come to mind. Sometimes the driving force for change may seem to be an individual councillor or officer, as with Brian Flood as leader in North Tyneside or Roger Paine as chief executive in the Wrekin, but support was required within the officer structure in North Tyneside and by the councillors in the Wrekin.

The impact of particular individuals in authorities is important in bringing about innovation, but the opportunities seized by those bringing about change cannot be detached from conditions in the authority. Change may be initiated by a particular crisis. Financial cutback may force reorganisation but the way it is carried out will reflect the impact of individual councillors and officers.

The arrival in power of a particular leadership or the appointment of a particular chief executive may reflect a wish for innovation. In some cases the leader is chosen after a period of political instability or as a reaction against past styles. The individual leader is likely to be part of a wider group seeking change. Innovators can be an important source of diversity, even though if successful their innovations may come to be more widely followed as they become known through the by-ways of local government communication.

There are two main forms taken by diversity in local government. One is associated with continuity and one with change. The continuity is grounded in the locality and the organisational context and the interaction between them. Change is associated with the innovators who may themselves be responding to change in the locality or to particular events in the organisational context.

To understand the nature of local government one has to appreciate both the forms and sources of diversity, but also the forms and sources of uniformity. In the interrelationships between them the workings of local authorities are played out.

## Towards the future

This book has been concerned with the past and with the present of local government. The future of local government contains new challenges for change. The Labour government's programme for modernising local government described in Chapter 7 is designed to change the workings of local authorities. The concluding part of this chapter considers the likely impact of those changes and the extent to which they will nurture diversity or enforce uniformity.

The Labour government's emphasis on community leadership will receive a ready response from those local authorities which are already pursuing that role. The new duty of community concern and the requirement to undertake community planning will legitimate their initiatives. There is a danger, however, that in some authorities, inherited structure and process will limit the development of community leadership, resulting in it being a peripheral activity rather than a central role of the local authority.

Attitudes nurtured by the traditions of professionalism, departmentalism and committee reinforce the role of local authorities as agencies for the provision of a series of services, and although they have been modified by recent changes, they remain powerful. The role of local authorities in community leadership does not rule out the provision of services, but sees that as the local authorities' contribution to community needs. The local authority has to be organised for service provision – whether directly or indirectly – but that organisation must be geared to community leadership if the role is to develop as more than a peripheral activity. The extent to which the government's emphasis on community leadership leads to major change will depend upon change in the way of working, and the response is likely to be variable, as responses to previous changes.

The government's support for the community leadership role is an opportunity for the development of local government. Local authorities have to recognise the implication for their organisation and ways of working, if the opportunity is to be realised. If the opportunity is realised then it is likely to lead to a diversity of policy and practice as local authorities recognise and respond to the needs of their locality and give expression to their distinctive politics. Chapter 13 has shown the diversity of locality within a shared society and a shared economy. Community planning will give expression to that diversity. It will nurture diversity within necessary uniformity.

The government's policies emphasise best value, and local authorities will be under an obligation to show to their public that they have achieved best value, which must involve consideration both of quality and cost. The extent to which those policies involve change will depend upon the extent to which the authority is willing to challenge past practice. Best value requires local authorities to consider and evaluate alternative ways of working. Local authorities have tended to assume that given a responsibility they would carry it out themselves, employing their own staff – the assumption of self-sufficiency. CCT challenged that assumption but did not require a comprehensive evaluation of alternative ways of working, but rather the observance of procedures to enforce competitive tendering. Evaluation of alternative forms of service delivery can involve more alternatives than direct provision or competitive tendering: partnership, self-help, negotiated contracts, combinations of providers. Evaluation should involve many factors beyond cost and efficiency: probity, flexibility, responsiveness, capacity for learning. Evaluation will involve a judgement on the relative importance of different factors.

Whether best value leads to significant change remains unresolved. There are two external driving forces for change. Local authorities will be required to consult the public on the extent to which services provide best value in meeting their needs. They will also be subject to external inspection with the ultimate sanction of government intervention. Inspection will cover both the processes by which best value is sought and the results. There could be differences between the public views and the pressures of inspection. This could represent a tension between forces for diversity and for uniformity, although that will depend on the extent to which the public's views vary from area to area and the extent to which inspection enforces uniformity.

The government policies aim to strengthen local democracy by measures to encourage voting in local elections and to develop greater public participation. As already discussed, innovation in democratic practice has developed in some local authorities. There are authorities which have opposed such developments as well as some who have undertaken them. Some councillors see participation as undermining their role as elected representative, while others see participation as necessary to realise the potential of that role. Greater citizen participation does not turn the role of the elected representative into that of delegate. The public do not speak with one voice, but with many, and the role of the elected representatives is to seek to reconcile or to balance those views in political judgement. The extent to which this is recognised by councillors will determine their response.

If local democracy is strengthened, it will enhance the legitimacy of councils in pursuing their own policies, but also the need to ensure those policies have wide support amongst local people. It would therefore enhance the capacity of diversity, but the extent to which that capacity was realised would depend on the extent to which needs and aspirations varied between areas.

Community leadership, best value and democratic renewal require new ways of working if they are to be realised. The government will require all authorities to review their political structures. Such a review is necessary and should cover officer structures if the new policies are to be realised. The government also requires that the review of political structures should involve the separation of the executive role from the backbench role, and have put forward three options, as set out in Chapter 7, involving directly elected mayors, cabinets and/or city managers. With these new structures the government wishes to see the development of the scrutiny role of the backbencher. The government allows for the possibility of a local authority retaining existing structures based on the committee system, but can require that to be tested in a local referendum.

The government recognises that there will not be a uniform response, and argue that 'The scope for diversity, innovation and local choice will be even greater...than it is under the single model which exists today' (DETR, 1988b, p. 31). This is not merely because of the choice between the options but choices within the option. A study by the Institute of Local Government Studies (Stewart *et al.*, 1998) shows the wide range of choices, centring on the divisions of responsibility between the executive (whether in the form of the mayor, cabinet, city manager) and the council, and on the meaning of scrutiny. The government seeks uniformity in the separation of the executive, but accepts and even welcomes diversity in how it is achieved, although it will lay down certain 'key features' (DETR, 1998b). The extent to which the models will involve significant change in practice remains uncertain. The government hopes for and expects change. It considers that the models will enhance efficiency, transparency and accountability and will support the community leadership role. It remains to be seen whether this is the case. It could be argued that decisions by a cabinet or by a mayor will limit public access and therefore transparency, although much will depend on the form of the new models and how they operate in practice.

The extent to which the model leads to change also depends in part on how far attitudes and relationships are carried forward from existing practice. Change in political structures will have an impact, but it will be mediated, as past changes have been, by those attitudes and relationships. The role of a political executive will depend on the relationship with the political group. The effectiveness of scrutiny will be affected by that relationship and the extent to which group discipline is relaxed. The working of a cabinet will be affected by the relationship between its members and departments and may match the past relationship between chair and chief officer. The relationship between mayor or leader and the chief executive or council manager will remain critical.

Change in structure alters the rules of the game, but how the game is played is only partly determined by the rules. It also depends upon the experience and attitudes that are brought to the game. The actual outcome of the changes proposed by the government remain indeterminate. Advocates hope the changes will lead to effective community leadership and clarity for accountability. Opponents fear the concentration of power and the possibility of its abuse. What can be said with a high degree of probability is that the impact will vary from authority to authority, depending not merely upon the particular model adopted, but upon the personalities involved, inherited conditions, and the nature of the locality and local politics.

The changes contained in the White Paper (DETR, 1998b) are not the only changes proposed by or being implemented by the Labour government. The institutional setting is being changed by Scottish and Welsh devolution, by the creation of regional development agencies and by the establishment of a Greater London Authority. Their impact on existing local authorities is not clear. Thus in Scotland and Wales the new Parliament and Assembly could strengthen local authorities, but could equally weaken them as both the new bodies sought to establish their role.

Government policies for particular services will have their own impact, the cumulative impact of which may be as great or greater than the White Paper. Those policies involve in education a redefinition of the role of local authorities in sustaining education standards, an extension of the role of OFSTED in inspecting local education authorities, the requirement for a variety of planning processes and new powers to remove responsibilities from local authorities.

There is a tension in the government policies between a commitment to decentralisation and an emphasis on inspection, centrally developed procedures and powers of intervention. It is present within the proposals set out in the White Paper and in the relationship of those proposals to service policies. The tension can be analysed as the tension between building the capacity for diversity and a perceived necessity for uniformity.

Within a national system of government and a shared society there will always be a necessity for uniformity, but local government requires a capacity for diversity if it is to be more than an agency for the organisation of service delivery. That diversity can be an important element in the national system of government, increasing its responsiveness to local needs and aspirations. From diversity, both local and national government can learn. From uniformity, little may be learnt, except of policy failure, but in diversity both relative success and failure can be found and learning develop.

There are and can be no objective rules for defining the scope of uniformity and the capacity for diversity. There will always be political judgements to be made on both. Any system of government should encompass forces for uniformity and forces for diversity. The government policies recognise both. The emphasis on community leadership requires a capacity for diversity, but procedures and policies may impose uniformity. The test must be whether there is a sufficient capacity for diversity within the necessity of uniformity. That remains to be seen.

The lesson to be learnt from this book is that, in the working out of the government's programme, many factors will be at work. History and the inherited world will have its impact as experience and attitudes are carried forward from the past to the present. Both locality and local politics will have their part to play, as will personality. The government's legislation may set new rules of the game, but within those rules the game will be played in different ways. That should be welcomed as an expression of the diversity of local government.

# Bibliography

Alexander, A. (1985) *Borough Government and Politics: Reading 1835–1985* (London: Allen & Unwin).

Alexander, A. (1986) *Managing Local Socialism* (London: Fabian Society).

Arden, A. (1987) *Final Report to the London Borough of Hackney* (London: Hackney London Borough).

Audit Commission (1989) *More Equal than Others: The Chief Executive in Local Government* (London: HMSO).

Audit Commission (1997a) *The Melody Lingers On: A Review of the Audits of People, Pay and Performance* (London: HMSO).

Audit Commission (1997b) *It's a Small World: Local Government's Role as a Steward of the Environment* (London: HMSO).

Audit Commission (1997c) *Capital Gains: Improving the Local Government Capital Expenditure System Report on Inspection* (London: HMSO).

Audit Commission and Social Services Inspectorate (1997) *Report on Inspection of Barnsley Social Services* (London: HMSO).

Baddeley, S. (1989) 'Political Sensitivity in Public Managers', *Local Government Studies*, 15, 2.

Baggulay, P., Mark-Lawsons, J., Shapiro, D., Urry, J., Walby, S. and Warde, A. (1990) *Restructuring: Place, Gender and Class* (London: Sage).

Bailey, S. (1997) *Cross on Principles of Local Government Law* (London: Sweet & Maxwell).

Bains Report (1972) *The New Local Authorities: Management and Structure* (London: HMSO).

Bemrose, C. and MacKeith, J. (1996) *Partnerships for Progress* (Bristol: The Policy Press).

Beuret, K. and Stoker, G. (1986) 'The Labour Party and Neighbourhood Decentralisation: Flirtation or Commitment', *Critical Social Policy*, 17.

Birmingham City Council (1875) *Proceedings of the Council 9.3.1875*.

Blair, T. (1998) *Leading the Way: A New Vision for Local Government* (London: Institute of Public Policy Research).

Bolton, J. E. (1974) *Corporate Management in Action* (London: Local Government Chronicle).

Boyne, G., Griffiths, P., Lawton, A. and Law, J. (eds) (1991) *Local Government in Wales* (York: Joseph Rowntree Foundation).

Boynton, Sir John (1986) *Job at the Top: The Chief Executive in Local Government* (Harlow: Longman).

Branson, N. (1979) *Poplarism, 1919–1925: George Lansbury and the Councillors' Revolt* (London: Lawrence & Wishart).

Bridges, L., Game, C., Lomas, O., McBride, J. and Ranson, S. (1987) *Legality and Local Politics* (Aldershot: Aylesbury).

Briggs, A. (1952) *History of Birmingham Vol. II* (Oxford: Oxford University).

Bristow, S. (1982) 'Rates and Votes – the 1980 District Council Elections', *Policy and Politics*, 10.

Broady, M. and Hedley, R. (1989) *Working Partnership: Community Development in Local Authorities* (London: Bedford Square).

Brooke, R. (1998) 'Tales of the old Town Titans', *Local Government Chronicle*, 9 Jan. 1998.

Bulpitt, J. (1967) *Party Politics in English Local Government* (London: Longmans).

Bulpitt, J. (1983) *Territory and Power in the United Kingdom* (Manchester: Manchester University Press).

Burns, D., Hambleton, R. and Hoggett, P. (1994) *The Politics of Decentralisation: Revitalising Local Democracy* (London: Macmillan).

Campbell, A. (1991) *The Role of the Centre* (Luton: Local Government Management Board).

Caulcott, T. (1996) *Management and the Politics of Power: Central and Local Government Compared* (London: Local Government Chronicle Communications).

Central Regional Council (1995) *Change in Central*.

Chandler, J. A. Gregory, M. and Hunt, M. (1995) *Decentralisation and Devolution in England and Wales* (Luton: Local Government Management Board).

Chester, D. N. (1951) *Central and Local Government* (London: Macmillan).

Christie, N. B. (1991) 'The Present and Future Position of Councils with the Competitive Market', *Local Government Studies*.

Clarke, M. and Hunt, J. (1997) *Political Leaders and Chief Executives* (Birmingham: Institute of Local Government Studies).

Clarke, M. and Stewart, J. (1990) *The General Management of Local Government* (Harlow: Longman).

Clarke, M. and Stewart, J. (1997) *Handling Wicked Issues* (Birmingham: School of Public Policy).

Clarke, M. and Stewart, J. (1998) *Diversity and Choice* (Birmingham: School of Public Policy).

Clements, R. V. (1969) *Local Notables and the City Council* (London: Macmillan).

Cohen, E. (1952) *Autonomy and Delegation in County Government* (London: Institute of Public Administration).

Collinge, C. and Leach, S. (1995) 'Building the Capacity for Strategy Formation in Local Government', *Local Government Studies*, 21, 3.

Collinge, C. and Leach, S. (1997) *Strategic Planning and Management* (London: Pitman).

Conservative Political Centre (1996) *Local Government: The Conservative Approach* (London: Conservative Political Centre).

Cooke, P. (1989) *Localities: The Changing Face of Urban Britain* (London: Unwin Hyman).

Council of Europe (1985) *European Charter of Local Self-Government* (Strasbourg: Council of Europe).

Davies, E. M., Game, C., Gibson, J. and Stewart, J. (1983) *Grant Characteristics and the Budgetary Process* (Birmingham: Institute of Local Government Studies).

Department of the Environment (1991) *The Internal Management of Local Authorities in England* (London: Department of the Environment).

Department of the Environment, Transport and Regions (DETR) (1998a) *Local Democracy and Community Leadership* (London: DETR).

Department of the Environment, Transport and Regions (DETR) (1998b) *Modern Local Government: In Touch with the People* (London: HMSO).

Dickson, M. B., Miller, W. L. and Murray, I. (1995) *Seeing Us How Others See Us: Comparative Public and Elite Attitude to Local Government*, Paper presented to ESRC Local Governance Conference 19 and 20 September.

Donaghue, B. and Jones, G. W. (1973) *Herbert Morrison – Portrait of a Politician* (London: Weidenfeld & Nicholson).

Doogan, K. (1997) *Marketization of Local Governance and Labour Market Fragmentation*, End of award report to ESRC.

Dunleavy, P. (1980) *Urban Political Analysis* (London: Macmillan).

Dunleavy, P. (1981) *The Mass Politics of Housing* (London: Macmillan).

Dunleavy, P., Dowding, K., King, D. and Margetts, H. (1995) *Regime Politics in London Local Government*, Paper presented to ESRC Local Governance Conference, 19 and 20 September.

Elcock, H., Jordan, G. and Midwinter, A. (1989) *Budgeting in Local Government* (Harlow: Longman).

Exeter, C. and Newchurch Consultants (1996) *Enhancing the Tiers of Local Government* (Luton: Local Government Management Board).

Finer, H. (1933) *English Local Government* (London: Methuen).

Flynn, N. and Leach, S. (1984) *Joint Boards and Joint Committees: An Evaluation* (Birmingham: Institute of Local Government Studies).

Foster, C., Jackman, R. and Perlman, M. (1980) *Local Government Finance in a Unitary State* (London: Allen & Unwin).

Fowler, A. (1995) *Human Resources Management in Local Government* (London: Pitman).

Fraser, D. (1976) *Urban Politics in Conservative England* (Leicester: Leicester Press).

Game, C. and Leach, S. (1989) 'The County Councillor in 1889 and 1989', in Young (1989).

Game, C. and Leach, S. (1993) *Councillor Recruitment and Turnover: An Approaching Precipice* (Luton: Local Government Management Board).

Game, C. and Leach, S. (1995) *The Role of Political Parties in Local Democracy* (London: Commission for Local Democracy).

Garvin, J. L. (1932) *The Life of Joseph Chamberlain* (London: Macmillan).

Gaster, L. (1995) *Management Skills in Decentralised Environments* (Luton: Local Government Management Board).

Geddes, M. and Wahlberg, M. (1996) *The Value of Public Enterprise* (Coventry: The University of Warwick).

Gill, C. (1952) *History of Birmingham, Vol. 1* (Oxford: Oxford University Press).

Goss, S. (1988) *Labour and Local Government* (Edinburgh: Edinburgh University Press).

Green, D. (1981) *Power and Party in an English City* (London: Allen & Unwin).

Greenwood, R., Hinings, C. R., Ranson, S. and Walsh, K. (1997) *In Pursuit of Corporate Rationality* (Birmingham: Institute of Local Government Studies).

Greenwood, R., Norton, A. and Stewart, J. (1969) *Recent Reforms in the Management Arrangements of County Boroughs in England and Wales* (Birmingham: Institute of Local Government Studies).

Greenwood, R. and Stewart, J. (1974) *Corporate Planning in English Local Government* (London: Charles Knight).

Griffith, J. A. E. (1966) *Central Departments and Local Authorities* (London: George Allen & Unwin).

Gyford, J. (1991) *Does Place Matter? Locality and Local Democracy* (Luton: Local Government Management Board).

Gyford, J. (1993) 'Professionalism, Managerialism and Politics: an Uneasy Coexistence' in Stoker (1993).

Gyford, J., Leach, S. and Game, C. (1989) *The Changing Politics of Local Government* (London: Unwin Hyman).

Hall, D. and Leach, S. (1996) *Changing Forms of Local Politics*, Final Report ESRC Local Government Programme.

Hall, D. and Leach, S. (1998) 'Party Influence on Local Authority Decision-Making', in Stoker (1998).

Hall, D. and Stewart, J. (1997) *Citizens Juries: An Evaluation* (Luton: Local Government Management Board).

Hambleton, R. (1978) *Policy Planning and Local Government* (London: Hutchinson).

Harrop, K., Mason, T., Vielba, C. A. and Webster, B. A. (1978) *The Implementation and Development of Area Management* (Birmingham: Institute of Local Government Studies).

Hasegowa, J. (1992) *Replanning the Blitzed City Centre* (Buckingham: Open University Press).

Hasluck, E. G. (1936) *Local Government in England* (Cambridge University Press).

Hay, C. and Jessop, G. (1995) *The Governance of Local Economic Development and the Development of Local Economic Governance*, Paper presented to the annual meeting of American Political Science Association.

Hayes, N. (1996) *Consensus and Controversy: City Politics in Nottingham 1945–66* (Liverpool: Liverpool University Press).

Headrick, T. E. (1962) *The Town Clerk in English Local Government* (London: Allen & Unwin).

Hennock, E. P. (1973) *Fit and Proper Persons* (London: Edward Arnold).

Hodgkinson, G. (1970) *Sent to Coventry* (London: Robert Maxwell).

Hoggert, K. (1991) *People, Power and Place* (London: Routledge).

Horton, I. (1978) *Directory of Liberal Party Resolutions* (London: Liberal Publication Department).

Hunt, Lord (Chairman) (1996a) *Select Committee on Relations between Central and Local Government, Vol. I, Report* (London: HMSO).

Hunt, Lord (Chairman) (1996b) *Select Committee on Relations between Central and Local Government, Vol. II, Oral Evidence and Associated Memoranda* (London: HMSO).

Jackson, R. M. (1958) *The Machinery of Local Government* (London: Macmillan).

John, P. (1996) *The Europeanisation of British Local Government: New Management Strategies* (Luton: Local Government Management Board).

Jones, G. W. (1969) *Borough Politics* (London: Macmillan).

Jones, G. W. and Travers, T. (1996) 'Central Government Perceptions of Local Government', in Pratchett and Wilson (1996).

Laffin, M. (1986) *Professionalism and Policy: The Role of the Professions in the Central–Local Relationship* (Aldershot: Gower).

Laffin, M. (1989) *Managing Under Pressure* (London: Macmillan).

Laffin, M. and Young, K. (1985) 'The Changing Role and Responsibilities of Local Authority Chief Officers', *Public Administration*, 63.

Lamb, C. and Geddes, M. (1995) *The Scope for Choice and Variety in Local Government* (York: Joseph Rowntree Foundation).

Laski, H. (1935) 'The Committee System in Local Government', in Laski *et al.* (1935).

Laski, H., Jennings, I. and Robson, W. (1935) *A Century of Municipal Progress: 1835–1935* (London: George Allen & Unwin).

Layfield, F. (Chairman) (1976) *Report of the Committee on Local Government Finance* (London: HMSO).

Leach, S. (1996) *Mission Statements and Strategic Vision: Symbols or Substance?* (Luton: Local Government Management Board).

Leach, S., Clarke, M., Campbell, A., Davis, H. and Rogers, S. (1996) *Managing Fragmentation* (Luton: Local Government Management Board).

Leach, S. and Collinge, C. (1998) *Strategic Planning and Management in Local Government* (London: Pitman).

Leach, S., Davis, H., Game, C. and Skelcher, C. (1991) *After Abolition* (Birmingham: Institute of Local Government Studies).

Leach, S., Pratchett, L. Wilson, D. and Wingfield, N. (1997) *All You Need is Trust: The Changing Relationship between Members and Councillors* (Luton: Local Government Management Board).

Leach, S. and Stewart, J. (1990) *Political Leadership in Local Government* (Luton Local Government Management Board).

Leach, S. and Stewart, J. (1992) *The Politics of Hung Authorities* (London: Macmillan).

Leach, S., Walsh, K., Game, C., Rogers, S., Skelcher, C. and Spencer, K. (1993) *Challenge and Change: Characterstics of Good Management in Local Government* (Luton: Local Government Management Board).

Lee, J. M. (1963) *Social Leaders and Public Persons* (London: Oxford University Press).

Lee, J. M., Wood, B., Solomon, B. and Walters, P. (1974) *The Scope of Local Initiative: A Study of Cheshire County Council 1961–74* (London: Martin Robertson).

Le Grand, J. and Bartlett, W. (eds) (1993) *Quasi-Markets and Social Policy* (London: Macmillan).

Lipman, V. D. (1949) *Local Government Areas* (Oxford: Basil Blackwell).

Lister, E. (1995) *Local Limits: Cutting the Costs of Good Councils* (London: Conservative Political Centre).

Livingstone, K. (1987) *If Voting Changes Anything, They'd Abolish It* (London: Collins).

Local Government Commission for England (1997) *The Future Local Government of Sefton: Recommendations* (London: HMSO).

Local Government, Information Unit (LGIU) (1996) *Community Involvement: Southampton Case Study* (London: LGIU).

Local Government Management Board (LGMB) (1977) *Innovative Models of Local Authority Working* (Luton: LGMB).

Local Government Management Board (LGMB) (1993) *Managing Tomorrow* (Luton: LGMB).

Local Government Management Board (1995) *Survey of Organisational Change* (Luton: Local Government Management Board).

Local Government Management Board (LGMB) (1996) *Survey of Community Safety Activities in England and Wales* (Luton: LGMB).

Local Government Management Board (LGMB) and Society of Chief Personnel Officers (SOCPO) (1993) *Equal Opportunities in Local Government* (Luton: LGMB).

Loughlin, M. (1996) *Legality and Locality* (Oxford: Clarendon Press).

Lowenburg, P. (1997) *Partnering for Service Delivery* (Luton: Local Government Management Board).

Lowndes, V. (1999) 'We Are Learning to Accommodate Mess: Building New Institutionalism for the Management of Local Governance', in Stoker (1999).

Lucas, J. M. (1990) *The Wandsworth Story* (London: WTCA).

Macdonald, C. and Arnold-Foster, J. (1995) *Working Together: Joint Administration in Local Government* (Reading: Labour Initiatives for Co-operation).

Macintyre, S. (1980) *Little Moscows* (London: Croom Helm).

Marshall, A. H. (1960) *Financial Administration in Local Government* (London: Allen & Unwin).

Maud, Sir John (Chairman) (1967) *Committee on the Management of Local Government Research, Vol. 5, Local Government Administration in England and Wales*, by M. Harrison and A. Norton (London: HMSO).

Mill, J. S. (1904) *Considerations on Representative Government* (London: Routledge).

Miller, W. (1988) *Irrelevant Elections* (Oxford: Oxford University Press).

Moran, G. (1996) *Promoting Health and Local Government* (London: Health Education Authority).

Morphet, J. (1993) *The Role of Chief Executives in Local Government* (Harlow: Longman).

Newman, J. (1996) *Shaping Organisational Culture* (London: Pitman).

Nolan, Lord (Chairman) (1997a) *Committee on Standards in Public Life: Report on Local Government* (London: HMSO).

Nolan, Lord (Chairman) (1997b) *Committee on Standards of Public Life: Transcripts of Oral Evidence* (London: HMSO).

Norton, A. (1989) *The Role of the Chief Executive in British Local Government* (Birmingham: The Institute of Local Government Studies).

Norton, A. (1991) *The Role of the Chief Executive in British Local Government* (Birmingham: Institute of Local Government Studies).

Page, H. (1936) *Co-ordination and Planning in the Local Authority* (Manchester: Manchester University Press).

Painter, J. M. and Goodwin M. (1996) *British Local Government in the Transition from Fordism*, Final Report ESRC Local Governance Programme.

Parkinson, M. (1985) *Liverpool on the Brink* (London: Policy Journals).

Peters, T. and Waterman, R. (1980) *In Search of Excellence* (New York: Harper & Rav).

Pinkney, R. (1983) 'Nationalising Local Politics and Localising a National Party: The Liberal Party in Local Government', *Government and Opposition*, 18.

Poole, K. P. and Keith-Lucas, B. (1994) *Parish Government 1984–1994* (London: National Association of Parish Councils).

Pratchett, L. and Wilson, D. (eds) (1996) *Local Democracy and Local Government* (London: Macmillan).

Quirk, B. (1997) *Managing Lewisham: Refining, Reforming and Refocusing the Role of Managers* (London: Lewisham London Borough).

Rallings, C. and Thrasher, M. (1994) *Explaining Election Turnout, a Secondary Analysis of Local Election Statistics* (London: HMSO).

Rallings, C. and Thrasher, M. (1997) *Local Elections in Britain* (London: Routledge).

Rallings, C., Temple, M. and Thrasher, M. (1994) *Community Identity and Participation in Local Democracy* (London: Commission for Local Democracy).

Ranson, S. and Stewart, J. (1994) *Management for the Public Domain* (London: Macmillan).

Rao, N. (1993) *Managing Change* (York: Joseph Rowntree Foundation).

Rao, N. and Young, K. (1995) *Coming to Terms with Change: The Local Government Councillor in the 1990s* (York: Joseph Rowntree Foundation).

Redcliffe-Maud, Lord (Chairman) (1969) *Royal Commission on Local Government in England 1996–1969, Vol. 1 Report* (London: HMSO).

Redlich, J. (1903) *Local Government in England*, edited with additions by F. W. Hirst (London: Macmillan).

Rhodes, G. (1981) *Inspectorates in British Government* (London: Allen & Unwin).

Rhodes, R. (1981) *Control and Power in Central–Local Relations* (Aldershot: Gower).

Rhodes, R. (1988) *Beyond Westminster and Whitehall* (London: Allen & Unwin).

Rittel, H. and Webber, M. (1973) 'Dilemmas in a General Theory of Planning', *Policy Sciences*, 4.3.

Robson, W. A. (1931) *The Development of Local Government* (London: Allen & Unwin).

Rose, G. (1988) 'Locality, Politics and Culture: Poplar in the 1920s', *Society and Space*, 6.

Sabin, P. (1989) 'The Role of the Chief Executive and the Management of County Councils', in Young (1989).

Saunders, P. (1982) 'Why Study Central–Local Relations?', *Political Studies*, 24.

Schulz, M. (1948) 'The Local Government Act of 1929 and Subsquent Legislation', in Wilson (1948).

Sharpe, L. J. and Newton, K. (1984) *Does Politics Matter?* (Oxford: Clarendon Press).

Shaw, A. (1895) *Municipal Government in Great Britain* (New York: The Century Company).

Simon, S. (1938) *A Century of City Government: Manchester 1838–1938* (London: Allen & Unwin).

Smellie, K. (1957) *A History of Local Government* (London: George Allen & Unwin).

Smith, J. Toulmin (1851) *Local Self-Government and Centralisation* (London: John Chapman).

Snell, Lord (1935) 'The Town Council', in Laski *et al.* (1935).

Stanyer, J. (1976) *Understanding Local Government* (London: Fontana).

Stanyer, J. (1989) *A History of Devon County Council* (Exeter: Devon Books).

Stewart, J. (1981) *Local Government: The Conditions of Local Choice* (London: Allen & Unwin).

Stewart, J. (1995) *Innovation in Democratic Practice* (Birmingham: The Institute of Local Government Studies).

Stewart, J. (1996) *Further Innovation in Democratic Practice* (Birmingham: School of Public Policy).

Stewart, J. (1997) *More Innovation in Democratic Practice* (Birmingham: School of Public Policy).

Stewart, J. and Stoker, G. (eds) (1995) *Local Government in the 1990s* (London: Macmillan).

Stewart, J. Clarke, M., Hall, D. and Taylor, F. (1998) *Practical Implications: New Forms of Political Executive* (London: Local Government Association).

Stoker, G. (1991) *The Politics of Local Government* (London: Macmillan).

Stoker, G. (1993) 'Professions, Accountability and the New Local Governance' in Stoker, G. (ed.) (1993) *The Future of Professionalism in Local Government* (Luton: Local Government Management Board).

Stoker, G. (ed.) (1999) *The New Management of Local Governance* (London: Macmillan).

Travers, T., Biggs, S. and Jones, G. W. (1995) *Joint Working between Authorities* (York: Joseph Rowntree Foundation).

Travers, T., Jones, G. W. and Burnham, J. (1993) *Impact of Population Size on Local Authority Costs and Effectiveness* (York: Joseph Rowntree Foundation).

Travers, T., Jones, G. W. and Burnham, J. (1997) *The Role of the Local Authority Chief Executive in Local Governance* (York: Joseph Rowntree Foundation).

Treasury, The (1998) *Stability and Investment for the Long Term*, Cm 3978 (London: HMSO).

Vickers, Sir Geoffrey (1972) *Freedom in a Rocking Boat* (Harmondsworth: Penguin).

Wainwright, H. (1994) *Arguments for a New Left* (Oxford: Basil Blackwell).

Walker, D. (1997) *Public Relations in Local Government* (London: Pitman).

Wall, Sir Robert (1993) 'Head to Head', *Local Government Management*, Spring 1993.

Walsall Metropolitan Borough Council (1997) *Neighbourhood Governance in the Borough of Walsall*.

Walsh, K. (1995) *Public Services and Market Mechanisms* (London: Macmillan).

Walsh, K. and Davis, H. (1993) *Competition and Service: The Impact of the Local Government Act 1988* (London: HMSO).

Webb, S. (1891) *The London Programme* (London: Swan Sonnenschien).

Wendt, R. (1983) 'Working in a Hung Authority', *Local Government Studies*, 9, 3.

Wendt, R. (1997) 'The Strength of County Government', *County Councils Gazette*, February 1997.

Widdicombe, D. (Chairman) (1986a) *Committee on Conduct of Local Authority Business: Report* (London: HMSO).

Widdicombe, D. (Chairman) (1986b) *Committee on Conduct of Local Authority Business Research, Vol. I, Political Organisation of Local Authorities*, by S. Leach, C. Game, J. Gyford and A. Midwinter (London: HMSO).

Wilson, C. H. (ed.) (1948) *Essays on Local Government* (Oxford: Basil Blackwell).

Woods, M. (1997) 'Discourses of Power and Rurality in Somerset in the 20th Century', *Political Geography*, 16, 6.

Young, K. (1988) 'The Challenge to Professionalism in Local Government', *Policy Studies*, 9, 1.

Young, K. (ed.) (1989) *New Directions for County Government* (London: Association of County Councils).

Young, K. (1995) Portrait of Change (Luton: Local Government Management Board).

Young, K. and Rao, N. (1994) *Coming to Terms with Change* (London: LGC Communications).

# Index